EXODUS
REVISITED

Exciting New Research Challenges Traditional Beliefs

by
Thomas Bordelon

authorHOUSE®

AuthorHouse™
1663 Liberty Drive
Bloomington, IN 47403
www.authorhouse.com
Phone: 1-800-839-8640

Published by AuthorHouse 11/17/2014

ISBN: 978-1-4184-8166-7 (sc)

Library of Congress Control Number: 2004095152

ACKNOWLEDGEMENTS

To John M. Allegro for igniting the spark which led to this book. I wish I had been fortunate enough to have met him before his death.

To my wonderful parents, Henry and Odette, who listened and supported my efforts even though they chose to cling to their individual beliefs.

To my cousin, Debbie, for showing me the way to publishing my manuscript.

To my dear wife, Dorothy, for her encouragement, patience and valuable assistance while I completed a most difficult task.

I also feel honored to dedicate my book to the numerous scholars and historians who produced the noble works that were the backbone of this book. Unfortunately, those works continue to lie unread on dusty bookshelves throughout the world. My publication is only a resurrection of their magnificent efforts to enlighten their fellow humans. The author has surely built upon the shoulders of giants.

Contents

LIST OF MAPS

LIST OF CHARTS

LIST OF ILLUSTRATIONS

LIST OF ANCIENT HISTORIANS

ANTONIUS AELIAN (Claudius Aelianus) – 170-235 A.D.
Greek writer of popular science and philosophy

BEROSUS – 3ʳᵈ century B.C.
Chaldean priest

CHAEREMON – 1ˢᵗ century A.D.
Superintendent of library at Alexandria

CTESIAS OF CNIDUS – 416 B.C. (in the court of Aetaxerxes)
Greek physician and historian. Born in Cnidus, Caria. His works were the only historical writings of his time based on official Persian sources. Physician to the Persian court for 17 years, under Darius II and Artaxerxes Mnemom. His works: *Persicha – A History of Assyria-Babylonia* in 23 books (non-existent).

GERMANICUS (Nero Claudius Germanicus) – 15 B.C.-19 A.D.
Roman imperial prince and Latin poet, astronomer and orator.

HECATAEUS (of Abdera) – Circa late 16ᵗʰ century B.C.
Greek geographer, mythologist, and forerunner of the historians. Born in Miletus, Ionia (western Asia). His works: *Journey Around the World* and *Histories*.

HERODOTUS – 480-415 B.C.
Greek historian. Born in Halicarnassus, Caria. His works: *History, Books 1-9*.

HYGINUS, GAIUS JULIUS – Circa 64 B.C.
Latin scholar and writer. His works: *Genealogies* and *De Astronomia*.

JOSEPHUS, FLAVIUS – 37-94 A.D.
Jewish notable and Greek historian. His works: *Wars of the Jews*, *Antiquities of the Jews,* and *Against Apion*.

LUCIAN (Lucianos) – 120-180 A.D.
Greek author and pamphleteer. Born in Samosata, Comagene.

LYCOPHRON, of Chalcis/Cilician – Circa 285 B.C.
Greek poet and scholar. Worked in Alexandrian library.

LYSIMACHUS – 360-281 B.C.
Of Greek origin. Companion and successor of Alexander.

MANETHO – Circa 300 B.C.
>   Egyptian priest and historian. Wrote a history of Egypt for Ptolemy I (305-282 B.C.). His division of the rulers of Egypt into 30 dynasties is still accepted.

OVID (Publius Ovid Naso) – 43 B.C.-17 A.D.
>   Latin poet. Born in Sulmo, Italy. His works: *Causes*, *Metamorphoses*, and many works of love.

PAUSANIAS – 143 – 176 A.D.
>   Greek traveler and geographer.   Traveled in Asia Minor, Syria, Palestine, Egypt, Macedonia, Epirus, and Italy.

PLINY, the Elder – 23-79 A.D.
>   Roman official and author. Wrote the renowned work titled, *Natural History*.

SCHEDIUS, ELIAS – Circa early 17th century A.D.
>   German historian, poet and scholar.

SICULUS, DIODORUS – Circa early 1st century B.C.
>   Greek historian. Traveled in Egypt during 60-57 B.C. His works: *Bibliotheca Historica* (a universal history).

STRABO – 63 B.C.-21 A.D.
>   Greek historian and geographer. Born in Asia Minor, moved to Italy. His works: *Historical Sketches* and *Geography*.

TACITUS, PUBLIUS CORNELIUS – 56/57-117 A.D.
>   Latin historian, orator and public official. His works: *Germania*, *Agricola*, *Dialogue on Orators*, *Histories*, *Annals*, and others.

VIRGIL (Publius Vergilius Maro) – 70-19 B.C.
>   Latin poet. Born in Andes, Italy. His works: *Eclogues*, *Aeneid,* and *Georgics*.

PREFACE

In the 18th century A.D. (1700s), the Christian church was under siege. Not from a foreign invader, nor from a philosophical belief, but from the rapidly advancing army of knowledge.

With the extinction of the Western Roman Empire in the fifth and sixth centuries A.D., the western world had plunged into the Medieval Era, commonly referred to as the Dark Ages. The various barbarian nations, left unconquered by the Romans and unrestrained, continually struggled for supremacy over the continent until the establishment of the first European states of Italy, Germany, and France around the ninth century A.D.

During this time, the Roman church gradually extended control over the periodic rulers and monarchs of the indigenous clans in Europe. By the 11th century A.D., western Christianity had been established over kingdoms, kings, and commoners alike. With Rome as the seat of Christian power, the Roman Pontiff was accorded infallibility in all matters of faith over what would become the Holy Catholic Church of the new Christian empire.

The Christian monasteries of the medieval period were the source of the true character and form of modern Christianity. Century after century, monkish scribes recorded, rewrote, and embellished ancient Biblical scriptures, and, on numerous occasions, exorcised passages and even whole books of the old Bible that were not acceptable to Church interpretation.

Then, in the 16th century A.D., Martin Luther's attempts to correct the many injustices being perpetuated by the Catholic Church led to the Protestant movement, or the Reformation. Unfortunately, this split resulted only in a division of intolerance and did little to bring peace, harmony, and enlightenment to the peoples of Europe, and it also doubled the plague of Bible alterations. History claims that this schism would herald the end of the Medieval or Dark Ages. Unfortunately, for many, its effects would be felt for decades.

In the 17th century A.D., like an exorable tide, an undercurrent of rebellion against the church's suppressing authority began to creep across the continent. For centuries, the nations' scholarly communities had been suffocating under threat of excommunication or death from expressing anything that would challenge the clergy's concept of Biblical scripture or their arcane religious beliefs. But this engagement of wills would not be postponed any longer, for the forces of free expression had spread throughout Europe.

By the dawn of the 18th century A.D., Europe was in a revival of knowledge and development. This time of enlightenment could no longer be restrained by the bastion of the church – it was as though the continent had awakened from a long slumber. Questions abounded not only of the future, but also of antiquity. In the light of this new insight, the very foundation and beliefs of Christianity did not escape the scrutiny of the questioning academics. Of paramount debate among skeptics and believers was the veracity of one particular Bible story, which seemed to fly in the face of reason: EXODUS.

The church clergy, however, would not be the ones to combat the challenge to this most sacred of Christian traditions. It would ultimately be the fundamental Christian Bible scholar of both Catholic and Protestant persuasions who would take up the banner for God's word. These learned disciples came forward to the front ranks of the Faith, deciding that this heresy could be defeated only by proving that the Exodus did actually take place. With this revelation, the religious devotees from the nations of England, France, Germany and others, dispatched archaeological expeditions to Egypt – fabled site of the roots of Israel.

For decades, excursions dug, poked, and prodded the desiccated sands of the Egyptian Nile delta, assuming that they would unearth the ancient rubble of the places told about in the Bible story. Year after year, individual scholars pilgrimaged to the "land of the Pharaohs," confident they would be a defender of the Faith by finding at least one of the fabled sites. Eventually, the featureless landscape of the eastern Nile delta began to give up the long forsaken remnants that once were – what archaeologists dared not to believe – the actual sites through which Moses was supposed to have led his people.

The work continued unabated through the 1800s and into the 20th century A.D., only interrupted by the advent of two world wars. Eventually, the explorers from the various nations were to publish their findings. The information presented in countless volumes opened new vistas for understanding and enlightenment into the origins of religious belief, human mythology, and diverse cultures. Unfortunately, the books giving this knowledge were so vast, enigmatic, and unsettling in nature to the religious community that they were unceremoniously relegated to dusty library bookshelves and all but forgotten.

Fate, however, was to play a capricious role with the results of the scholars' discoveries. Since the archeologists and historians were from different countries, there had been little collaboration between them; therefore, the knowledge was not shared, much less ever correlated. But when the findings from all the books were combined and reviewed as one effort, a vastly divergent picture was revealed than the one hoped for by the participants – the Exodus was, in fact, really only a legend.

Up until the mid 20th century A.D. (1900s), these European books were unobtainable in the United States. But with the advent of the inter-library loan, a vista of research opened up the floodgates of knowledge into every subject imaginable. Thus, with the ability of obtaining European books, it was in the early 1960s A.D. that this author was led into a forty-year study of religious history, which culminated in this analysis of the Exodus story.

This book will present the facts, discoveries, and other evidence from historians and archaeologists, from Egyptian and Middle Eastern history, and from the Judeo-Christian Scriptures themselves, establishing that the Exodus story is only mythology. Ironically, the information presented by the author reveals that the story, to its credit, does use many historical facts and locations to build the account, but this same information, however, does not substantiate what has been taught to Christians and Jews for centuries.

The key to this esoteric tale lies in the phrase, "land of Rameses" (GENESIS 47:11), which has always been openly evident, but which no scholar, to date, has been fully willing or able to grasp. The author has finally, for the first time, positively placed the Exodus tale in the proper chronological time frame, which hinges upon the pharaonic title, "Ramesses".

First, it is necessary to present an explanation of Egyptian political and religious history from the Hyksos invasion (about 1720 B.C.) to the XIX Dynasty (about 1305 B.C.). This, then, will establish the basis for the abandonment of the typically ethnic Egyptian Pharaonic titles and the subsequent unprecedented adoption of a title of Asiatic origination: Ramesses I, first pharaoh of Dynasty XIX.

Next, the author examines the convoluted and esoteric ancient mythology surrounding the title, "Ramesses," then proceeds to reveal the fact, which is virtually unknown to western scholars to this date, that the name, "Rameses," had its origin in the far-off land of India.

During the remainder of the book, the author examines the Exodus story from many accounts, placing the Judeo-Christian Scriptures in juxtaposition with historical evidence, revealing:

1. Why the Exodus fable had to take place no earlier than Dynasty XIX.

2. What pharaohs would have ruled during the story.

3. The true source of the Exodus legend.

4. Where the Israelites would have gone, according to the Judeo-Christian Scriptures, Egyptian history, and archaeological discoveries.

5. When the Exodus would have taken place according to all available evidence.

6. That, according to Judaeo-Christian Scriptures, the "promised land" is not today's Israel.

7. How the centuries-old Bible land maps of the Exodus route were surreptitiously altered to reflect modern archaeological discoveries.

8. Other facts about the clan of Israel, which put in question the teachings of the Christian and Jewish faiths.

The title "God" is not used in this work, except for direct quotes. "God" is the English term for the Christian creator and does not represent the creator names of the Egyptians or Hebrews. "Deity" is used in place of the title God.

All quotes from the Judeo-Christian Scriptures are taken from the "King James Version," 1972, Thomas Nelson, Publishers. Italics used in the quotes are those of the author and are not from the scriptures.

FOREWORD

The Exodus Account from the Judaeo-Christian Bible

The Exodus story, as related in GENESIS of the Old Testament, really begins in lower Canaan where the Hebrew Jacob (also called Israel) was living. Of all his children, Jacob loved his son, Joseph, the best.

The other sons, jealous of Joseph, plot his death, but later sell him to Midianite traders, who take him into Egypt. There he is sold to the Egyptian Potiphar, an officer of the pharaoh. Later, Potiphar's wife accuses Joseph of mocking her. Joseph is thrown in jail and, while there, interprets the dreams of two fellow prisoners.

Two years later, while Joseph is still in prison, the pharaoh of Egypt has disturbing dreams. He asks his wise men to tell him their meaning, but the wise men fail to do so. Eventually, pharaoh hears about Joseph's ability to interpret dreams, and pharaoh sends for him. Joseph tells the king his dreams mean that Egypt will have seven years of plenty followed by seven years of famine. Then Joseph tells pharaoh that he should appoint officers over the land to collect one-fifth of the produce during the seven years of plenty and then store the grain for the coming famine. Pharaoh makes Joseph governor over the land of Egypt to carry out this plan.

Famine finally arrives and extends into Canaan. After two years of drought, Joseph sends for his father, Jacob, and family, who are starving and whose flocks are dying.

When his kin arrive in Egypt, Joseph settles them in the "land of Goshen." Later he brings Jacob (Israel) before pharaoh, who officially gives Jacob a possession in the "land of Rameses."

Eventually, the famine is so severe that the money fails and the people are destitute. Joseph then buys all the land of Egypt for pharaoh, moves the people into cities, and distributes to each peasant a plot of land, of which he takes one-fifth of the harvest for pharaoh.

During this time, the tribe of Israel flourishes, growing and multiplying exceedingly in the "land of Rameses."

Jacob passes away after living in Egypt for 17 years. Then later, Joseph's life ends after his sojourn in Egypt for over 80 years. The Hebrews continue to multiply after Joseph's death and fill the land.

"Now arose a new king over Egypt" who was afraid the Hebrews were so numerous that they might join pharaoh's enemies in an uprising. So pharaoh places them under bondage to build the cities of Pithom and Raamses. When this does not work, pharaoh commands that every Hebrew son born should be cast into the river.

This, then, is when the Hebrew child (called Moses) is born. He is placed in a basket on the river, where a daughter of pharaoh finds him. He is given to a Hebrew woman to raise but eventually is brought up in the house of pharaoh.

When Moses was grown, he murders an Egyptian for beating a Hebrew slave. Realizing that he is in trouble with the king, he flees to Midian. After a long time in Midian, Moses' deity tells him that the pharaoh who was seeking his life has died. His deity then commands him to return to Egypt and lead the Hebrew/Israelite slaves in an Exodus from the Land of the Pharaohs.

Progress of a Story

"When first told, it was said to be a lie.
A few years later, it was referred to as a fake.
After 25 years, it had become a fable.
After two centuries, it was called a myth.
After five centuries, it was tradition.
One thousand years had made it into an accepted belief.
And at the end of two thousand years it had been
Proclaimed as a dogma of faith."

Anonymous

Egyptian Mural

CHAPTER I

Setting the Stage for the Exodus Story

Ramesses I

Somewhere around the year 3000 B.C., Pharaoh Menes united Upper and Lower Egypt under one ruler. Many centuries passed, with each succeeding pharaoh taking various and all manner of ethnic names such as: Cheops (Khufu), Shepseskara, Pepy, Neferkara, Menthu-hotep, Sesostris, Taa-ken, Tuthmosis (see Egyptian King List, pages 4-5). Even with the conquest of Lower Egypt between 1720-1575 B.C. by a Semitic people called the Hyksos, the ethnic name quality did not change. This occurred later after the reconquest and return of Egyptian authority by Taa-aa, first king of Dynasty XVII, 1575 B.C.

With the assumption of Amenophis IV (Akhenaten) in 1364 B.C., Eastern influence in Egypt reached its zenith, causing a time of crisis for the Egyptian religious order. The Pharaoh Akhenaten abandoned the pantheon of deities worshipped for so many centuries in a revolutionary effort to reform the Egyptian mythology by integrating abstruse Middle Eastern contemporary religious thought of a pronounced single deity or savior. This was based upon the shift of belief in a new savior that was to rule over a new astrological period every 600 years, which had originated in India thousands of years earlier. This revolution was short-lived, however, with the established priesthood engineering Akhenaten's demise. In the waning years of Dynasty XVIII, Egypt was rift by a time of upheaval from the internal turmoil caused in returning to the ancient ways of worship and from military campaigns to repulse the invasion of the Nile Delta by Assyrian warriors. This period from 1374-1305 B.C., which included Smenkhkare, Tutankhamun (the boy king), Ay, and Horemheb left Egypt in a state of impotence and ineptitude, unable any longer to retain its vassal states or rule itself. Out of this chaos came a rebirth of purpose and will in Egyptian nationalism with the assumption of a new pharaoh who was to be the creator of a new order, a new dynasty, Dynasty XIX of Egypt.

With the investiture of Ramesses I to the throne, the Ramesside name first appeared in the Egyptian King List. It had no inherent or genealogical relationship to the old pharaonic indigenous national purity. Where did this interloping name originate, and by what process did it become subtly absorbed into the Egyptian hierarchy? How did it emerge as the title to be carried by more pharaohs than any other in Egyptian history? To properly understand the etymological interpolation, it is necessary to review the geopolitical and religious scene of preceding centuries.

From Hyksos Invasion to Dynasty XIX

The natural isolation offered to the inhabitants of the Nile river valley crucible by the surrounding torrid deserts not only kept them from military intrusion, but allowed them the unique ability to retain their ways and beliefs, uninterrupted throughout Egyptian history – that is, until the Hyksos invasion. For many hundreds of decades, the upper caste of Egypt had meticulously retained a purity of race, customs, and mythology. This ethnically sterile practice was so prevalent that all non-Egyptians were considered unclean, and it was emphatically forbidden to as much as share a meal with such impure people.

Eventually, however, as Egypt's power and influence spread throughout the Middle East and Mediterranean area, they were drawn into trade with the very peoples whom they thought of as so disgustingly unclean. Egyptian ideas, theologies, and customs were exchanged with the contemporary inhabitants of the Aegean, Mediterranean, and a host of Middle Eastern societies.

Then, in the year 1725 B.C., an invasion of Semitic nomads, later labeled the "Hyksos," swept down upon the seemingly invincible Egyptian people. Within a short period, these Semitics (probably Arabian) had conquered and occupied the entire Nile delta region, extending their control as far south as the town of Cusae, 25 miles south of Hermopolis (see Land of Egypt Map, next page). Their astonishing triumph over the army of the Nile, which for centuries had been invincible, was due to the devastating effects of chariot warfare used by these aliens against the overconfident Egyptians who had never seen this revolutionary weapon of battle.

This humiliating occupation of the Hyksos, loosely interpreted as "Shepherd People," derived from the phrase Hegau-khasut ("the rulers of foreign countries", taken from the Egyptian writings called the "Story of Si-nuhe"), lasted for approximately 150 years. During this time, as written by Egyptian scribes, "all type and manner of crimes were committed to the holy places which were an abomination against the deities." Their reign, for those many humiliating decades, saw the spread of Semitic religious practices into the once unadulterated, timeless land of the pharaohs. Unencumbered, trade was conducted by the interlopers with the diverse inhabitants of the Mediterranean. No longer could Egypt's military might and natural sheltering topography inhibit the dispersion of foreign mythology and worship among the conquered natives. It also could not stop the eventual assimilation and intertwining of Semitic legends with the pantheon of deities that were worshipped in the country of the red and white feather, symbols of Lower and Upper Egypt.

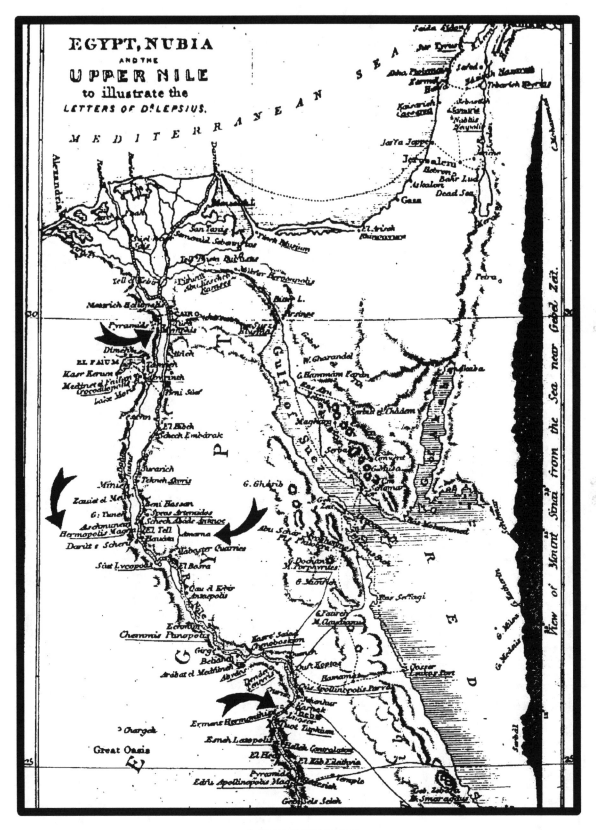

LAND OF EGYPT

EGYPTIAN KINGS LIST
ARCHAIC PERIOD: 3200 TO 2680 B.C.

Dynasty I: 3200-2980 B.C.

Narmer }
Aha   } Menes
Zer (Ity): 19 + years
Zet
Wedymu (Khasey)
Az-ib (Mer-pa-ba): 20 + years
Semerkhet (Shemsu?) 9 years

Qay-aa (Sen-mu)

Dynasty II: 2980-2780 B.C.

Ra-neb
Hetep-sekhemuwy

Netery-mu: 22 + years
Peribsen (Sekhem-ib Per-en-maat)
Sened
Kha-sekhem

Kha-sekhemuwy: 17 years

Dynasty III: 2780-2680 B.C.

Zoser (Neterkhet): 19 years
Sa-nekht
Kha-ba (Tety ?)
Neb-ka (Neb-ka-ra)
Huni (Hu): 24 years

OLD KINGDOM: 2680 TO 2258 B.C.

Dynasty IV: 2680-2565 B.C.

Sneferu: 24 years
Cheops (Khufu): 23 years
Radedef: 8 years
Chephren (Khafra): 25(?) years
Bikheris (Ba-ka-ru?): 1(?) year
Mycerinus (Menkaura): 28(?) years
Shepseskaf: 4 years
Thampthis (Dedef-ptah?): 2 years

Dynasty V: 2565-2420 B.C.

Weserkaf: 7 years
Sahura: 14 years
Neferirkara: 10 years
Shepseskara (Isy): 7 years

Neferefra: ? years
Ne-user-ra: 30(?) years
Men-kau-hor: 8 years
Isey (Zedkara): 39(?) years
Unas: 30 years

Dynasty VI: 2420-2258

Tety: 12 years
Weserkara: 1(?) year
Pepy I: 49 years (Mernera probably co-regent
Mernera: 14(?) years; 5 years of reign alone
Pepy II: 94(?) years
Mernera II: 1 year

FIRST INTERMEDIATE PERIOD: 2258 TO 2052 B.C.

Dynasty VII: Interregnu
Dynasty VIII: (Memphite) 2258-2232 B.C.
Dynasty IX: (Heracleopolitan): 2232-2180 B.C.
  Khety I (Mer-ib-ra): 2232-2215 B.C.
  5 kings of Turin Papyrus: 2215-2140
Dynasty X: (Heracleopolitan): 2180-2152 B.C.
  5 kings of Turin Papyrus: 2180-2040 B.C.
  Neferkara: 2140-2120 B.C.
  Khety II (Wah-ka-ra): 2120-2090 B.C.
  Merikara: 2090-2070 B.C.
  Khety III (Neb-kau-ra): 2070-2052 B.C.
Fall of Heracleopolis to Menthu-hotep II: 2052 B.C.

Contemporary with Dynasties IX-X:
  Intefs: Princes of Thebes: 2232-2134 B.C.

Dynasty XI in South: **2134-2052**

  Intel I   (Seher-tawy): 2134-2130 B.C.
  Intel II   (Wah-ankh): 2130-2081 B.C.
  Intel IIII (Nekht-neb-tep-nefer): 2081-2079 B.C.
  Menthu-hotep I (Se-ankh-ib-tawy):2079-2061 B.C.
  Menthu-hotep II (Neb-hepet-ra): 2079-2052 B.C.

Fall of Heracleopolis to Menthu-hotep II: 2052 B.C.

MIDDLE KINGDOM: 2052 TO 1786 B.C.

Dynasty XI: United Egypt: 2052-1991 B.C.

  Menthu-hotep II: 2052-2010
      Menthu-hotepIII(Se-ankh-kara):2010-1998B.C.

Civil wars plus short reign of
  Menthu-hoptep IV (Neb-tawy-ra): 1998-1991 B.C.

Dynasty XII: 1991-1786 B.C.

  Amenemhat I (Sehetep-ib-ra): 1991-1961 B.C.
  Sesostris I (Keper-ka-ra): 1971-1928 B.C.
  Amenemhat II (Neb-kau-ra): 1929-1895 B.C.
  Sesostris II (Kha-kheper-ra): 1897-1878 B.C.
  Sesostris III (Kha-kaura): 1878-1842 B.C.
  Amenemhat III (Ny-maat-ra): 1842-1797 B.C.
  Amenemhat IV (Maat-kheru-ra): 1798-1789 B.C.
      Queen Sebek-neferura: 1789-1786 B.C.

SECOND INTERMEDIATE PERIOD: 1786 TO 1570 B.C.

Dynasties XIII-XIV: 1786-1680 B.C.
Period of political disintegration: circa 30 kings
Dynasties XV – XVI (Kyksos): 1720-1570 B.C.
(Local rulers at Thebes forming Dynasty XVI)
Khian (Se-weser-en-ra)
Apepi (Aa-weser-ra)

Aa-seh-ra
Apepi (Aa-kenen-ra)
Dynasty XVII: 1600-1570 B.C.
Taa-aa
Taa-ken (Sekenenra)
Kamose (Waz-kheper-ra)

NEW KINGDOM: 1570-1985 B.C.

Dynasty XVIII: 1570-1349 B.C.
Ahmose I: 1570-1545 B.C.
Amenhotep I: 1545-1525 B.C.
Tuthmosis I: 1525-1508 B.C.
Tuthmosis II: 1508-1504 B.C.
Hatsheput: 1504-1483 B.C.
Tuthmosis III: 1504-1450 B.C.
Amenhotep II: 1450-1423 B.C.
Tuthmosis IV: 1423-1410 B.C.
Amenhotep III: 1410-1372 B.C.
Semenkhkara: 1364-1362 B.C.
Tut-ankh-amen: 1362-1353 B.C.
Ay: 1353-1349 B.C.
Horemheb: 1349-1314 B.C.

►►*Dynasty XIX: 1349-1197 B.C.*
Ramesses I: 1314-1313 B.C.
★Sety I: 1313-1301 B.C.
Ramesses II: 1301-1234 B.C.
Merenptah: 1234-1222 B.C.
Amen-meses: 1222 B.C.
Siptah (Merenptah): 1222-1216 B.C.
Sety II: 1216-1210 B.C.
Siptah (Ramesses)
Irsu (?) 1210-1197 B.C.
Dynasty XX: 1197-1085 B.C.
Sety-nekht: 1197-1195 B.C.
Ramesses III: 1195-1164 B.C.
Ramesses IV-XI: 1164-1085 B.C.

PERIOD OF DECLINE: 1085-603 B.C.

Dynasty XXI: 1085-950 B.C.

(Tanite Dynasty; priest kings in Thebes)
Smendes:
Herihor (Thebes): 1085-1054 B.C.
Psusennes I (Pasebkhanu):
Paynozem (Thebes): 1054-1009 B.C.
Amen-em-ipet: 1009-1000 B.C.
Sa-amen: 1000-984 B.C.
Psusennes II (Pasebkhanu): 984-950 B.C.
Dynasty XXII: (Bubastite) 950-730 B.C.:
Libyan kings
Sheshonq I: 950-929 B.C.
Osorkon I: 920-893 B.C.
Takelot I: 893-870 B.C.
Osorkon II: 870-847 B.C.
Sheshonq II: 847 B.C.
Takelot II: 847-823 B.C.
Sheshonq III: 823-772 B.C.
Pami: 772-767 B.C.
Sheshonq V: 767-730 B.C.
Partly contemporaneous with Dynasty XXII:
Dynasty XXIII: 817(?)-730 B.C.
(Dates only approximate for following kings):
Pedibast: 817-776 B.C.

Sheshonq IV: 763-757 B.C.
Osorkon III: 757-748 B.C.
Takelot III:
Rud-amen: 748-730 B.C.
Osorkon IV:
Dynasty XXIV: 730-715 B.C.
Tef-nekht: 730-720 B.C.
Bocchoris (Bakenrenef): 720-715 B.C.
Partly contemporaneous with Dynasties XXIII-XXIV:
Dynasty XXV: (Kushite: Ethiopian) 751-656 B.C.
Kashta
Piankhy: 751-716 (Conquest of Egypt: Circa 730)
Shabako: 716-701 B.C.
Shebitku: 701-690 B.C.
Tahurqa: 690-664 B.C.
Tanwetamani: 664-653 B.C.

Assyrians in Egypt; 671 B.C., sack of Memphis under Esarhaddon; 663 B.C., sack of Thebes by Ashurbanipal; 638-631 B.C., Psamtik I gains control of country.

SATI PERIOD: 663 TO 525 B.C.

Dynasty XXV: (Kushite: Ethiopian) 753-656 B.C.
Psamtik I (Wah-ib-ra): 663-609 B.C.
Necho (Nekau, Wehem-ib-ra): 609-594 B.C.
Psamtik II (Nefer-ib-ra): 594-588 B.C.

Apries (Haa-ib-ra): 588-568 B.C.
Amasis (Ahmes-sa-neith, Khnum-ib-ra): 568-525
Psamtik III (Ankh-ka-en-ra): 525 B.C.

During that time, the foreign rulers abolished all the ancient political and religious deities and supplanted instead a similar pantheon that was indigenous to the invaders.

The banishment of the old deities and introduction of the Hyksos national deities was eventually to prove the lesser concern of the two issues. The dismal reality of being disenfranchised from ruling politics in everyday existence for the Egyptians far overshadowed the self-induced integrity of their spiritual beliefs. Their national pride was the preeminent force that made foreign domination intolerable and continually separated the two societies.

The Egyptians chafed under the rule of the Hyksos occupation of the lower Nile; however, as the decades wore on, the split in Egyptian religious continuity came to be filled as each new generation was exposed to the cult practices of the captors. Since politics and religion are inextricably intertwined, the Egyptians found it expedient to look favorably on the Hyksos guardian figures. Eventually, the belief in the purity of their own worship and abhorrence toward foreign deities began to wane as it became evident that, except for proper names, the similarity in categories and duties of the opposing pantheons had, in fact, sprung from a common root. Whether it be dispensing protection from evil spirits, punishment of evildoers, nurturing of the earth, control of life and death, or myriad other areas affecting human life, the counterpart to the Egyptian deity performed the same task and only the name was dissimilar. Again, all this was related to humans assigning an ethereal connotation to natural but unexplainable phenomena of life.

By the 17th century B.C., Asiatic deities had begun to infiltrate the Egyptian deity system and, by the 15th century, an abundance of these formerly abhorred divinities were firmly entrenched in the daily life of the Nile Delta inhabitants. Most prominent of these was the deity Set (Seth). This one deity alone was to have major influence in reshaping the religious pantheon of Lower Egypt.

Prior to the Hyksos invasion, the female and male co-divinites, Isis and Osiris (heaven and earth), were in a preeminent position in the Delta region. As time passed and the Asiatic deity Set (patron divinity of the Hyksos) assumed a more dominant role over all the delta inhabitants, there arose a relationship of conflict between the Asiatic deities and the time-honored deities still worshipped by the Egyptians living under the unconquered pharaohs of the XV and XVI Dynasties, who ruled Upper Egypt from their capital, Thebes. The decades of struggle between Egyptian and Asiatic political factions was reflected religiously in the struggle between Set (Seth) and Osiris.

Eventually, the Egyptians in the Nile valley rebuilt their army and resolved as a nation to wrest their land back from the hated Asiatics. The revolt took place around 1600 B.C., under the Pharaoh Taa-aa (Dynasty XVII). In 1575 B.C., after a series of battles, the Egyptians successfully drove the Hyksos back into the deserts of Sinai.

The religious significance of the Egyptian's victory over the Semitic shepherds was to be seen from the 16th century on, where Set (Seth) became the Egyptian equivalent of an Asiatic enemy deity. Conversely, when the Hyksos were driven out, Osiris (who, mythologically, had been killed by the Asiatic Set or Typhon and replaced by him during the Hyksos rule) was reborn as a prominent deity in "Horus" (see G. Higgins, *Anacalypsis*, Volume I, page 102 for Osirian mythological story). It is evident how far the infiltration of Asiatic mythology had penetrated the Egyptian religion and life over the centuries because the very name Horus (Hor-us) is of Assyrian derivation (G. Higgins, *Anacalypsis*, Volume II). The deities of the Asiatic nomads in the delta were of the wilderness whom the Egyptians identified with Seth, the enemy of Horus, who was the deity representing the cultivated land.

After undisputed control had been extended over the delta by the Egyptians and national allegiance reestablished, a new order or "New Kingdom," as it came to be called, arose under the title "Dynasty XVIII".

With the expulsion of the Hyksos, Upper and Lower Egypt were once again reunited under one government and absolute political power of the red and white feather. Remaining, however, were foreigners who had come to call the Nile Delta home, whether they were the remnants of the former Asiatic conquerors, who had sworn allegiance to the victorious Egyptians, or peoples from the diverse countries ringing the eastern Mediterranean basin, who had come to settle in the Delta during those years of the Hyksos reign. However, the Egyptians were incapable of driving the old deities and practices from the minds of these alien inhabitants as well as from their many Egyptian-born offspring and from older Egyptians who had embraced the foreign pantheon for one reason or another.

The expediency of political and commercial reality was eventually to overpower the millennia of the Egyptian inhabitants' narrow cultic belief, which had espoused religious purity of thought and culture resulting in their abhorrence of all things foreign. Prior to and during the Hyksos occupation, commerce among the countries of the eastern Mediterranean had gradually increased to the point that by Dynasty XVIII it was a flourishing business. The Asiatics had opened the formerly tightly sealed gates of the "Land of the Nile" to traders who actively sought the many products of the Delta region, such as linen, glass, textiles, and a substance on which Egypt almost held a monopoly: papyrus.

The reoccupation of the Delta brought the victorious pharaonic rulers of Dynasty XVIII face to face with an obvious fact that they could no longer ignore, and that was: Commerce is the life's-blood of a nation. The formerly puristic Egyptians could now relax their standards, especially under the incentive of such lucrative overseas business pouring gold into Pharaoh's treasury.

The depth of Asiatic influence on religious thought in Egyptian life became abundantly obvious during Dynasty XVIII as people of non-Egyptian origin slowly began to infiltrate the political offices of the land. The geographical and political seat of power also began to shift gradually toward the Delta, the religious seat remaining in Thebes in Upper Egypt, as commerce between Egypt and her Mediterranean and mid-Eastern neighbors assumed more and more importance to the country's wealth and prestige.

Akhenaten and Eastern Influence

All doubt was vanquished as to the depth of foreign religious impact on Egyptian belief with the ascension of the tenth pharaoh of Dynasty XVIII, carrying the title of "Amenhotep IV," or, as he later retitled himself, "Akhenaten."

From within their own system arose a king who rejected the accepted pantheon of deities, and abandoned the priesthood and temples consecrated to the ancient divinities. He turned, instead, to a heretical belief that revolved around a single deity, who he called "Aten" (this belief was another form of sun worship which was the result of the belief in astrological cycles of the zodiac).

As strange and ambiguous as this deviation seemed for an anointed pharaoh of ancient lineage to postulate, it only reaffirmed the contention that Eastern transcendental thought and belief had now become an integral constituent of Egyptian life. Even though it may seem that way to contemporary scholars, Akhenaten's single-deity worship was not new or original – he had only fallen sway to an ancient theology, which had gradually found its way into the Nile Valley.

Akhenaten's belief had its roots firmly established in astrological worship prevalent throughout the Middle East. This theology was based upon centuries of astronomical observations of the Earth's phenomenon called the "precession of the equinoxes" by a mystical clan living in northern Indian in very ancient times. They had devised a system to divide the precession time into 12 periods, each beginning when the sun entered into a new zodiacal sign. Later, even another astrological system arose that encompassed a 6,000 year era based upon 10 luni-solar periods of 600 years (Avatars). Each period had begun at the vernal equinox on March 25.

Ancient Observance of Vernal Equinox

The vernal equinox takes place when the sun's center crosses the equator and coincides with the equinoctial point about March 21st, making the hours of darkness and light of equal length. This time heralded the celebration of the spring rite. Ancient mythology relates that the fertility deity was put to death with vegetation during the winter season. At the vernal equinox (spring), the deity is resurrected from the underworld in all growing things.

Because of the precession of the equinoxes, the date of the vernal equinox continues a gradual change until it eventually returns to the same date after 26,000 years. In 45 B.C., during the reign of the Roman emperor Julius Caesar, the date of the vernal equinox was March 25th.

The Hebrew Passover is to have originated during the Israelites time in Egypt (Exodus 12). Coincidentally, it was the exact time that the Jewish/Christian Jesus was to have been crucified and resurrected. Using the old lunar calendar, this celebration was supposed to fall on the 14th day of the full moon in the month Nisan (the Christian month of March). The determination of this date was a secret process jealously guarded in the Jewish temple. (The Encyclopedia Americana; 1962: page 506.)

Later a dispute arose between the eastern and western Roman Christian churches, about the time of celebrating Easter. In the First Council of Nice (Nicaea) convened under Constantine I (claimed to be the first Christian emperor), Easter day was placed on the first Sunday after the full moon that falls on, or next after, the 21st of March, the vernal equinox. If the full moon happens on Sunday, Easter is celebrated one week later. (New Catholic Encyclopedia, II Edition, Volume 5, page 12.) This dating was accomplished by using the more accurate solar calendar.

At Nicaea, it was decided that the announcement of Easter day be referred to Alexandria, Egypt, the citadel of astronomy, where the bishop there was to declare the date each year. (Church History; Wharey; page 37. Published by the Presbyterian Board of Publication.)

Whether it be the date of the Hebrew Passover (deliverance, also supposed death of Jesus) or the Christian Easter (supposed death and resurrection of Jesus), the fact is plainly evident that what is being celebrated is the ancient passing of the vernal equinox or spring rite at the end of March or early April. This time was part of a religious system that had originated in the sub-continent of India, millennia prior to the time of either Hebrews or Christians (Anacalysis, Higgins; Volume II, Chapter III, pages 24-25, 801. Volume I, Book II, Chapter II, Section 10, page 83.)

In time, the system was formulated into a religious practice. The priesthood of this belief eventually came to develop a doctrine that proclaimed that each new cycle was the beginning of an era of renewal, instituted by a messiah or savior who would to rule over that period.

Just prior to Akhenaten's reign, a new cycle had begun. Throughout the ancient world, a new Messiah was being heralded. Of course, no accurate records are available to show who the new Messiah was during this period; however, strong evidence points to a mystery cult prophet/teacher, Zoroaster, who was later deified by his followers and lived in the area later known as Persia. As usual, the existing myths and allegory revolving around its originator, whose name was rendered in earlier times as "Abraham Zoradust," has made it almost impossible to pinpoint his chronological origin.

Evidence shows that the cult of the Magi (Persian astronomers) became corrupt and was reformed before the time of Cyrus the Great, King of Persia (circa 529 B.C.) by this individual later called Zoroaster. Because of the strong presence of Asiatics in his court, Akhenaten was undoubtedly influenced by India/Middle Eastern astrological belief, which revolved around sun worship, already an integral constituent of the Egyptian faith.

Akhenaten's radical departure from the accepted religious practices of Egypt was swiftly truncated, however, between 1364-1347 B.C. His reign was to expose the first solid evidence of how far other Asiatic philosophies had penetrated the religious system of the Nile Valley. After closing the temples and confiscating the vast estates of the priests who administered the worship of the popularly accepted pantheon of deities headed by Amun, Akhenaten came into direct conflict with that entrenched priesthood. This purely Egyptian-originated cult, developed over millennia, had guaranteed financial security to that host of self-anointed authorities over the unknown who rely upon the general populous for their subsistence. This challenge to their power and influence over the Nile inhabitants was to unite them in a coalition of jealousy and hatred guaranteed to ensure that not even pharaoh, "Son of Amun, an earthly representative of the deities," could succeed in banishing "the only true deities" and their divinely appointed ministers for some heathen imposter.

The reigning clergy almost assuredly held a typical stranglehold on worship in all the communities along the Nile, so it can be strongly assumed that regardless of his quasi-divinity, which all pharaohs claimed (unfortunate, because that divinity placed them in that realm the priesthood governed), Akhenaten undoubtedly met with the vehement animosity of Amun's priesthood whenever he attempted to establish the worship of his new deity within a city.

Undeterred in his belief, Akhenaten resorted to an unprecedented course of action by proceeding to build a new capital city dedicated to his deity, "Aten." To dwell in this metropolis he called "Akhenaten" (modern-day Tell Armarna – see Land of Egypt map, page 3), he brought and invited all those who would give allegiance to this new faith. He built many magnificent temples and staffed them with a new priesthood consecrated to the worship of pharaoh's munificent heavenly benefactor. The whole municipal area was guarded by strong detachments of mercenaries, among whom, strangely enough, were large numbers of Nubian and Asiatic foreigners.

It is unlikely that "Aten" was widely accepted among the Egyptians, and, therefore, it is debatable as to what ethnic background the general population of Akhenaten belonged. It is evident that his homeland did not totally reject his right to be Pharaoh, even though he had rejected the popular deities (maybe they were tired of them anyway), but Akhenaten was obviously under a strong influence of Eastern mythological thinking. This fact is unmistakable, for many of his administrative officials and even his own wife were of Asiatic origin. It seems likely that, in the unprejudiced atmosphere toward those of Asiatic heritage, this type people gravitated to Akhenaten, where the center of power in Egypt resided and chances of achievement in wealth and influence existed without hindrance from the existing structure. History does not leave us an accurate account of the concluding years in Amenhotep IV's (Akenaten's) reign. Officially, most historians have now agreed that the regnal dates should be 1364 to 1347 B.C., but records also indicate that another pharaoh, a son-in-law of Akhenaten, officially ruled during the period 1351 to 1347 B.C. under the title "Semenhkhara." Because of the highly ambiguous political and religious situation at the time, exact events are shrouded in mystery, leaving open the speculation: "Did Amun's priesthood wreak revenge upon the upstart pharaoh?"

The consummation of Dynasty XVIII carries with it an air of derision and political unrest as confirmed by the discovery of the extant "Amarna Letters", uncovered during the early years of the 20th century A.D. An event which added to the problems was that, some time in the mid-fourteenth century B.C., a tidal wave of Semitic barbarians began sweeping into Canaan and Syria from the Northern Arabian deserts, achieving a tenuous hold on mostly undisputed territories. The choice Mediterranean coastlands were firmly held by the Phoenicians or the newly arrived Philistines. This is verified by ancient records discovered in Amarna, the capital of Pharaoh Akhenaten, the heretic king. The rule of the remaining four pharaohs, after Akhenaten, was to be uneventful, marked only by the restoration of the Amun cult and its priesthood to their position of religious preeminence. Another heir of Amenhotep IV, who took the scepter of office following Semenkhara, was not to be just another enigmatic figure in the pages of history. It was due to the persistence of an amateur archaeologist named Howard Carter that this pharaoh's fabulously wealthy tomb was discovered during the early 20th century A.D., giving him the decided honor of being the most popularly known king in the history of Egypt. His rule, under the title, "Nebkheprure Tutankhamun" (1347-1337) originally Tutankhaten but changed his name under duress as Atenisum was obliterated, should be considered the last true pharaoh of Dynasty XVIII. The first of the remaining two rulers was "Ay" (1337-1333), known as "Title Father of the God" and "Inspector of the Chariot Troops." He had been guardian of the royal couple, because Tutankhamun and his wife were only children. Ay was followed by "Horemheb" (1333-1305), commander-in-chief and governor-general-autocrat in Memphis. Both Ay and Horemheb were personages of dubious lineage, immersed in the ineptitude and confusion signaling the death throes of Dynasty XVIII.

It is certain that Egypt had plunged into turmoil when Horemheb assumed office as regent. Obscure records seem to reveal that the Egyptian army was handed a defeat at the hands of the Assyrian king, "Adad-nirari I" (1307-1275 B.C.), at about that time. Due to rivalry between in-country political factions, it is uncertain and only speculation whether Horemheb was to represent the last of a series of inept monarchs, concluding in the demise of Dynasty XVIII, or was instrumental in leading his nation from the shadows of disintegration and occupation.

Out of the ashes left from the years of religious and political upheaval arose the dawn of a new era, one that melded Egyptian-Asiatic belief and aspiration: Dynasty XIX. The first pharaoh chose a composite name reflecting many societies, a name of decidedly non-Egyptian origin, a title that was to be assumed by so many pharaohs to follow: Ramesses (Ramses) I.

Dynasty XIX

The rise of Dynasty XIX in 1305 B.C. brought a temporary resurgence in Egyptian power, when the pharaohs reestablished their hold over all worthwhile property from Canaan into Syria; however, this was to last only until around 1200 B.C. After the death of the third pharaoh of Dynasty XIX, Ramesses II (the Great), Egyptian power and possessions disintegrated rapidly.

Egyptian History – Basis for the Exodus Story

In the reign of Ramesses II's successor, Merneptah (1224-1204 B.C.), a plague broke out in the area of the Egyptian capital of Memphis. To halt the spread of disease, the pharaoh banished the leprous and unclean people, but allowed them to occupy the Mediterranean coastal town of Avaris (the old Hyksos capital) just outside the eastern frontier of Egypt. A large number of these outcasts, with the assistance of other Hebrew Semites from lower Canaan, were able to mount a rebellion against Egypt. After some years, this insurrection was crushed under Merneptah's son, Sety II (1204-1198 B.C.). The Hebrew Semites were driven "from the land of Ramesses" into the wilderness of Sinai, from where they returned to their homeland in Edom, known in modern times as the Negev Desert. They were seemingly under the leadership of a learned, charismatic individual who kept them together during this journey.

The Hebrews of the Exodus Story and their Beliefs

By Dynasty XXI, a period of decline, Egypt's power and influence in the Middle East waned into non-existence. The mainly *arid and uninhabited* hill country of lower Canaan was abandoned to a state of small tribal bickering over control of the few trading centers. Then, in the first part of the 10th century B.C. (900s), the predominately Hebrew tribes of Moab and Edom began making military incursions into lower Canaan. After many years, they were successful in obtaining a foothold over the hill country north of and around the old Ammorite city of Uru-Salim or Salem, later renamed Jeru-salem.

These Hebrew-Semites worshipped a varied pantheon of deities, representing the male and female principle. As a whole, these nomadic desert people were followers of the "Linga," or male principle. The generally accepted male deity of worship in Canaan was titled "El or Elon," meaning "Most High One". The Hebrew-Semites eventually absorbed the *clan title of Israel,* meaning champion of El, which had been used for centuries by the Phoenicians. In time, the Hebrew-Semite clans in the north intermixed with the older Canaanite-Semites, who were followers of the Yoni, or female principle, and eventually adopted their agrarian lifestyle and form of worship to keep harmony with the local population. For many years, the northern and southern clans squabbled to determine which principle of worship would prevail, the Yoni or Linga.

Although the northern tribes, known as Samaritans, lived in the most desirable fertile lands of the hill country, this was to place them at a great disadvantage in the power struggle with their southerly antagonists. Not only were they in the direct path of warring armies from Assyria, Mesopotamia, or Egypt, which frequently swept through the area, but their land was often occupied by these foreign powers, whose kings ruled the territory and forced the inhabitants to produce food for them. Finally, the militarily stronger clans, living in the isolated country around Jerusalem, were to establish dominance over the unwanted mountainous area of southern Canaan.

Unlike the image portrayed by most modern historians, the Hebrew-Semites had little impact upon the larger political arena. They were pawns of the larger nations of Egypt, Syria, Hittite, and Babylon, who controlled all worthwhile property and left the Hebrew-Semites to their towns in the *barren hill country* – as long as they paid taxes to the occupying nations and caused no disturbance.

Close examination of the Old Testament will clearly reveal that, as a whole, they worshipped the commonly accepted deities of the area and were never a nation that was monotheistic. The very diverse names given to their deity in the Old Testament of the Judaeo-Christian Bible – Jehovah, Yahweh, El, Elon, Jah, Adonis, Sabaoth, and Iao were applied to their protector at different periods during their history. These were titles that had been venerated anciently throughout the Middle East.

In the early 6th century B.C. (500s), after continual insurrection against Babylonian authority, the last of the disruptive Hebrew-Semites, called the Judah clan in the Old Testament, were removed totally into Mesopotamia (Babylon).

At the time that the patriarchal, or Linga-worshipping, Hebrew-Semites were brought to the land of the Tigris-Euphrates river valley, the Babylonians had been long-standing disciples of a more advanced religious philosophy. Based upon an ancient Indian astrological system of adoration, this philosophy had brought the male and female principles into a hermaphrodite union. The Hebrews were to come into direct confrontation with this method of worship.

Many centuries earlier, the individual worship of either male or female principle had given way to the concept of joint connection. This had been dictated by a prominent heavenly constellation (see Chapter II), gaining religious importance.

For decades, the Hebrews (the Judah clan of the Old Testament) had thought themselves a select group by retaining this early or pure form of male principle worship without images, while other societies around them were considered heathen because they practiced the idolatry of Yoni or Yoni-Linga worship. After many years attempting to hold themselves apart from their captors, the Hebrews were slowly to begin reverting to Babylonian worship and ways. In order to retain a hold on their clan, the Hebrew priesthood sought to instill the idea that their tribe was a chosen people and that they must remain separate in association and worship. Over time, this attitude was to take concrete form by translating their old traditions and new philosophies into written manuscripts. Within the body of this literature was incorporated not only the vague remembrances of 400-year-old oral tribal tales, but also the universally accepted ancient mythology of India.

A major proof that the Exodus story is mythology can be established when it becomes evident that the story of Moses' birth was identical to the birth of the great Babylonian conqueror and lawgiver, King Sargon of Akkad, who was born about 2370 B.C., as well as similar to many other religious cult heroes.

LANDS OF THE STORY

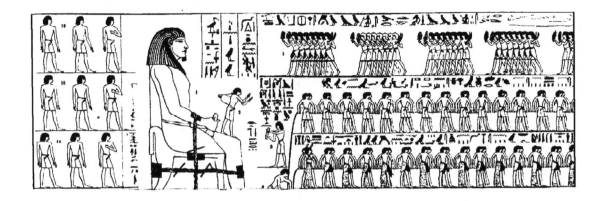

CHAPTER II

Origin of Ramesses Title

The previous chapter has clearly revealed that it was the continual infusion of Asiatic belief, beginning with the Hyksos invasion in 1725 B.C. that gradually restructured the purism of ancient Egyptian thought through a combining of diverse philosophies out of political and social necessity.

A new Egypt would arise by Dynasty XIX, a melting pot of many beliefs represented by a mingled society not only of those of Nile valley origin, but of people with roots in many foreign countries. It seemed logical, if not expedient, that this new "politic" should be identified with a new title reflecting this coalition, a symbol or banner, as such, where all would find allegiance for common support. The first pharaoh who was to assume rulership over this new era and society chose his appellation wisely, one that would represent all aspects of the diverse populous. That title would be one of an ancient lineage from far-off Asiatic lands: Ramesses I, first pharaoh of Dynasty XIX.

How the title Ramesses came into use can be readily understood only by presenting the origin of the Ramesside name. It will not only reveal how, but why, it came into use in Egypt. One will also glean unique knowledge into how the Hebrew-Israelite faith drew so abundantly upon earlier mythologies for its own development.

The convoluted etymology of the Ramesses (Ramses) title is so deeply enmeshed in a vast spectrum of Asiatic religious belief, covering such far-flung geographical areas and societies, that neither precise understanding nor totally clear source can be extracted from existing records. However, the many credible isolated facts that are available, when gathered together, present a preponderance of evidence leaving little doubt that the origin of "Ramesses" extends back into the subcontinent of India.

One of the primary sources of knowledge giving insight into the origin of "Ramesses" comes from the ancient southwestern Asian history, legend, and mythology surrounding the esoteric name of "Semiramis (Semi-Ramis)".

Semiramis (Myth or Fact)

The legendary "Semiramis" appears first in the works of Greek historian, Ctesias. He writes:

> "The progeny of mythological figures; after her birth from an egg, Semiramis was miraculously fed by doves, until she was found by 'Simmas,' the royal shepherd, who brought her up and married her to 'Onnes'."

The historian Diodorus Siculus expands the story in his work *Diodorus of Sicily, Book II,* 1-20, with:

> "Some time in the early second millennium [B.C.], Ninus, king of Assyria, having conquered the Caldeans [Babylonians], then proceeded for the next 17 years to subrogate all of western Asia, then the northern territory of the *Egyptian delta,* between Tanis and the Nile ...

> "It was during this campaign siege against Bactriana that Ninus beheld Semiramis, wife of Onnes, one of his generals. Ninus had Onnes killed by placing him at the forefront of battle, thereupon, Ninus took Semiramis to wife. Not long after Ninus died, leaving a son, Ninyas." [The pattern for the future tale of David & Bathsheba]

Siculus' tale continues with:

> "During her son's minority, Semiramis assumed the regency ... during her reign she built the city of Babylon ... left many memorials of her power and munificence ... which retained her name for ages. After this, she invaded Egypt and conquered Ethiopia, along with the greater part of Libya. Having accomplished her wishes ... she directed her forces toward the kingdom of India."

In both Greek and Hindu histories, it states:

> "This mythical queen is said to have fought a battle on the banks of the Indus River, with a king called Strabrobates,

which she was defeated, whereupon, she was crucified and
her soul then flew away in the *form of a dove*."

Semiramis' precise legendary or mythical origin is obscure. Some writers claim
she was the daughter of "Venus-Ataryatis, a fish deity, and "Oannes," a Babylonia deity of
wisdom. Semiramis was said to have been born at Ascalon, a coastal city in Canaan, but
her mother, Venus-Ataryatis was worshipped there under the name "Dagon" (half man, half
fish), the principal deity of the Philistines.

Many memorials were preserved at Ascalon, Hierapolis, and Babylon in Syria. These
memorials related to a history of which the *dove* was the principal type. It was upon the same
account that Semiramis was said to have been changed into a dove because she was always
found depicted and worshipped under that form.

Dove Mythology – Hindu Religious Astronomy

To all appearances, it would seem that the Semiramis legend had its roots in the
Middle East; however, in reality, its source was deeply embedded in Hindu religious belief
based upon a very ancient system of astronomical observations stretching back in time to at
least the 5th millennium B.C. (4000s) or even earlier.

Precession of the Equinoxes

Very anciently, an unknown race living in northern India had discovered and began
measuring the earth's wobbling phenomenon called "the precession of the equinoxes." At some
period antedating 5000 B.C., ancient astronomers of this society had divided the precessional
circumference consisting of 25,960 years into 12 periods. One of these periods, which began
around 4680 B.C., seemed to be the start of these observations. How they did this or for what
purpose caused them to choose 4680 B.C. as the beginning of their system is so difficult to
understand that it is the reason no one in the west is even aware of its existence.

Taurus-Buddha (Male Principle); Pleiades-Dove (Female Principle)

A very brief explanation of this mythology will be made because a detailed study is
beyond this work. In a future book, the complete study will reveal all details of this religious
system. At some time prior to 4680 B.C., the observations made by these ancient astronomers
were developed into a religious belief. Eventually, a priesthood arose that devised a pantheon
of deities to rule over an individual period. Again, at some unknown time, this priesthood
constructed a zodiacal system when the sun entered a new constellation every 2160 years.
Between 4680-2540 B.C., the sun was in the constellation Taurus. This was to become the
male principle of that arcane system.

It was also at this time – several millennia B.C. – that the worship of Buddha
originated. Contemporary scholars are mistaken in their belief that Buddha's birth and

subsequent veneration began much later, in about 600 B.C. (This enigma will be explained in a subsequent book). The son of the deity Maya, Buddha became the savior of that period. His life history was to be the model for the Christian savior, Jesus.

During that time, the ancient astronomers discovered that there was another star cluster, within the constellation of Taurus, which was eventually called "Pleiades". This star cluster gradually took on the function of the "female principle," with the dove as its emblem.

In very early times, clans of India became divided into an almost inconceivably large number of sects dedicated either to the male or female principle. The system of Buddha, or renewed incarnation, revolved around the principles of the Yoni (female) or Linga (male). Because its adherents believed this would end in a remote Grand Millennium some 6,000 years in the future, the jealousies and divisiveness of the Indian people were held in check.

However, some time around the third millennium B.C. (2000s) certain religious sects sought to bring these opposing principles into union. The conflicting philosophies sparked long and bloody cult wars, varying in different times and different states, called the Maha-barat. This ended a supposed golden age – the age of universal religion. During these conflicts, various sects, under different titles, were expelled to the west.

The Numbers 12 and 7

In one of these sects, either driven out of or emigrated from India, was to be found the ancient "Ionians". These people were chiefly found in Attica (modern Turkey) and on the most western coast of Asia Minor. They had a very fine country divided into twelve (12) states or tribes, in a confederacy, which all assembled at stated times to worship at a temple built by them in common. The story of the twelve tribes of Israel was developed after the Ionians.

The historian, Lucian, in *The Goddesse of Surrye* (Vol. IV, pages 379-80), states concerning the worship of the deity Juno at Hieropolis in Syria:

> "There are two Priapuses (pillars) in front of the temple, 300
> fathoms high, on which devotes went, at certain seasons, and
> remained seven (7) days." [This was the pattern for the later
> Hebrew temple.]

The number twelve (12) was anciently venerated because it was related to the twelve astrological symbols or twelve periods of time. The number seven (7) related to the seven prominently observable bodies in the nighttime sky, which were: Sun, Moon, Venus, Jupiter, Mars, Mercury, and Saturn. (See next page for astrological symbols.)

The Ionian cult deity was "Helen," which like Semiramis, was supposed to have been born out of a "waterfowl's egg". Her or his identification with Semiramis, or their mythological characters, can scarcely be doubted. The Septuagint version of Hebrew

The Sun, the Moon, Venus and the Host of Heaven,
on a Babylonian monument of the Twelfth Century, B.C.

Šamas (Sun)   Sin (Moon)   Ištar (Venus)

BABYLONIAN ZODIAC

Scripture (ordered under Greek rule in 270 B.C.) repeatedly translates the "sword of the dove" into "from the Hellenic sword" (Bryant, *Anal.* Vol 3, page 160).

Helen – Ione

Helen and Ione had the same meaning: "female generative power." Her visible form was that of a dove as well as that of a woman, who was "IO" of the Ionites or Ionians of Syria. The priests of Menes in Egypt were said to have been changed into doves because they were Ioanian (Bryant, *Anal.* Vol 3, pg 290). The learned historian Lycophron calls "Helen" a dove by two names of that bird: "Pleiades" (the star grouping in the constellation of Taurus) and "Oinas," or the "Bacchic Dove".

Greece was anciently divided between the "Hellenes" and the "Ionians". Since "Helen" has the same meaning as "Ioni," and both names are synonymous with the female generative power, it appears they were the same ethnically connected people but under different appellations. They were the descendents of the historical king figure, "Helen and Ion", two names of the same personage. He was styled "Ion, Ionan or Ionichus" and was supposed to be the author of magic.

Ebn Batrick states:

> "The historical evidence shows that the name of the Iranian
> prophet, Zoroaster, is styled, "Iuna," which is Helen or another
> form of the India Buddha."

The dove is the admitted emblem of the female procreative power. Hence, in Sanskrit, the female organ of generation is called Yoni, which in Hebrew is also Iune. The Syrian female deity, "Dodonna", had a dove on her head and was called Dione or Di-<u>iune</u>, which is the holy Iune or Helen.

The Babylonians, who were immigrants from Ionia, had the same name "Ionium". They were originally followers of the Yoni, the female generative principle, the symbol being an inverted pyramid. By the 10th century B.C. (900s), they had reverted to worshipping the union of the male principle, or "Linga", the symbol being an upright pyramid, and the female principle (see illustration). Here, again, it can be seen how the Hebrew incorporated ancient symbols for their own cult.

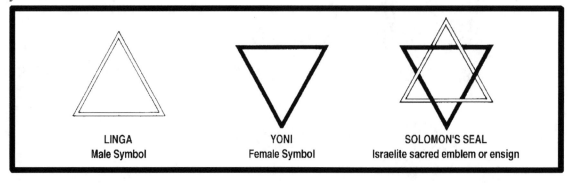

LINGA	YONI	SOLOMON'S SEAL
Male Symbol	Female Symbol	Israelite sacred emblem or ensign

Ramesses of India Origin

Semiramis was an emblem. It signified "The Divine Token" or "Sword of the Dove" (which was used in the Septuagint), a type of providence or divine guidance. As a military ensign (banner) for which it was used, it could be interpreted. The Standard of "The Most High," which is almost identical to "The Most High God" (Genesis 14:18). It consisted of the figure of a dove encircled with an iris outline. All who went under this standard or who paid allegiance to it were called *Semarins* or *Samorins*.

The Z(s)amorin of Cape Comorin, at the southernmost point of India, was where the "Bali-i-Cama" – or "Como," as it is spelled in the country of Java – was adored. At this location was an ancient temple dedicated to the deity, *"Siva or Shiva," but was also known as "Sama" or "Cama"*. This temple was frequented by Hindu pilgrims, at least two thousand years before Christianity. Cama was a corruption of the ancient word "Sani," which was another name for that fiery celestial orb, the sun.

Faber, in *The Origin of Pagan Idolatry,* states:

> "In the temple at Hierapolis was the female statue, with a *dove* upon its head, called *"Sema"*. This was the "Semi-ramis" of the Assyrians converted into a *dove*, as well as the Bama-Sema or *Sema-Rama* of India."

In Hindu mythology, the deity *"Rama"* was either the sixth, seventh, or eighth incarnation of "Vishnu". *Rama* had a direct relationship to the constellation of Aries (the lamb or ram) when the sun was in that precessional equinoxal sign for 2160 years between 2540 to 360 B.C.

The Israelite *Samaritans* were also attracted to the worship of the dove. Their origin can be directly traced back to southern India, the country where can be found the roots of Mosaic mythos (G.H. Higgins, *Anacalypsis).* Evidence shows that they took their name "Sama-ritans" from the worship of the Sama or Cama of the Hindus. The animosity between the Judah (Israelite) and the Samaritan (Israelite) clans resulted from this worship of the female as opposed to the male principle worshipped by the Judah (Israelites).

Conclusion

The story of Semiramis or Semi-rama-isi has been shown to have its roots deep in ancient Indian mythology. She is the female principle of her counterpart, the male principle, which was originally Buddha. Her story is integrally connected with the mythology of the Egyptian deities Horus-Isis mythology in the Nile Delta region, where the first Ramesside pharaohs built resplendent monuments to them.

The following simple comparison will show how the mythological names came from India to Egypt:

INDIA	ASSYRIA
Pleiades (bird) (female principle).	.Dove (female principle)
Buddha – Iuna (dove)	Iuna (Ionian) (dove)
Sama (sun)	Rama-Sema (the sun)
Sama	(Sama)ritans
Samarama (deity)	Sēmi-rama-is (deity)

SEMIRAMIS (ASSYRIA)	HORUS (EGYPT)
The Standard of the Most High	.The High One
Renewal (generative power)	Renewal (generative power)
(Arising from death)	(The son of dead Osiris)
(Reborn every 600 years)	.(Reborn every 600 years)
Crucified Dove (encircled by iris)	.Crucified Osiris (the eye of Horus
	Wounded by Set (evil principles)

Prior to Dynasty XIX, there is no name that even closely resembles the title, Ramesses. Its origin is clearly established as coming from the results of the 150-year Hyksos occupation and the Asiatic influence in the courts of the pharaohs in Dynasty XVIII. It can now be concluded that the time of the Exodus fable could not have taken place prior to Dynasty XIX in 1305 B.C., when the title Ramesses was assumed for the first time *ever* by a pharaoh that reflected this influence. The use of the phrase, "Land of Ramesses" in the Old Testament book EXODUS that was given to the children of Israel, locks the time of the story chronologically to this period or later. It could not be earlier, however, because the title "Ramesses" was not used until then. The many works produced previously that attempted to prove an ancient heritage of the Israelite clan by comparing them to the Hyksos all fall short because they fail to take this phrase into account. For how could there be a "Land of Ramesses" without a Ramesses?

In the following chapters, conclusive evidence will be presented that reveals how the origin of the Exodus story was based upon actual historical events in the Nineteenth Egyptian Dynasty.

CHAPTER III

Geography of the Delta – History and Cities

In the span of some three thousand years, the Delta has undergone considerable change; the Nile's final dispersion was much more complex. Even in the time of the fifth century B.C., the Greek historian, Herodotus, states (Vol. I, Book II, page 17):

> "The Nile divides [Egypt] … flowing … as far as Cercasorus [some ten miles north of modern Cairo], in a single stream, and below that city, splitting into three branches, of which one trends eastward and is known as the mouth of *Pelusium*, and another trends westward and is called the mouth of *Canopus*. There remains the third branch, which coming down from the Southward to the tip of the Delta, flows straight on and cuts it in two on its course to the sea. This branch, issuing at what is called the mouth of *Sebennytus*, is neither the least in volume, nor the least famous of the three. In addition, there are two other mouths, the *Saitic* and *Mendesian*, which split off from the Sebennytic, and so runs into the sea. The *Bolbintine* and *Buccolic* mouths are not natural branches, but excavated channels." [See Nile Delta Rivers Branches, next page, during the time of Dynasty XIX]

AUTHOR'S COMMENTARY

One major branch that is not mentioned in the Herodotus account is the Tanitic branch, which separates from the Mendesian branch above old Athribis (modern Benha), then proceeds northeastward until flowing into the "Horus Lake" (modern Lake Menzalah). On this branch, just south of the Horus Lake, is located Tanis (modern San e-Hagar) which will be discussed later.

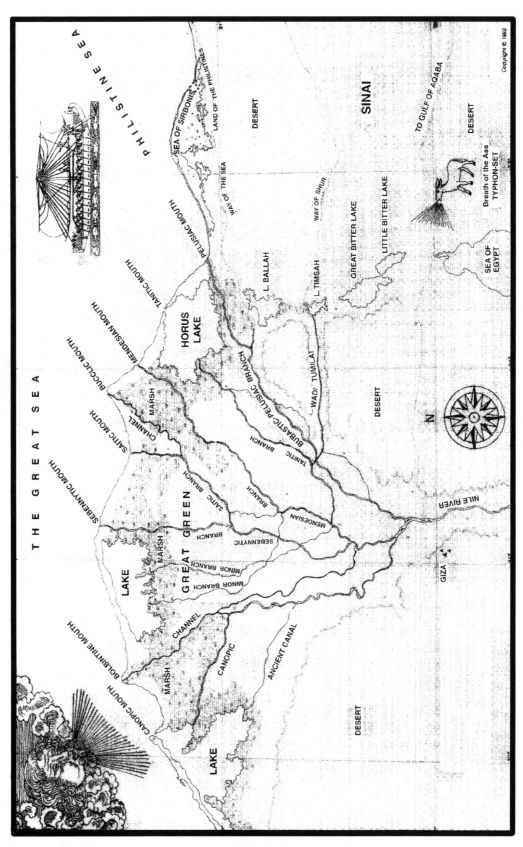

NILE DELTA RIVER BRANCHES

It is quite certain that Herodotus was telling the truth about these branches, because not only are they affirmed by other sources, but in recent years aerial photography has helped in revealing the faint traces of the original beds along which they flowed. Herodotus' description, "...one trends eastward and is known as the mouth of Pelusium", corresponds perfectly with one specifically eastward course that can be traced as having had its exit at the old Roman coastal town of Pelusium, the ruins of which are today three miles inland because of silting. Just how much this silting has changed the appearance of the Delta can be gauged from the 30-foot depth of silt that has accumulated during the past 6,000 years. There were also serious subsidences in the coastal area during the first millennium A.D. Deep core samples taken in areas subsequently given over to swampy water and salt marshes have revealed pollens indicative not only of abundant reeds, bulrushes, ferns, asphodel, and lotus, but also characteristically dry-ground flora such as tamarisk and acacia.

The lesson of these findings is that, quite aside from human activity in about the second millennium B.C. (1000s), the Delta seems to have been distinctly different in appearance from its rather featureless character today. Unlike the predominantly agricultural Upper Egypt to the south, the Delta was mainly pastoral, offering lush grazing to large herds of cattle, sheep, goats, and any number of pigs. But there were also cities, as is quite obvious from Egyptian records, and it is only because of silt accumulations and the use of perishable, reusable mud brick as building material that today's Delta lacks the impressive ancient monuments so abundant in the south.

> The barren desert sands, menacingly perch like some thirsty
> specter upon the very threshold of the Delta, as though glaring
> covetously at the living landscape beyond; its verdant essence,
> drawing generously from the fan of watery veins which branch
> forth from the apex of that lengthy meandering aorta, the Nile,
> after it has split the dissected body of Egypt.
>
> Author Unknown

As on the west, the eastern side of the Nile Delta is bordered by the parched environs of shifting sands, blistering heat, and furnace-like winds. From modern Cairo, east to the Great Bitter Lake, the desert offered a formidable barrier to any traveler in those ancient times. On the northern boundary of this area lay a valley-like depression called "Wadi Tumilat", connecting the Delta, just east of ancient Bubastis, to Lake Timsah, on the edge of western Sinai. To the north of this wadi (a low valley-like depression) and south of the Nile branch previously referred to as "Mouth of Pelusium", lay a generally uninhabited semi-arid land during the period of Dynasty XIX. The northeastern sector of the Delta was occupied by the Horus Lake (modern Lake Menzalah), with marshy low areas adjacent to the south extending as far as Lake Balah. The line of the modern day Suez Canal was considered by ancient Egyptians as the eastern border or frontier of "the Land of the Nile".

Memphis and Area

By the dawn of the Ramesside period, the apex of the Nile had become the seat of power. Commerce with its Mediterranean neighbors, the growing animosity of the kings toward the far-distant capital at Thebes, and the pretensions of the priests of Amun placed Memphis in a good position. The interracial populace had found a passive balance and, with this accomplished, it was business as usual.

A new age had begun for Memphis with the New Kingdom, in the course of which the city rose to be the second capital of the empire. The weak kings of Dynasty XVIII, who had come close to utterly destroying the unity of the two lands, had introduced a division between the southern capital, Thebes, and Memphis, which was the administrative center for Lower Egypt. Each received a vizier as head of the administration. This innovation stimulated activity at Memphis during the widening circumstances of the Empire. Furthermore, there was the additional fact that in the reign of Tuthmosis I (1506-1494 B.C.), at the time of the first great Syrian campaign, the crown prince resided at Memphis as commander-in-chief of the army and particularly of the chariot guards who were organized on Asiatic lines and equipped with Asiatic horses. The broad and level stretches of land on the edge of the desert between Saqqara and Giza [see map, Nile Delta City Locations, page 28] were available for maneuvers of the horse-drawn units.

Colonies of foreigners were to be found, especially in Memphis, on the estates and in the workshops. Most of these foreigners were settled prisoners of war hence, these colonies were later often called camps. In the early years of Amenophis III's reign (1402-1364 B.C., Dynasty XVII), who seemed to favor Memphis before Thebes, the Asiatic deity, Astarte, was appointed the female deity of the royal estate in Perunefer, near Memphis. Foreigners were put to work in the quarries of Masara, on the opposite side of the Nile from Memphis, as attested by the Chief Architect Minmose. It is no surprise, therefore, to find that in the reign of King Amenophis IV, Akhenaten (1364-1347), a Semite was High Priest of Amun, Baal, and Astart in Perunefer. Memphis had just begun to be a cosmopolitan city and was to a far greater extent than the far-distant Thebes.

As with the mercenaries of the army, so with the foreigners there came alien deities. The patron deities of the chariot troops were the Syrian Reshef and Astarte, as we learn from the stela at the Sphinx, which throws significant light on the composition of these troops. The association of the Great Sphinx, located at Giza, opposite from modern Cairo, with the sun deity was principally based on the ancient legend that the kings of Dynasty V were born as sons of Rē, by the wife of a priest from a place called Sahebu (the female name for lord in the female tense), which was apparently near Giza. Although the origin of the Sphinx still mystifies historians to this day, the purpose of this anomalous recumbent monument can be easily revealed. The body, which is the representation of a lion, was the solar emblem of Horus and El. The Nehbkao symbol has wings and the head of a man. In this case, the face is the likeness of Pharaoh Chephren (Dynasty IV), 2680-2565 B.C. It was at the time thought to be the representation of Re-Harakhate, the sun deity of Heliopolis (located just north of modern Cairo). This monument functions as the vivifier of the body of the dead. The Egyptologist Petrie says, "It is the symbol of eternal circulation."

The balance tipped increasingly in favor of the northern capital for two reasons. More Memphite families secured leading positions, even in Thebes itself, and more dependents of the army gained control of the State, especially foreign mercenaries who had been rewarded for their services. Moreover, the persecution of the Amarna Period affected Memphite families far less severely than those of Thebes. Consequently, when Horemheb, who had been commander-in-chief under Tutankhamun and Ay, started from Memphis and seized the royal power, Memphite art moved into first place, consciously replacing what the reforms of Akhenaten in Thebes had removed. Many Theban craftsmen evidently migrated to Memphis; for, at Memphis, one found overseers of craftsmen who owned tombs comparable to nothing that Thebes had seen at that time.

The more that foreign policy demanded the presence of the king in the North, the more Memphis fulfilled the role of second capital. Memphis continued to fulfill this role throughout the Ramesside Period, although Ramesses II built a new residence north of the western end of Wadi Tumilat, called Per-Ramesses-meri-Amun, on the Pelusiac branch, which will be located later.

Heliopolis

Heliopolis, "the city of the sun; the city of temples", was another major site of importance to the Israelite Exodus myth. It, too, was located at the Nile apex, only twenty miles northeast of the political capital of Memphis but on the opposite side of the Nile. Memphis and Heliopolis were both some distance away from the Nile, but ship canals connected the two centers with the river and its traffic (see Nile Delta City Locations, next page).

The Heliopolitan religious belief first made its appearance during Dynasty II (2980-2780 B.C.) as is suggested by certain royal theophanic names like that of "Nebra – Rē [the sun deity] is lord." Asiatic (stemming from ancient India) influence or origination of this city name is again evident because Heli or Helis in Sanskrit means "Sun". However, it was not until the accession of Dynasty V, with the accompanying predominance of the Heliopolitan worship of the sun, that it was to receive prominence. During the old Kingdom (2680-2258 B.C.), the city of the sun preached the teaching that Atum (At-om (Buddha)) was the creator of the world. At the same time, the Heliopolitans declared the sun deity, Harakte (hara (lord)), to be the divine king of the existing world, born of the earth deity, Geb, and the female deity of heaven, Nut, who daily rose regenerated from the primeval ocean and the underworld as the rising sun.

In Heliopolis there also flourished many kinds of cults connected with natural things such as sacred trees, the "Mnevis" bulls, and the pair of lions, that had their own proper place of worship in Leontopolis (modern Tell el-Yahudiyah) north of Heliopolis. The particular worship peculiar to Heliopolis was, however, that of the stars. The principal Heliopolitan

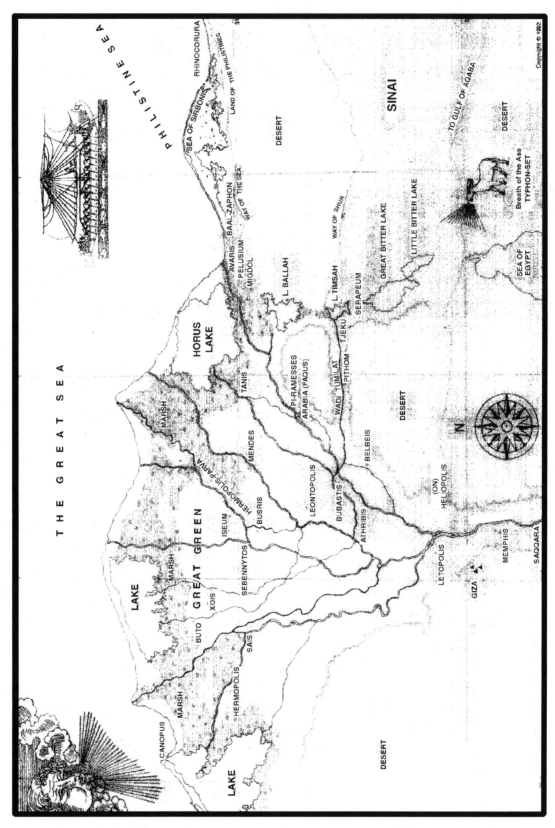

NILE DELTA CITY LOCATIONS

holidays were the festivals of the sky, the divisions of the lunar month, the New Moon, the sixth day of the month (being the start of the second week), Full Moon and the Last Quarter. These festivals remained unaltered through the ages. From the worship of the stars evolved the worship of Rē in the form of "Horus of the Horizon" (in Egyptian, Harakhate is the deity of the morning sun). This conception must have been developed at a time when Horus, the deity of the Egyptian king, played a dominant role. During Dynasty V (2565-2420 B.C.), the kings were erecting sanctuaries near their residences in Memphis to serve for the worship of Rē, which, by then, had become the state faith.

The chief Heliopolitan sanctuary was situated on the "high sand" north of Heliopolis, an artificial mound that mythology regarded as the primeval hill, "the place of the first becoming", which rose out of the primeval waters of chaos. In the same system of symbolization, stress was laid on the ben-ben stone that stood in the open court as the cult image; it was the forerunner of the obelisk. At sunrise every day, when the sun's rays touched the gilded tip of the stone, the sun deity took his seat there, an act that was the never-ending repetition of the first rising of the sun, the time of creation of the world. Associated with this system was the myth of the "Phoenix", whose return to the sanctuary from a far-distant land of the deities symbolized the appearance of the primeval divinity on the primeval earth. The House of the Phoenix and the House of the Obelisk were of equal importance in the eyes of Egyptian theology; the Egyptian words for the Phoenix and obelisk (more exactly, the ben-ben stone) were formed from the same root, which meant rise up or something similar (see illustration of Sun Temple, next page).

Hathor

As was mentioned earlier, the "Semiramis" myth, legend, and emblem representing the female generative power were assimilated into the Egyptian pantheon under the title "Hathor" (cow-female deity). Cow worship existed at all times in the borderlands of Egypt and to the west as far as Cyrenaica in Libya, either under the name of Hathor, the mother of Horus (the deity of heaven) or subsequently under the name of Isis. As sky female deity, she wore a solar disk; as mother female deity, she was represented with a cow's head. The male counterpart aspect of Hathor was the golden bull, Apis, at Memphis, or Mnevis at Heliopolis (which related to the bull constellation Taurus). The particular cult worship – fertilizing energy or ancient fertility rites – became so predominant and sophisticated by Dynasty XVIII that eventually, upon the death of the sacred bull of Memphis during the reign of Amenophis III, it was buried in its own chapel near where the temple of Serapeum (dedicated to the Apis) was ultimately built in the desert west of Memphis next to the Stepped Pyramid. A complicated theological system grew up around the figure of the Apis Bull that was designed to associate it with the chief divinities as "the living Apis-

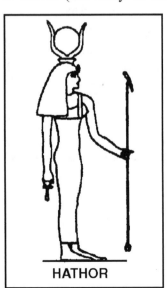

HATHOR

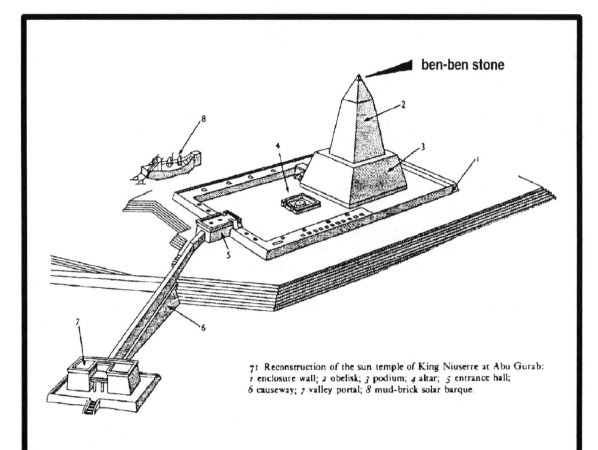

ben-ben stone

71 Reconstruction of the sun temple of King Niuserre at Abu Gurab:
1 enclosure wall; *2* obelisk; *3* podium; *4* altar; *5* entrance hall;
6 causeway; *7* valley portal; *8* mud-brick solar barque.

The great innovations of the age are the sun temples of which the badly
dilapidated example built by Niuserre at Abu Gurab near Abusir remains
the most complete. They are presumed to be based upon the design of the
temple of Re at Heliopolis. The main feature of these temples was a court
open to the sky with a colonnade around two of the walls, sheltering reliefs
and giving access to a large courtyard with a great altar positioned in front of
an abstract symbol of the cult - the gilded **ben-ben** elevated upon a podium
like a squat obelisk. The most striking feature of the complex, however, was
a long narrow chamber, now known as the "Room of the Seasons" from
the subject of its reliefs which portray all the activities during the Egyptian
agricultural year as a kind of visual hymn of praise to the sun god
for all his country.

SUN TEMPLE

Osiris, Lord of Heaven, Atum, whose two horns are upon his head", which made it what it was later called: "king of all sacred animals".

In a number of cases as early as mid-Dynasty XVIII and even under Ramesses II in Dynasty XIX, the same person was high priest both in Memphis and Heliopolis, and this merging of offices was repeated in regard to the worship of the sacred bull of Mnevis at Heliopolis and of Apis at Memphis.

At Heliopolis, there could also be seen the "ished tree", the tree of life (another direct tie to the tree worship of Mesopotamia-India). On its leaves it was said: "the deity set down the names and years of the kings to serve as their annals." Even the cow female deity, Hathor, received the title, "Lady of the Southern Sycamore". Next to Ptah, she was the oldest deity in Memphis.

Trees were supposed to grow around the borders of heaven, and under them sat the celestial deities, like shepherds sitting at the edge of the pasture. In the famous but misunderstood Egyptian *Book of the Dead*, this philosophy is stated as follows:

> "At the beginning of the world, the sacred ished tree in Heliopolis
> unfolded itself on the appearance of the sun-deity on the eastern
> edge of the world."

This is where the solar theology placed the "Field of Reeds of the Blessed", the Egyptian paradise, where the blessed tilled and harvested, admittedly in divine proportion. It seems, even in paradise, the Egyptians could not fully free themselves from their earthly chores. In this paradise, the *Book of the Dead* also states:

> "… stood the two sycamores from Turkis, between which Rē goes
> forth, which have sprung up from the seed sown by Shu [Egyptian
> sky deity, son of Rē] at that eastern door, out of which Rē goes
> forth."
>
> (*Book of the Dead*, chapter 109)

Common, too, were local deities with names such as "He under His Olive Tree" and, in Memphis, Hathor was also venerated as "Mistress of the Southern Sycamore".

This bewildering array of Asiatic-Egyptian metaphysical belief was the heritage that Joseph, of the story, would have been exposed to, when Pharaoh, Sety I (Sethos I):

> "45 And Pharoah called Joseph's
> name Zặph'nặth-pā-a-nēah; and he
> gave him to wife Asenath, the
> daughter of Potipherah, priest of On[1]. "
> (GENESIS 41:45)

---

[1] On is Heliopolis.

Other Delta Cities

The Delta, as a whole was difficult of access especially the northern districts and the area lying between the two principal arms of the Nile. It was, in ancient times, quite unsuitable for agriculture on the large scale for which today it is the outstanding region of Egypt. In very ancient times, in fact, we hear very little about the Delta except in one respect: the deities and shrines of the "Land of the Papyrus", an echo of the fame that comes down to us in the ritual and religious texts of the Old Kingdom, with its traditions derived from the Thinite Period (Dynasty II).

Some of the well known cities of the Middle and Western Delta were:

Buto (modern Tell el-Fara'in)
> The "place of the throne" (ancient Pe), the old capital of the kingdom of the West Delta, situated deep in the marshes.

Xois   (modern Koum Farayn)
> The capital of the Sixth Xoite nome with the symbol of a desert bull.

Sais   (San el-Hagar)
> Further to the south and near the canopic arm of the Nile, the home of the arrow deity, Neith.

Busiris (Abusir)
> In the middle of the Delta, south of the start of the Saitic arm of the Nile, the home of Osiris and the djed-pillar (a degenerated form of phallic worship).

Iseum (Behbeit el-Hagar)
> Further to the north in the Sebennites Nome is the city Iseum, acquiring its name, "The Divine", from the sacred lake from which, according to ancient rituals, water for purification was drawn, as from the alleged source of the Nile at Elephantine.

(See map of Nile Delta Nomes, page 40.)

* * * * * *

Egypt's isolationist policy rapidly disintegrated after liberation of the "Land of the Nile" from the Hyksos yoke. Under the aggressive, expansionist campaigns by kings of early Dynasty XVIII, commerce began to flourish with the newly acquired Asiatic vassal states, from Canaan to Syria and Mesopotamia. The route between the political and religious hub at the Delta apex in Egypt and its far-flung provinces soon was a burgeoning, well-trodden path for emissaries, traders, travelers, artisans, and armies alike.

For centuries, the life-giving Nile had been the undisputed pathway for all movement between Upper and Lower Egypt. Its ever-present wind-gorged, white cotton sails, silently propelled all manner of river craft through its turbid waters, transporting products and people to various points along its distant, meandering course to the sea.

Pelusiac / Bubastic Branch of the Nile

At Memphis, the hub of activity in the New Kingdom, the road to the frontier and mysterious Asia beyond veered northeastward, past Heliopolis, then along the boundary of the Delta, at the edge of the desert. Here, again, the mighty Nile was not to fail the weary traveler to distant lands, for it continued to provide a convenient avenue of transport for the journey to the very eastern border of Egypt.

The "Pelusiac" or "Bubastic" (see map of Egyptian Delta, page 35), an ancient branch had been developed into a main channel for shipping. Exiting the Nile immediately west of Heliopolis, it was to be an answer to the footsore individual's dreams. As if by design, it would seem, more than by natural occurrence, the course of this rivulet threaded its way toward the eastern frontier, past the entrance of Wadi Tumilat, and then to the beginning of the northern Sinai desert. It finally emptied into the Mediterranean Sea at the old coastal town of Pelusium. The river traffic, which had moved down the Nile from the south, could continue unabated to this port at the end of Egypt. Likewise, the caravans from the east need not continue their plodding overland trek but complete the remainder of the journey relaxing under the billowing sail of some river craft as it glided serenely over the placid surface toward its destination somewhere up the Nile.

At various periods of history, this artery highway branch was to be given various titles, such as She-Hor (Shi-Hor), Waters of Horus, Waters of the Sun, Canal of Horus, or Waters of Rē. Because this branch became so essential in the lives of the Egyptians, it eventually gained an almost mystical quality similar to its trunk, the very source of life, the mighty Nile.

All the great conquerors from the east, like the Egyptian kings returning to their country from abroad, made use of the Bubastic arm of the Nile from the Egyptian frontier posts onward into the heart of Egypt. They, therefore, appeared officially in Egypt at Memphis and not at the old capital of Thebes in Upper Egypt itself. Along this waterway also lay Bubastis, the ancient capital of the Eastern Delta.

Wadi-Tumilat

Before commencing with the location of the specific cities and sites – Rā-am′sēs, Pīthom and the Land of Goshen – there remains one geographical area that needs to be examined: Wadi Tumilat. In Dynasty XIX, the Isthmus of Suez, land bridge between Egypt and the Sinai Peninsula was heavily defended by the Egyptians, who allowed only two points of passage through these fortifications. The first crossing was the northern route at the southern edge of Horus Lake (modern Lake Menzalah), which was used by Egyptian armies marching into Asia, but was also utilized by all Asiatic conquerors to invade Egypt. The lesser-used southern route, coming through the neighborhood of modern Ismailiyah on Lake Timsah, was along the thinly populated Wadi Tumilat. But Lake Timsah, in the center of the Isthmus, could be reached only from the east along the difficult desert trek from Syria or from the desert region of the Moab/Edom, where a watch could easily be kept over the few wells that made the trip even possible.

Although there is some confusion among the historians – Aristotle, Diodorus Siculus, Strabo, and Pliny – there is a consensus that a canal through its depression existed connecting the Nile's Pelusiac/Bubastic branch with Lake Timsah. From all evidence, it was probably initiated by Sesostris (Sety I) and completed under Ramesses II. How far this canal reached is not totally certain, but it was reported that work was interrupted before its completion to the Sea of Egypt (modern Gulf of Suez), because the water level was discovered to be higher than the land.

Herodotus in Vol. I, Book II, page 158, states:

> "It was first undertaken by Nekos or Necho (titled Nekau, Wehem-ib-ra, 609-594 B.C.); however, work was interrupted. Afterwards, the Persian king, Darius (522-485 B.C.), took up the work."

The connection actually existed in the time of Herodotus, as we learn from his words:

> "This canal, like many others cut by this king, [Ramesses II], had particular purpose; he acquired thereby a considerable portion of the desert. But, if we consider the special attention which Sesostis also paid to shipbuilding since he first navigated the Arabia Gulf [Red Sea] with warships (Herod. ii; 102), it could not have appeared to him a very strange idea to cut through the narrow Isthmus between the Sea of Egypt and the Bitter Lakes. The Egyptians had for ages possessed the art of leveling in the greatest perfection and practiced it more than ever in the reign of Sesostris."

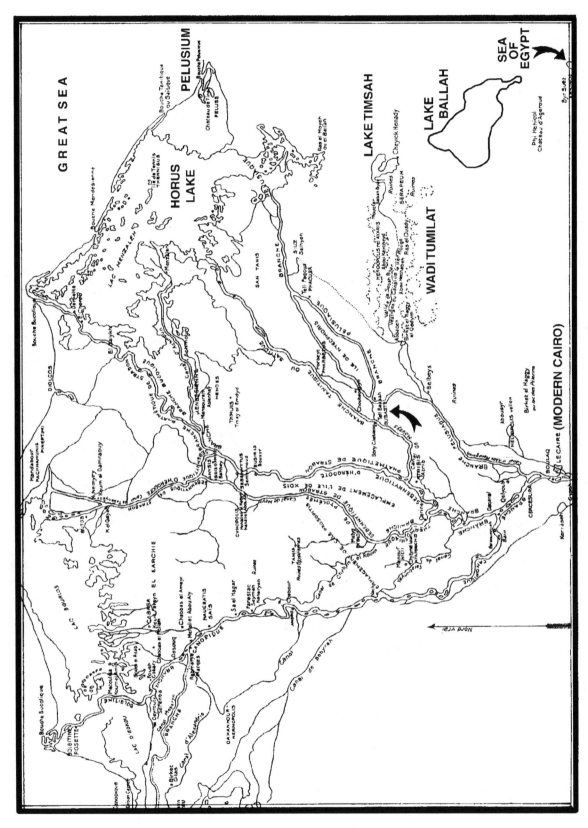

EGYPTIAN DELTA

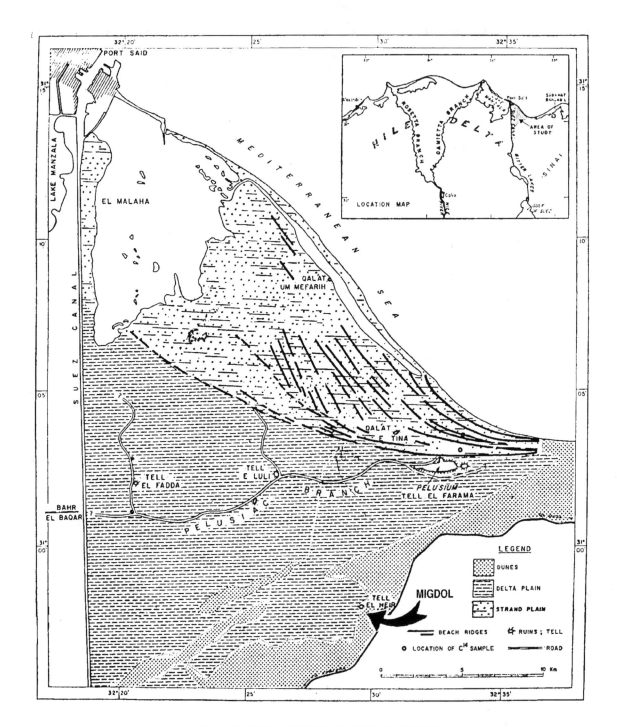

NORTHEAST CORNER OF NILE DELTA

CHAPTER IV

Joseph of the Story

To begin, the legend of the "Exodus of the Israelites" has its geographical location in the northeastern Nile Delta of Egypt, fabled Land of the Pharaohs; however, there is no chronological dating.

CHAPTER 1
"NOW these *are* the names of the children of Israel, which came into Egypt:
every man and his household came
with Jacob." (EXODUS 1:1)

The story of the Exodus is preceded by the life of Joseph, who is purported to be the forerunner or predecessor of the Israelite Hebrews into Egypt. Joseph is important to the story because his life, as told in GENESIS, the first book of the Old Testament of the Judaeo-Christian Bible, can place the story of Exodus in the proper time frame. In GENESIS Chapters 39, 40 and 41, the story relates how Joseph came to Egypt. It then goes on to relate the events that brought Joseph to interpret pharaoh's dreams of cows and corn. On his successful interpretation that Egypt would have seven (7) years of plenty, then seven (7) years of famine, pharaoh commands, in GENESIS 42:6:

6 "And Joseph was the governor over
the land, …"

As the story relates, when Joseph began his administering of Egypt, by the command of the Pharaoh, he was thirty years old.

46 "And Joseph was thirty years old
when he stood before Pharaoh king of
Egypt. …" (GENESIS 41:46)

During the years of his administration, his family and brethren joined him in Egypt, where they lived under Sety I (when he was coregent with Ramesses I) and later, under Ramesses II. Dynasty XIX of Egypt began with the reign of Ramesses (Ramses I) in 1305 B.C. Joseph's brethren lived in the area called "Goshen" or "Land of Ramesses" (geographical location of this area will be examined later). This very fact places the Exodus myth within the chronological period of the Ramesside era, which began at 1305 B.C., and axiomatically prevents it from happening at any earlier period.

The story goes on. Just as Joseph had interpreted the dream of the king, the land of Egypt experienced 7 years of "plenty" and then began 7 years of "lean", during which all the corn stored away was exhausted and the money failed. The Hebrew book of "GENESIS", 47:20-27, states:

"20 And Joseph bought all the land of Egypt for Pharaoh: for the Egyptians sold every man his field, because the famine prevailed over them: so the land became Pharaoh's.

"21 And as for the people, he removed them to cities from one end of the borders of Egypt even to the other end thereof.

"22 Only the land of the priests bought he not; for the priests had a portion assigned them of Pharaoh, and did eat their portion which Pharaoh gave them; wherefore they sold not their lands.

"23 Then Joseph said unto the people, Behold, I have bought you this day and your land for Pharaoh: lo, here is seed for you, and ye shall sow the land.

"24 And it shall come to pass in the increase, *that ye shall give the fifth part* unto Pharaoh, and four parts shall be your own, for seed of the field, and for your food, and for them of your households, and for food for your little ones.

"25 And they said, Thou hast saved our lives: let us find grace in the sight of

my lord, and we will be Pharaoh's ser-
vants.

"26 And Joseph made it a law over the
land of Egypt unto this day, that
Pharaoh should have the *fifth part*; except the land of the priests only, which
became not Pharaoh

"27 ¶And Israel dwelt in the land of
Egypt, in the country of Goshen; ..."

Among the verbiage in which the story's chronicler attempts to establish the foundation
of the Israelite cult history, there is embodied sufficient facts that can be corroborated by
other independent historical records. They set this part of Joseph's life in the chronological
period at the beginning of Dynasty XIX. This fact would seem to give the story credence;
however, as will be evident later, this method of introducing random historical events to give
the Exodus narrative credibility in reality works towards its detriment.

Conjunction of the Story and History

The preceding passages offer no evidence to establish under which pharaoh Joseph
first would have served. But now the evidence is given that has always existed, revealing that
events in the story of Joseph are exactly like the acts of Pharaoh Sety I.

Diodorus Siculus says, in his *Bibliotheca Historica*, Vol. I, Book I, paragraph 54, of
King Sesoosis that:

> "He divided the whole country into thirty-six parts called
> Nomes; over these he placed Nomarches, who had the charge
> of the Royal Revenues, ..." (See map of Nile Delta Nomes,
> next page.)

Herodotus states in his Book II:

> "... It was they [prisoners] who were forced to drag the
> enormous masses of stone which were brought during *Sesostris'*
> reign for the temple of Heaestus, and to dig the dykes which
> one finds there today, thereby depriving Egypt, though it was
> far from their intention to do so, of the horse and carriage
> which were formerly in common use throughout the country.
> All the Delta is flat; yet, from that time onwards, it was unfit
> for horses or wheeled traffic because of innumerable dykes,
> running in all directions,

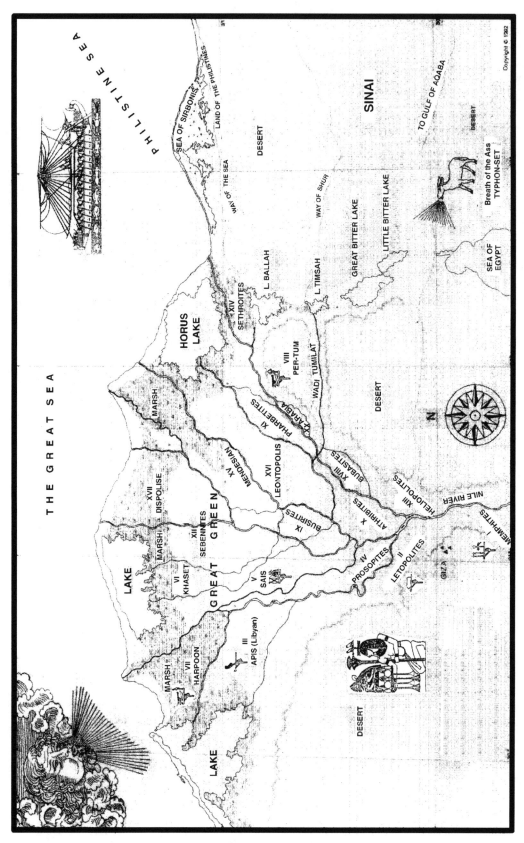

NILE DELTA NOMES

which cut the country up. The king's *Sesostris'* object was to supply water to the towns that lay inland at some distance from the river; for previously the people in these towns, when the level of the river fell, had to go short and drink brackish water from wells. It was this king, moreover, *who divided the land into lots and gave everyone a square piece of equal size, from the produce of which he extracted an annual tax"*. *(Works of Sesostris*, pp 100-110).

Josephus, in *Antiquity of Jews*, Vol. I, Chapter IX, states:

> *"Sesostris* (Sety I) made the Hebrews cut great number of channels for the river [Nile], build walls for cities and ramparts, to restrain the river, to hinder its waters from stagnation."

Herodotus' "Sesostris", who divided the Delta lands and extracted an annual tax, is virtually identical to the Exodus story's Joseph, who bought all the land of Egypt (actually, only the Delta). If it can be proven that "Sesostris" is, in reality, one in the same "Memare Sethos I" or "Sety I" of Dynasty XIX, it establishes both a chronological pivot point by which all the events in the Exodus story can be placed in historical continuity beginning with Dynasty XIX and the beginning of the Ramesses title. All events of the Exodus story prior to this point and after will be shown to fit perfectly in line with historical facts as well as with all other events in the story itself.

The Herodotus account is ambiguous, especially considering that Dynasty XII (1991-1786 B.C.) had three pharaohs named Sesostris and is the only dynasty containing pharaohs of that obvious name (examine pharaonic king list, Chapter I). A meticulous examination of his Book II, however, reveals that there is little doubt this, Sesostris is Sethos (Sety) I.

Sesostris is Sesoosis is Sety I – Sethos is Sety II

Herodotus, in *Works of Sesostris*, states that he additionally received the following information directly from the Egyptian priests themselves. Herodotus would have received his information from priests in Dynasty XXVII, since he lived between 450-425 B.C.

A.   "Min was the first king of Egypt." (Vol. I, Book II, paragraph 4)

B.   "The priests then read to him names of three hundred and thirty monarchs ... all of them Egyptians except eighteen, who were Ethiopian kings, and one other, who was an Egyptian woman" [called Nitocris] (Vol. I, Book II, paragraph 100).

AUTHOR'S COMMENTARY ON A AND B

Menes was the first king, which is similar to the name of "Min". The most contemporary pharaonic list contains approximately 200 kings in the entire Egyptian history, which includes Ethiopian kings of Dynasty XXV. The Ethiopian period, lasting from 751-656 B.C. (only 95 years) had only 6 kings, not 18 kings. Oddly, Herodotus mentions nothing concerning the Hyksos kings. Since the Hyksos ruled Lower Egypt for some 150 years, it would have been enough time for 18 kings. It seems obvious that there was confusion in the period of the Hyksos reign, which was somehow taken to be Ethiopian. Also, when the king list is reviewed, it can be seen that after Dynasty XII, there is no Sesostris. This dynasty preceded the Hyksos period (1720-1570 B.C.) so Herodotus' Sesostris would have to be later than Dynasty XII.

In Book II, Herodotus goes on:

C.   "As none of the kings [Ethiopians] on the priests' roll left any memorials at all, I [Herodotus], will pass on to say something of Sesostris, who succeeded them.

D.   "*Sesostris* had a *powerful army* and *navy* and he marched across the continent, reducing to subjection every nation in his path. ... Thus, his victorious progress through Asia continued, defeating the Scythians and Thracians in Europe.

E.   "*Sesostris* was the *only Egyptian king to rule Ethiopia.*"

AUTHOR'S COMMENTARY ON C, D AND E

The Hyksos left no memorials of their reign because they did not use stone. All their buildings were constructed out of mud bricks (like the ones the Hebrews made), which deteriorated in a short time.

Sety I (also known as Seti or Sethos) of Dynasty XIX was known to have a large army and navy. He also made extensive, successful campaigns into Asia, according to Manetho.

The historian Manetho, from *Ancient Fragments* by I. P. Cory, states that Ethiopia was a vassal state of Amenophis (Merneptah), 4th pharaoh of Dynasty XIX, who was Sety (Sethos) I's grandson.

Then Herodotus goes on in Book II with a list of the kings that followed Sesostris, who are given below:

1. *Sesostris*   4. Rhampsinitus   7. Mycerinus
2. Pheros   5. Cheops   8. Anysis
3. Proteus   6. Chephren   9. *Sethos*

Later, in the same work, Herodotus mentions the following kings:

Neco, Psammetichus, Necos (Psammetichus' son, who began the canal in Wadi Tumilat), Apries, and *Amasis*

AUTHOR'S COMMENTARY ON NINE KINGS

Of the nine kings, the only other recognizable name besides Sesostris is Sethos. Herodotus connects the Assyrian king *Sennacherib* (704-681 B.C.) with this particular Sethos. However, Sennacherib's reign was contemporary with the Egyptian pharaoh Sebitku (701-690 B.C.) in Dynasty XXV of the Ethiopian era. There is no Sethos mentioned in the pharaonic list during this period (see Kings List, Chapter I).

The fifth and sixth kings mentioned were pyramid builders in Dynasty IV (2680-2565 B.C.). This would make them totally out of place. Obviously, these names have been interpolated from some unknown mistake or were nicknames for other pharaohs somewhere between Dynasties XIX and XXVI, possibly to connect them with their ancient forbearers, but lost later in time. It is plainly apparent that no Sesostris existed prior to Cheops and Chephren in Dynasty IV. (See Kings List, Chapter I).

The name that gives some slight indication of the general chronology of Sesostris is the fourth king, Rhampsinitus, which loosely connects Sesostris with the Ramesside period beginning with Dynasty XIX.

Both Herodotus and Diodorus Siculus claim that Sesostris is also the name "Sesoosis". Diodorus Siculus states in his Book I, pg 54, that Sesoosis:

> "... *divided the whole country into thirty-six parts*, which the
> Egyptians called Nomes; over these he placed the Nomarchs,
> *who had the charge of the Royal Revenues*, and ruled everything
> besides in their provinces."

According to Dr. Richard Lepsius in his *Egypt, Ethiopia, and Sinai*, the historian Germanicus Nero stated:

> "**Sesostris** was the name of **Sethos I**" (Sety I).

In Flavius Josephus' account of Israelite history, he states:

> "**Sethosis** and Ramesses followed Amenophis." [Merneptah,
> fourth king of Dynasty XIX.]

AUTHOR'S COMMENTARY

A. H. Sayce states:
"The pharaoh Amenophis, the son of Ramesses and father of Sethos, is Merneptah, the son of Ramesses II and father of Sety II."

Since Josephus' "Sethosis" (as in Sethosis and Ramesses, above) is "Sety II" and Germanicus' "Sesostris" is "Sethos (Sety) I", then the reasonable conclusion would be that Herodotus' "Sesostris" (Sesoosis) is Menmare Sethos I (Sety I), second king of Dynasty XIX. (See list, Chapter I). The following will graphically show this relationship:

Sesoosis:	moved cities and dug canals in Delta	
Sesoosis:	conquered Ethiopia (Nubia)	Diodorus Siculus
Sesoosis:	divided Delta into Nomes (36)	
Sesostris:	had powerful army and navy	Herodotus
Sesostris:	ruled Ethiopia	Herodotus
Sesostris:	divided land into lots for taxing	Diodorus Siculus
Sesostris is Sesoosis		Herodotus; Diodorus Siculus
Sety I:	Ethiopia his vassal	Manetho
Sesoosis is Sesostris is Sethos I (Sety I)		Germanicus

It can now be determined that the only pharaoh who could have ruled Egypt during a period exactly similar to the dividing up of Egypt in the Exodus myth would have been Menmare Sethos I (Sety I, also called Sesostris). Through exhaustive study, historians now readily agree that Sesostris was Menmare Sethos I (Sety I).

It is important to note that the unnamed pharaoh who placed Joseph as governor over the land of Egypt was also the pharaoh who gave Joseph's brethren, the Hebrews, the "land of Ram' e-sēs" (GENESIS; 47:11). This could mean one of two possibilities: that Egypt was called the "land of Ram' e-sēs" or that a specific designated area was called the "land of Ram'-e-sēs". In either case, the fact must remain that this phrase referred to the area that was under domination of a reigning Ramesside pharaoh or land that had been previously named after a Ramesses pharaoh – in other words, in Dynasty XIX or later.

A Review

It has been established that Menpehtyre Ramesses I, whose one-year reign was approximately between 1305-1303 B.C., was the first of the Ramesside kings and founder of Dynasty XIX.   There are many Egyptologists who agree that due to the truncated reign of Ramesses I, his successor-son, Sety I (1303-1289 B.C.), was made co-regent. The Hebrew story "EXODUS" reveals that no exact chronology exists as to the time of Joseph's entry into Egypt. Even the king who placed Joseph as governor over "the land of Egypt" has no specific name, only pharaoh. The first glimmer of historical relationship arises when, in GENESIS 47:11, it is related that pharaoh gave Joseph's brethren, the Hebrews, the "land of Ram' e-sēs". This very statement axiomatically places the story no earlier than Dynasty XIX.   Then GENESIS 47:20-27 relates that pharaoh appropriated the land for the state then redistributed it in parcels to the citizenry, thereby taxing the same. This corresponds identically to independent accounts by later historians, who recount the political policies of Menmare Sethos I (Sety I), also called Sesostris. These same policies were carried on and eventually completed by his successor, Usermare Ramesses II. It must be remembered that Joseph, according to the story, served under Pharaoh Sety I for a minimum of 14 years. This being the case, the similarity between Sety I's (Sesostris') 14-year reign (1303-1289) and the seven years of plenty and seven years of lean, totaling 14 years, has astonishing parallels.

As has been mentioned, Sety I's successor, the Great Ramesses II (1289-1224 B.C.), ruled over Egypt for some 65 years. His reign is marked by expansion, reconstruction, and a monumental building program. The history books are rich with accounts of this grand pharaoh. Records of his achievements are deeply inscribed upon monuments and temple walls from one end of Egypt to the other. Under his regency, the Land of the Nile was to reach its zenith in power and influence. To this very day, the grandeur and brilliancy of his monarchy are lauded because the remains of artifacts and records attesting to the power of his rule are in such abundance.

The continuity of parallels between Egyptian history and the Exodus myth is still undisturbed by Ramesses II's phenomenal rule. By applying a simple formula, it will reveal that the myth continues to follow recorded history.

A. Joseph came to Egypt at approximately the same time as origination of Dynasty XIX. (His age is unknown, but he was still young.)

B. Joseph was 30 years old when he came before pharaoh.

C. Shortly after this, Joseph's brethren were given the "Land of Ram' e-sēs" (at the time of famine).

D. During this same period, Joseph was governor of Egypt for the 14 years of plenty and lean, *corresponding to the 14-year reign and similar history of Sety I (1303-1289 B.C.)* This would make him approximately 44 years of age.

The story does not state whether Joseph served under one or more pharaohs; however, it does state that Joseph was 110 years old at the time of his death. Since Joseph was about 44 years of age at the end of the 14 years of plenty and lean, then there are 66 years remaining to be accounted for, and, as if by some unassociated coincidence, this number coincides almost exactly with the number of years in the reign of Usermare Ramesses II (the Great) (1289-1224 B.C. or 65 years).

GENESIS, the first book in the Old Testament of the Judaeo-Christian Bible, concludes with the death of Joseph. During the reign of Sety I and Ramesses II, meticulous records were kept of the officials in office. *Those records, still extant, give no mention of a Zaphnathpaaneah (Joseph) being governor over the land of Egypt.*

Ramesses II passes into the pages of history, according to the Egyptian pharaonic chronology, at about 1224 B.C., and he was followed by Baenre Merneptah (Siptah) (1224-1204 B.C.). The magnificence of the preceding era rapidly dims, possibly because Ramesses

II, in his waning years, was prone to rest on his laurels. He would enjoy the fruits of his earlier glory while leaving the affairs of state in the inept hands of underlings.

There is a period of disorder during the remaining years of Dynasty XIX (about 1217-1186 B.C.). There is anarchy and invasions by Libyans and Mediterranean coast peoples, ending in a usurpation by a Syrian.

Hebrew Affliction

The Second Book of the Old Testament called "EXODUS" opens with a reaffirmation that Joseph was truly dead. It also adds in EXODUS 1:6 that:

> "6 And Joseph died, and *all his breth-ren, and all that generation.*"

The same first chapter, verse 8, states:

> " 8 ¶Now there arose up *a new king* over Egypt, which knew not Joseph."

As it has been shown, the Hebrew chronicler toes the mark by faithfully following Egyptian history to this point. Since this has been shown to be accurate, then the new king, which knew not Joseph, would seemingly be Baenra Merneptah (1124-1204 B.C.), or was it?

The Exodus story continues:

> "7 And the children of Israel were fruitful and *increased abundantly*, and *multiplied,* and *waxed exceeding mighty*; and *the land was filled with them.*"

Then it states:

> "8 ¶Now there arose up a new king over Egypt, which knew not Joseph.

> "9 And he said unto his people, Be-hold, the people of the children of Israel are more and mightier than we:

> "10 Come on, let us deal wisely with them; lest they multiply, and it come to pass, that, when there falleth out any war, they join also unto our enemies,

and fight against us, and so get them up
out of the land.

"11 Therefore they did set over them
taskmasters to afflict them with their
burdens. And they built for Pharaoh
treasure cities, Pī'thom and Rā-am'sēs.

"12 But the more they afflicted them, the
more they multiplied and grew. And
they were grieved because of the children
of Israel.

"13 And the Egyptians made the children of Israel to serve with rigour:

"14 And they made their lives bitter
with hard bondage, in mortar, and in brick,
and in all manner of service in the field:
all their service, wherein they made them
serve, was with rigour."

Even though there are no years in the story between Joseph's death and Moses' birth, it must have been quite some time simply because the original 70 Israelites that came with Jacob (Israel) into Egypt would need many years to multiply and fill the land.

Ramesses II and the City of Raamses

Joseph's time in Egypt has been shown to correspond to Egyptian history with a fair degree of accuracy up until the commencement of what has been titled *The Second Book of Moses*. From this point, it would seem from the passage in EXODUS 1:11 that if the enslaved Hebrews were building the treasury city of Rā-am'sēs, then they would not be under the reigning Pharaoh, "Baenra Merneptah," but under Ramesses II, who had already died.

There are two important factors that need to be considered when examining this seeming contradiction.

First: There is little doubt remaining, as already proven by many historians and the author's personal examination, that the two accounts, GENESIS and EXODUS, were written by entirely separate individuals at disassociated periods.

Second: The events in the story cannot be relied upon to be totally accurate in content or historical chronology (in other words, poetic license was employed).

Overlapping of accounts can readily be assumed, since the Hebrew chroniclers are not attempting to record history but are only developing cultic infallibility by weaving together diverse societal elements.

Unquestionably, Ramesses II was a builder on a huge scale, inevitably using slave labor, leading one to believe he must be the pharaoh of repression. With a great flair, it was he who built the famous colossal rock-cut statues of Abu Simbel, set 200 miles beyond the country's southern border, to warn any potential northward-bound Nubian invaders that they should stray no further. It was his thousand-ton, sixty-foot-high statue in the Ramesseum at Luxor that inspired Shelley's famous poem, "Ozymandias," which the author feels compelled, at this point, to insert because of its prophetic message and compelling verse:

> "I met a traveller from an antique land
> Who said: "Two vast and trunkless legs of stone
> Stand in the desert . . . Near them, on the sand,
> Half sunk, a shattered visage lies, whose frown,
> And wrinkled lip, and sneer of cold command,
> Tell that its sculptor well those passions read
> Which yet survive, stamped on these lifeless things,
> The hand that mocked them, and the heart that fed:
> And on the pedestal these words appear:
> 'My name is Ozymandias, king of kings:
> Look on my works, ye Mighty, and despair!'
> Nothing beside remains. Round the decay
> Of that colossal wreck, boundless and bare
> The lone and level sands stretch far away."
>   Percy Bysshe Shelley

At no point does the Exodus story reveal the identity of which pharaohs were reigning during the extended events. However, an in-depth study has unraveled the contradiction and reveals that historic continuity can be maintained.

There are two factors that give us the key to unlock the puzzling contradiction that stem from the penchant of the Egyptians to record their history.

First: Although there has been endless squabbling among 20th century religious historians as to the exact location of the Treasure City Rā-am′sēs of the Exodus myth, there is little doubt that the general area around the western end of Wadi Tumilat would be the site, because many ruins, unearthed by archaeologists, carried the name Ramesses II.

Second: The *Anastasia Papyrus*, circa sixth/seventh century A.D., reports that it was *Ramesses II, who began the city, Per-Ramesses-meri-Amun,* (just north of Wadi Tumilat) but it was his son, *Merneptah, who completed the task.*

CHAPTER V

Hidden Chronology

Although there are no years mentioned in the story between the death of Joseph and enslavement of the Israelites to build the cities of Pithom and Rameses, the story does not lose continuity even if it is vague.

Seldom mentioned from church pulpits and synagogues is the reason for the Israelites' enslavement after Joseph's death, which is stated in EXODUS 1:7:

> "7 And the children of Israel were fruitful and increased abundantly, and multiplied and waxed exceeding mighty; and the land was filled with them."

This one paragraph not only gives the reasons for enslavement but also reveals a hidden chronology that determines when the Israelites were pressed into forced labor to build the treasure (store) cities of Pī′thom and Rā-am′sēs.

Goshen

Before commencing to locate the two cities, it is necessary to place them in a geographical area where the Israelites would have certainly been to verify that those "Bible Lands Maps" were accurate.

In GENESIS 46:28, it speaks of Jacob and his son, Judah:

> "28 ¶And he sent Judah before him unto Joseph, to direct his face unto

> *Goshen*; and they came into the *land of Goshen*."

Then further, in paragraphs 31-34, it states:

> "31 And Joseph said unto his brethren, and unto his father's house, I will go up, and shew Pharaoh, and say unto him, My brethren, and my father's house, which were in the land of Canaan, are come unto me;
>
> "32 *And the men are shepherds, for their trade hath been to feed cattle*; and they have brought their flocks, and their herds, and all that they have.
>
> "33 And it shall come to pass, when Pharaoh shall call you, and shall say, What is your occupation?
>
> "34 That ye shall say, Thy servants' trade hath been about cattle from our youth even until now, both we, and also our fathers: that ye may dwell in the land of Goshen; *for every shepherd is an abomination unto the Egyptians*."

In these paragraphs lay two facts of primary importance that relate to historical evidence.

First: That Joseph's brethren were shepherds who owned and herded cattle. It has already been established that the Delta region was ideal for raising cattle and was used extensively for that purpose.

Second: Since every shepherd was an abomination to the Egyptians, it would axiomatically relegate them to limited numbers and confine them to a specific area, sequestered from the mainstream of Egyptian life. This can be seen even in the story, when the mythical Joseph became so completely Egyptianized that he would not eat at the same table with his brethren and only speak to them through an interpreter.

The Septuagint (Greek translation of the Old Testament of the Judaeo-Christian Bible produced in the third century B.C.), specifically refers to Goshen as "Gesem Arabias" in

GENESIS 46:34. Gesem/gsm is the ancient Egyptian equivalent of the Hebrew "Goshen" and also "Arabias", is linked with the city "Faqus." Pi-Ramesses was located just north of Faqus, which was known to have been the capital of Egypt's "Arabian" district in ancient times (see map of Land of Goshen, next page).

In 1884 A.D., Dr. Edouard Naville excavated Saft el-Henna, near the modern city of Zagazig, and Tel el-kebir (about 18 miles east of Zagazig, into Wadi Tumilat) and found ancient "Qosem or Qos", called "Pha-kussa" by Greek geographers, which was the capital of the Arabian Nome (see map of Land of Goshen, next page).

From all evidence, it can be safely assumed that "the Land of Goshen" was an area at the western end of Wadi Tumilat, stretching north to just below Faqus, on the west to Bubastis (close to the Tanitic arm), and on the south to Belbeis.

Rā-am'sēs (Pi-Ramesses)

Down through the years, those old faithful "Bible Lands Maps" have illustrated three separate locations of the origination site from which the Hebrews began their odyssey. This demonstrates the typical confusion about the account. These locations are:

A.   Tanis (modern San el-Hagar)
B.   Qantir (Tell el-Daba) just north of Faqus
C.   Some undetermined location at the western end of Wadi Tumilat, near the Bubastic branch.

However, in the Exodus story, it very plainly states that the Hebrew/Israelites started from a place that is related to the Ramesside period. EXODUS 12:37 states:

> "37 ¶And the children of Israel jour-
> neyed from Ram'e-sēs to Suc'coth, ...

Although there are Ramesside remains at Tanis (San el-Hagar), they have been proven to be of Dynasty XX or a later period. As far as the location at the western end of Wadi Tumilat, isolated Ramesside monuments have been found even from the period of Ramesses II; however, nothing was discovered to indicate that there existed a city of that exact name. With the plethora of Ramesses II monument ruins strewn throughout the eastern delta, the chances of an exact location at this late date seem impossible.

Interestingly enough, however, in 1966 A.D. an Austrian archaeological team under an Egyptological specialist, Dr. Manfred Bietak, began excavation of a site four miles north of "Faqus," as mentioned earlier, the capital of the Arabian district, Gesem Arabis-Goshen. This site was by the village of Qantir, called Tell el-Dab'a. By 1980, Dr. Bietak had found sufficient evidence to identify this site as the eastern delta capital of Ramesses II, called "Pi-Ramesses" (see map of Pi-Ramesses, page 53). This site is geographically about halfway between each of the other suggested locations for the origination city. It is quite obvious,

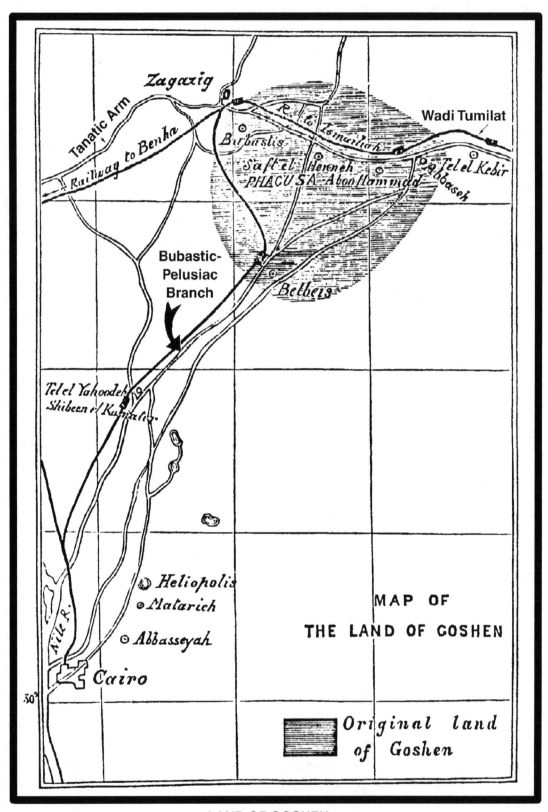

LAND OF GOSHEN

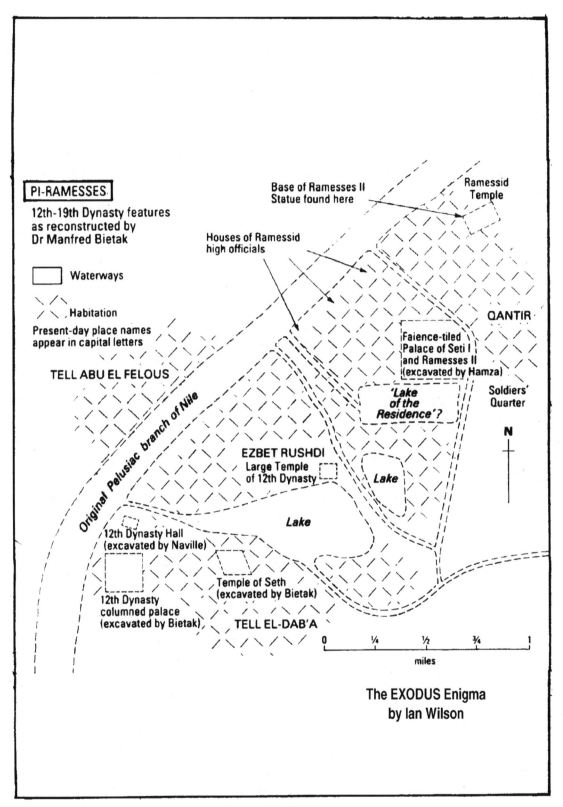

PI - RAMESSES

from Dr. Bietak's findings, that Tell el-Daba / Qantir had a history much earlier than the time of Ramesses II. It has been suggested that because of certain remains found that relate strongly to the Hyksos, that this site was probably their old capital of Avaris or Abaris. This claim has little substance, however, for the historical facts point out otherwise, as will be seen in Chapter VII.

Ramesses II's own father, Sety I, must have built quite extensively at this site because some monument remains have been found to be his. Building at Pi-Ramesses or, for that matter other sites in the eastern Delta, did not halt with the death of the Great Pharaoh, for extant records such as the so-called "*Anastasi Papyri*", in the British Museum, sycophantically praise Ramesses II's successor, Pharaoh Merneptah, for apparently having built "Pi-Ramesses-meri-Amun …. The forefront of every foreign land, the end of Egypt, …"

More clarity can be brought to the subject when an examination is made of the spelling of this site during the progression of the story. Extracts are presented as follows:

> "…………….. the land of Ram'e-sēs, …"　　(GENESIS 47:11)
> "………. cities, Pī'thom and Rā-am'sēs."　　(EXODUS 1:11)
> "… Israel journeyed from Ram'e-sēs …"　　(EXODUS 12:37)

On inspection, it can be clearly determined that from the spelling in EXODUS 12:37, the Hebrews did not leave from a city, as in EXODUS 1:11, but from a geographical area (the spelling is the same as EXODUS 47:11). The obvious conclusion would be the area called "Goshen" or "District of Ramesses", somewhere around the western end of Wadi Tumilat, since the Egyptians confined all shepherds to this remote location. The Hebrew/Israelites would hardly have been in Pi-Ramesses, the Nile Delta capital, where Egyptians would have had social contact with abominable cattle herders.

In the "Septuagint" version of the Hebrew Scriptures, the 70 translators mention the "District of Ramesses."

Pithom

It has been shown that if there ever was the Exodus treasure (store) city of Rā-am'sēs, other than Pi-Ramesses, there are no historical records revealing its location. However, enough evidence still remains to place historical significance to the other treasure city of "Pithom" that the story claims the Hebrews labored so hard to build.

According to Herodotus, in his Book II, page 158, the canal of Sesostris branched off a short distance above Bubastis (modern Zagazig), ran eastward past the village of Patamos (Pithom), and then went through Wadi Tumilat (see map of Wadi Tumilat, next page). The location of the city of Pithom (known also as Athos or Heroonpolis), has generally been accepted by historians, Egyptologists, and archaeologists alike to be the site now called Tell er-Retabeh in Wadi Tumilat. The Egyptian name Pithom; it was a sacred city dedicated to "Tum or Thoum", the ruler of the setting sun. *Monuments found at Tell er-Retabeh showed the founder to be Ramesses II.*

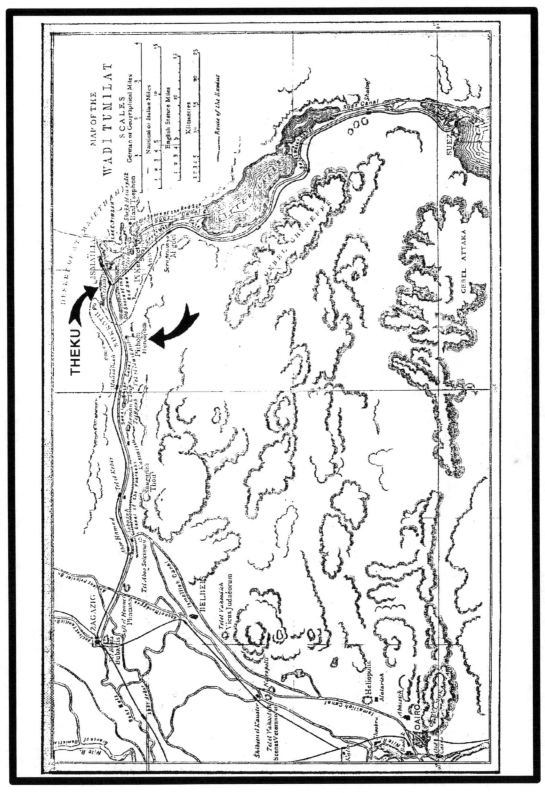

WADI TUMILAT

There remains a copy of a classroom text that provides a rare mention of this Per-Atum. It takes the form of the sort of a report an official might send back to his Pharaoh:

> "Another communication to my [Lord], to [wit: We] have finished letting the "Shosu" tribes of Edom pass the fortress [of] Merneptah-Hotephirma, which is [in] Tjeku [Theku], to the pools of Per Atum of Merneptah-Hotephirma in Tjeku, in order to sustain them and their herds, in the domain of Pharaoh, ..." (*Ancient Records of Egypt III*; James H. Breasted).

The Egyptologist, Flindes Petrie, excavated Tell er-Retabeh in 1905-6 A.D. He discovered a temple dating to the time of Ramesses II and a double statue representing Ramesses and the deity "Atum". Other Egyptologists, such as Dr. Edouard Naville, Karl R. Lepsius and Alan Gardiner, made extensive excavation in Wadi Tumilat, uncovering many remains from the reigns of Ramesses II and Merneptah.

Moses and His Deity

In the second chapter of EXODUS, the story continues with the birth of Moses. The story concerning the events that follow his birth, as told in EXODUS 2:2-9, are well known from the Judaeo-Christian Bible. However, this story was but a new version of an ancient tale already in existence for centuries. It was told about "Sargon of Akkad" (2370 B.C.), the great Babylonian conqueror and lawgiver, that:

> "He was placed by his mother in an "ark of reeds", the mouth whereof she closed with *pitch*, and then launched it on the waters of the Euphrates. The child was carried to Akki, the irrigator, who adopted him as his son, and brought him up until the day came when, through the help of the goddess "Istar", the true origin and birth of the hero was made known, and he became one of the mightiest of Babylonian Kings." (A.H. Sayce; *The Early History of the Hebrews*.)

It is obvious that this myth was absorbed into Hebrew literature, because "pitch" was a substance gathered in Canaan and Mesopotamia, but was not used in Egypt at the time.

In EXODUS 2:10, Pharaoh's daughter adopts the child and gives him the name of "Moses", "because I drew him out of the water." According to the story, the Egyptian princess who adopted him used her knowledge of Hebrew to give him the name of "Mosheh" or Moses, employing a punning etymology in so doing. Moshen, it seems, is derived from the Hebrew word "Mashah (to draw out); however, it is similar to the Egyptian word "Messu," meaning "son".

Moses' early life would have been one of duality in faith and allegiance, for not only had he been suckled by his own Hebrew mother, Jochebeb, but he became a member of pharaoh's household, as shown in EXODUS 2:10. It is obvious also that contact with his people and their cultic beliefs did not terminate as he grew to manhood, for EXODUS 2:11 states:

> "11 ¶And it came to pass in those days, when Moses was grown, that *he went out unto his brethren ...*"

As a son of pharaoh, Moses would have received extensive tutelage. He would have been taught the Egyptian knowledge in many disciplines. He would have been familiar with Egyptian religion, history, literature, mathematics, etc. This knowledge would have influenced all of his actions and thinking in his relationship with his brethren, the Hebrews.

The Exodus chronicler now draws upon another piece of Egyptian history in EXODUS 2:11-15:

> "11 And it came to pass in those days, when Moses was grown, that he went out unto his brethren, and looked on their burdens; and he spied an Egyptian smiting a Hebrew, one of his brethren.

> "12 And he looked this way and that way, and when he saw that there was no man, he slew the Egyptian, and hid him in the sand.

> "13 And when he went out the second day, behold, two men of the Hebrews strove together: and he said to him that did the wrong, Wherefore smitest thou thy fellow?

> "14 And he said, Who made thee a prince and a judge over us? Intendest thou to kill me, as thou killedst the Egyptian? And Moses feared, and said, Surely this thing is known?

> "15 Now when Pharaoh heard this thing, he sought to slay Moses. But Moses fled from the face of Pharaoh,

and dwelt in the land of Mīd´ ĭ-an:
and he sat down by a well.”

Again, a similar story was related in Egyptian literature of an Egyptian official, living in the Middle Kingdom, named “Si-nuhe”, who fled from the Pharaoh Sen-Usert (1971-1928 B.C.) across Sinai to Palestine. On the point of dying of thirst, he found rescue in the traditional hospitality of desert nomads.

There is no description of the route that Moses was supposed to have taken to Midian, only that, upon his arrival there, the story relates that as he was sitting by a well, he meets and helps the daughters of “Rēu´el”, a priest of Midian (EXODUS 2:18). Now things get interesting, for Rēu´el eventually gives Zip-po´rah, his daughter, to Moses. Accordingly, Rēu´el would become Moses’ “father-in-law”.

Some time after this, while Moses is still in Midian, EXODUS 3:1 states:

CHAPTER 3
¨NOW Moses kept the flock of Jĕth´rō
his father-in-law, the priest of Mīd´ ĭ-an: …”
(EXODUS 3:1)

This would have been his *second* father-in-law.

When the same story is related in NUMBERS, a separate book in the Old Testament, another relation is uncovered. NUMBERS 10:29 states:

“29 ¶And Moses said unto Hō´băb, the
son of Ră-gū´el, the Mĭd´ĭ-an-īte, Moses’
father-in-law, …”

If two fathers-in-law were not bad enough, Moses adds a *third*, Ra-gū´el. This dalliance or polygamous situation is passed over in *Smith’s Bible Dictionary* as simply: “one of the names of Moses’ father-in-law”. Smith’s authority for this explanation was taken from Josephus, *who quotes no authority.*

The only propitious comment that should be made to this kind of apparent obscuration is: “Which one, there’s three.”

One fact is ascertained: when Moses took a daughter(s) of a priest of Midian, he axiomatically became a full-fledged member of the Semitic clan he married into, somewhere around the northern parts of the Gulf of Aqaba or Southern Edom. Naturally, he would have taken part in their cultish practices and beliefs in order to be fully accepted into their band. With three separate cultic persuasions wafting around in his head, it certainly would have made Moses one confused young man.

Bewildering as the above information is, the story's narrator goes on to state in EXODUS 3:1-2:

CHAPTER 3

"NOW Moses kept the flock of Jĕth´rō his father-in-law, the priest of Mid´ĭ-an: and he led the flock to the backside of the desert, and came to the mountain of *God*, even to Hô´rĕb.

"2 And the angel of the LORD appeared unto him in a flame of fire out of the midst of a bush: and he looked, and, behold, the bush burned with fire, and the bush was not consumed."

Here is a classic case of combining tree and fire worship that had been taken from other mythological works. This "Lord", referred to here, was rendered "Jehovah", which we will examine in another chapter.

In EXODUS 3:4, this particular deity states:

"4 And when the LORD saw that he turned aside to see, *God* called unto him out of the midst of the bush, and said, Moses, Moses. And he said, Here am I."

Later, in the same chapter (EXODUS 3:14), the deity that Moses is hearing states:

"14 And *God* said unto Moses, I AM THAT I AM: and he said, Thus shalt thou say unto the children of Israel, I AM hath sent me unto you."

The Hebrew Yehweh, El or Elohim was rendered "God" in English. Elohim, the plural of Eloah, is used as singular in their scriptures. In Phoenician mythology, the Auxiliaries of the deity, Kronus (ILus, IL or EL), were called Elohim. (I. P. Cory, *Ancient Fragments*.) The Egyptian name for this supreme deity was "Nuk-Pa-Nuk" or "I am that I am" (James Bonwick, *Egyptian Belief and Modern Thought*, page 395).

This seems strange, for GENESIS 22:14 states:

"14 And Abraham called the name of that place Je-hō´vah jī´reh: as it is said

to this day, In the name of the LORD
it shall be seen."

The "Jehovah" used in EXODUS is already established as the cult identity name for their "Lord" already in use by Abraham. Again, this clearly shows that the different books were written by separate individuals at unrelated periods and that Divine Inspiration or inerrancy is purely human concoction. The name "Jehovah," which was adopted by the Hebrews, was a name esteemed sacred by the Egyptians. They called it "Y-ha-ho" or "Y-ah-weh." (See S.F. Dunlap, *Vestiges of the Spirit History of Man*, and G. Higgins, *Anacalypsis*, Volume I, page 329 and Volume II, page 171.)

In EXODUS 4, Moses now hears his cult deity state:

"19 And the LORD said unto Moses in
Mĭd′ ĭ-an, Go, return into Egypt: *for all
the men are dead which sought thy life.*"

It is now necessary to place the personal examination of the cult hero, Moses, aside until Chapter IX. That will reveal which pharaoh would have been reigning at the time of his return to Egypt and when, eventually, he would have led his people, according to the fable, in an exodus out of the "Land of Ramesses".

CHAPTER VI

A Time of Unrest and Origin of the Hebrews in Canaan

In 1236 B.C., the 55th year of Ramesses' reign, Merneptah (Ramesses II's 13th son) became regent of Egypt. Ramesses II died twelve years later, and Merneptah succeeded to the throne. Merneptah inherited a difficult situation because, during his father's old age, vigilance on the frontier had slackened and the army had been sorely neglected.

By the time Merneptah assumed the throne in 1224 B.C. – it seemed likely he did so in order to move against a Libyan threat – Egypt was in trouble on all frontiers of the Delta. Famine had driven the Libyans (warriors coming across the western desert from Tunisia and Sicily) in roving bands into the western part, therein terrorizing the inhabitants. The Philistines, from the islands and coasts of the Ionian seas, settled in lower Canaan about this time, undoubtedly threatening Egypt's vassal state of Canaan. The Assyrians were also expanding their kingdom, placing more pressure upon territories held by the Egyptians. According to Merneptah:

> "Barbarian enemy [people of the Greek seas, Sardinians, Achaeans or Myceaeans and others from Asia Minor called Siculians] were harassing the frontier and devastating the seaports in the North. Also, rebels were destroying the country from within, 'their tents were pitched from Per-Berset on the West, to the Heliopolitan canal (near Memphis) on the east'."

The period of Merneptah's reign seemed to herald the end of a time of unrest and migration throughout that part of the world. After more than twelve or thirteen centuries of continuous historical records in Egypt and Mesopotamia, there is a complete interruption. Egyptian inscriptions virtually disappeared between 1730 and 1580 B.C. (the Hyksos period).

After the fall of Babylon around 1530 B.C., inscriptions also disappear in Babylonia and are not resumed until 1400 B.C. Hittite inscriptions suffer the same fate for more than a century. In short, a catastrophic hiatus occurred throughout the Middle East, a sort of Dark Ages, brought about by multiple invasions of iron-bearing, horse-drawn, chariot-riding barbarians of obviously terrifying mien and disposition. Coincidentally, the beginning of this period was again to herald the cyclic appearance of the anciently observed comet that might have caused the flood. It was also the time in which archaeologists claim there was a gigantic volcanic eruption on the island of Thera, south of Greece.

The great invasions of patriarchal warriors all over the civilized world wrecked countless states, kingdoms, and even empires, and destroyed more than one rudimentary civilization. Knossos, capital of Minoan Crete, collapsed into ruins at the close of the 15th century. The Mycenaeans, for a while, replaced the Minoan Empire with their own Achaean seapower and policed the seas as King Minos used to do. The final break in cultural continuity came in the 12th century, when the Dorian invasions took place – overwhelming Mycenae, destroying the Hittite Empire, sweeping away everything and everyone that stood in their path until they reached Egypt where, in 1188 B.C., they were stopped at the Battle of the Nile.

This great invasion had been preceded in the 14th century B.C. (1300s) by _tidal waves of Semitic barbarians sweeping into Canaan and Syria from the Northern Arabian deserts_ and, in the 13th century (1200s) by repeated invasions of the Nile Delta by warriors coming across the western desert from Tunisia and Sicily.

These invasions changed the entire ethnic landscape by triggering massive migrations: Cosseans rushed down from their mountains into Mesopotamia, while Hurrians invaded Syria; _non-Semitic invaders (refugees from Crete) flooded into Palestine to collide with the Semites_; the intrusion of Phrygian-speaking people into Asia Minor pushed the Carians down the Maeander valley, whose inhabitants, in turn, shoved the Lycians all the way down to the toe of the Anatolian peninsula. On the other side, the Dorians overwhelmed the Greek mainland, pushing the Ionians onto the Aegean Islands and Ionia on Anatolia's west coast. In Syria, the Semitic Amorites were drowned under waves of Hittite refugees who fled up the Orontes Valley, compounded by another tidal wave of Aramean Semites springing from northern Arabia.

Except for Phoenicia, the coast of Canaan was taken over by Philistine refugees fleeing the Aegean, while inland, the Hebrews streamed into Canaan (in the early 12th century [1100s]) about the time that the Exodus story was to have taken place. (See map of Warrior Invasions, next page.)

Israel Stela and the Origin of Israelite Cognomen

Before leaving Merneptah for his successor, there must be one erroneous theory laid to rest concerning the existence of the Hebrew/Israelites as a nation prior to Merneptah. At Thebes, in Egypt, was found a stela (stone pillar with inscriptions) from the fifth year of

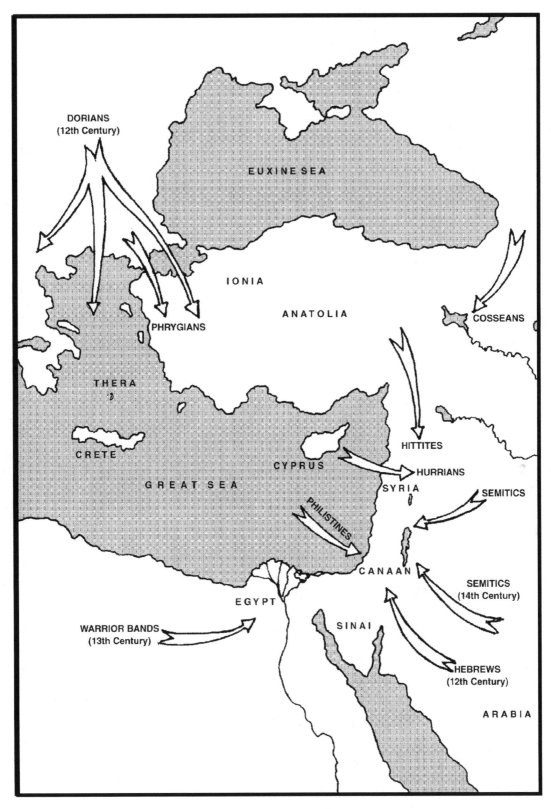

WARRIOR INVASIONS

Merneptah's reign, commemorating a victorious campaign in Libya and seeming to insinuate his successes in an earlier campaign in Asia (Breasted's *Ancient Records of Egypt, VIII*, pg. 256), commonly referred to as the "Israel Stela". Here can be found the earliest mention of the name "Israel" in historical records, excluding the Hebrew Scriptures themselves, and the only one in Egyptian history. Biblical scholars and many historians have concluded that this proves that the "Jacob clan" Israelites had left Egypt earlier and were in Canaan prior to Merneptah. By this inference, it gave them a more ancient heritage, preferably implying they were the Hyksos of some 300 to 400 years earlier.

During the reign of Sety I, there is no mention of even the name "Hebrew" when he destroyed the Shasu or Bedouin from the frontiers of Egypt to "the land of Canaan". So where and how did the name of "Israel" come to be on a stela in the reign of Merneptah? The answer is revealed by examining the history of those early seafarers who settled the Mediterranean Sea's eastern coast: the Phoenicians!

Kronos was named "Israel" (meaning champion of EL) in the land of Phoenicia. The Phoenicians yearly sacrificed their loved and first-born children to Kronos. It was said that an ancient king of that country assumed that name:

> "… in order that he might deliver his kingdom from the peril
> of an impending war. Rendering the gods propitious by
> immolating an only begotten son."

This only-begotten son, called "Ieud" (the word from which the Hebrew "Jehovah" was derived), was sacrificed in an annual ceremony, which was the method of seeking assistance from their deity.

> "When a very great danger of war threatened the country, the
> king had his son adorned with the royal dress (the purple robe
> which was later appropriated by the Church) and offered up."
> (Movers, 303; quotes Euseb. Praep. Ev.i.10)

The name "Israel" was assumed by many Phoenician kings, which they thought allowed them to share in a mystical sanction as a demi-deity, thereby enabling them to perform this yearly spring ritual of propitiation at the vernal equinox.

Of course, "EL" was a widely accepted cult deity throughout Syria. The title "Israel" is deeply intertwined with the mythology of the Syrian and Ionian people and it would not at all be in the scope of this work to attempt to unravel this enigma; however, a few examples of this subject will suffice to reveal the complexity.

A.   The Greek *Kronos* (Cronos) is identified with *Saturn*, an ancient deity of the seed-sowing. *Kronos* was named *Israel* among the Phoenicians. Kronos was also titled *Saturn Israel*. (S.F. Dunlap, *Vestiges of the Spirit History of Man.*)

B.   The Phoenicia Elon or Elion means "the highest god", like the Egyptian's Horus, Semiramis, or later Hebrew "I AM" or "The Most High". The old Phoenician and general Semitic chief deity was "Bel *Saturn,*" who was also the Canaanite national deity of the whole Semitic race.

When early Hebrew Scriptures are examined in the light of historical evidence uncovered, wider aspects of the existing religious systems in the Middle East are revealed. The evidence becomes overwhelming that, as the pastoral Hebrew/Semitics settled into Canaan and reverted to the agrarian life of the country, they absorbed the old Phoenician beliefs almost totally. Only later, as their historians developed a national identity, did they attempt to build their own system and try to disassociate themselves from the fundamental beliefs that they had appropriated earlier.

Now, for the first time, it can be revealed that this is where the Hebrew/Semitics derived the name of their clan and territory. The Hebrew figures Solomon, David and Abraham were only a more contemporized version of the ancient clan deity allusion from their early beginnings. This dawning had its roots deeply imbedded in India, many centuries prior to the period of the Exodus story.

* * * * * *

By closely examining the contents of the monument, it can be seen that the "Israel" mentioned *is not* a people or society. The stela's composition is one of a class common in   Dynasty XIX. The mention of "Israel" occurs in a clear-cut strophe of twelve lines, which forms the conclusion of the stela's message. The strophe opens and closes with a couplet containing a universal statement of the subjugation of foreign peoples in general. This inscription is evidence of Merneptah's campaign in Palestine during his third year. It is presented as follows:

> Concluding Strophe
> The kings are overthrown, saying: 'Salam!'
> Not one holds up his head among the Nine Bows.
> Wasted is Tehenu,
> Kheta is pacified,
> Plundered is Pekanan (Canaan) with every evil,
> Carried off is Askalon
> Seized upon is Gezer
> Yenoam is made as a thing not existing
> *Israel* is desolated, *his seed is not*;

Palestine has become a widow for Egypt
All lands are united, they are pacified.

Much has been made of the second phrase, "his seed is not" and referred to as the slaying of the male children or sons of the Israelites by the Egyptians. In other words, Israel is being alluded to as a nation. But this type phrase is found five times elsewhere in the stela inscriptions, where it refers to a number of other people, as follows:

A. "Those who reached my border are desolated, (*their*) seed is not."
B. "The Libyans and the Seped are wasted, (*their*) seed is not."
C. "The fire has penetrated us, (*our*) seed is not."
D. "Their cities are made ashes, … desolated; (*their*) seed is not."

These first four phrases mentioned above all concern "people or nations"; therefore, the plural pronoun "their" or "our" is used in connection with multitudes. However, when it comes to individual leaders, a singular pronoun is applied as in the fifth phrase, as follows:

E. "[Gored] is the chief of [Amor] … (*his*) seed is not."
    (similar to "Israel is desolate, (*his*) seed is not.")

Without the knowledge that Israel was another name for the Phoenician deity, Kronos, and that the king of Phoenicia assumed the name Israel, then it might seem that this part of the Strophe is referring to a country or clan. The phrase, "Israel is desolated, (*his*) seed is not," is referring to an individual or to a king named "Israel." More simply put: The king, "Israel," would be producing no more children because the Egyptians had captured and put him to death.

Pharaoh of Exodus – Not Merneptah

Now it is necessary to use Egyptian history again to dispel any doubt that it could not have been Pharaoh Merneptah who, according to the mythical story, chased the Israelites as they made their fabled exodus. Before resorting to Egyptian history, the stage will be set again by using the words of the story itself, as taken from EXODUS, Chapter 14:

> "8 And the LORD hardened the heart of *Pharaoh* king of Egypt, and he pursued after the children of Israel: and the children of Israel went out with a high hand."

Then in later paragraphs:

> "23 ¶And the Egyptians pursued, and went in after them to the midst of the sea, even all Pharaoh's horses, his chariots, and his horsemen.

> "28 And the waters returned, and cov-
> ered the chariots, and the horsemen,
> and all the host of Pharaoh that came
> into the sea after them; *there remained
> not so much as one of them.*"

It doesn't exactly state in unchallengeable words in Chapter 14 that the pharaoh was leading his troops into the watery tomb, but this is put to rest in Chapter 15, where it states:

> "19 For *the horse of Pharaoh went in*
> with his chariots and with his horse-
> men *into the sea*, and the LORD brought
> again the waters of the sea upon them; ..."
> (EXODUS 15:19)

Although assuming is dangerous, it must be assumed that the pharaoh was on his horse (or chariot), for monument inscriptions often lauded the exploits of the Egyptian kings by stating: "He rode before his troops leading them to victory." The only other conclusion would be that someone else rode his horse or the horse went into the sea by itself, but these ideas can be safely rejected.

The phrase, "there remained not so much as one of them," emphatically states that the pharaoh was drowned and that neither he nor his troops were recovered. Unlike the movie version of a drowned, floating body, a person sinks immediately to the bottom when drowned. The body floats only many days later because of the formation of gases, but by then it is unrecognizable. Therefore, under no stretch of the imagination could the Hebrew myth of the Exodus take place under the first four pharaohs of Dynasty XIX: Ramesses I, Sety I, Ramesses II, or Merneptah, simply because all of their mummified remains have been discovered and are extant.

Even if we assume that the Exodus story is mythology, it is still necessary to establish which pharaoh would have been reigning *if it were true*, because there are so many historical elements involved that can be used to establish a reasonable chronology. It is also necessary if only to reveal the outlandish claims made previously by biblical historians, and expose the fabrications of chroniclers.

One fact becomes disturbingly obvious, however, when searching for the pharaoh of the EXODUS. Even by looking at the Egyptian king list to determine that individual, one is in for a baffling, if not futile, quest to reveal that personage.

Merneptah was seventy at his death; the examination of his mummified remains found in 1898 A.D. showed he probably died of heart trouble. No records survive about the reign of Merneptah beyond his fifth year, but since he was in his mid-fifties when he assumed the throne, the remaining 15 years of his tenure can only be speculated about even though we know there was political intrigue.

Even to this date, evidence is so scant and anomalous that the immediate successor to Merneptah will probably never be conclusively established in the king lists. Records tend to reveal that a usurper was to grasp the throne from the aged king. This period will be examined in detail later. As far as the story is concerned, the statement in (EXODUS 2:23) –

> "23 And it came to pass in process of
> time, that the king of Egypt died: …"

– is referring to a pharaoh who had been ruling while Moses was hiding in Midian, after he fled from a pharaoh for killing an Egyptian. This was certainly not Merneptah, who had reigned long before the Israelites had been put into forced labor (see Chapter IV).

It will be shown in Chapter IX that Moses would not have returned to Egypt in Dynasty XIX but in Dynasty XX. It must be remembered that the Exodus story is a fable and even though historical events are used to construct the fable – it is still a fable. So to pinpoint who would have been the pharaoh is only conjecture and not historically viable.

The Roots of the Exodus Story – The End of Dynasty XIX

When order was restored some approximately twenty years later under Dynasty XX, Sethos II (Seti II) was looked upon as the only legitimate king between Merneptah and Sethnakhte (Sethankht) (1199-1185 B.C.), first king of Dynasty XX. The following list constitutes the names that Egyptologists have officially credited with having ruled during this period:

LATTER PART OF DYNASTY XIX

Baenre Merneptah (1224-1204 B.C.) then:

Amenmesses . . . . 4 years

Sekhaenra Ramesses Siptah . . . . .3 years

Userkeprure Sety (Sethos) II (Set-Necht) . . . . 6 years
Akhenre-setepenre Merneptah Siptah }

(Queen) Site-meryetamun Tewosret   } · · · · · · · · ·8 years

Yarsu (usurper) . . . . 4 years

BEGINNING OF DYNASTY XX

Userkhaure Sethnakhte . . . . 1186- B.C.

The confusion of this era may mask the very events that became the foundation for the fable of the EXODUS. Although there is no evidence of the Jacob-Israel/Joseph/Moses clan in Egyptian history, other independent records have much to say regarding this time and the origin of the fable. Fortunately, events of this period were set down by early historians, and, when placed in juxtaposition to pharaonic history and the EXODUS story, a clear sequence of events emerges.

The following is this author's reconstruction of what might very well be the proper order of Dynasty XIX, which historical accounts tend to reveal. Dates can have a variance of 20 years (plus or minus), since no exact dating exists.

DYNASTY XIX

I.   Menpehtyre Ramesses (Ramses) I . . . . 1305-1303 B.C.

II.   Menmare Sety-Merneptah (Sethos) I . . . . 1303-1289 B.C.
        a.   Also called Sesostris
        b.   Also called Miammous

III.   Usermare-Setepnere Ramesses-Meriamon II . . . . .1289-1224 B.C.
        a.   The Great Pharaoh
        b.   Also called Armesses
        c.   Also called Rampses

IV.   Binre-Meriamon Merneptah-Hotephirma . . . . 1224-1204 B.C.
        a.   Also called Amenophis
        b.   13th son of Ramesses II
        c.   Grandson of Sety I (his son, Sethos, called Ramesses)

V.   Amenmesses-Siptah (in Merneptah's reign) . . . . 1204 B.C.
        a.   Originally called Danaus or Hermeus
        b.   Usurped Merneptah's throne, during exile
        c.   Effaced Merneptah's monuments

VI.   Sekhaenra Ramesses Siptah (in Merneptah's reign) . . . . 1217 B.C.
        a.   Took Mernptah's throne, during sickness
        b.   Teworet, his Queen
        c.   Was assassinated by Sety II

VII.   Sethos (Seti) II . . . . 1204-1198 B.C.
        a.   Called Egyptus, Rampses, Sethosis
        b.   Aassassinated brother, Ramesses Siptah
        c.   Teworeet, his consort

VIII.   Ikhenre-Setepnere (*Merneptah Siptah*) . . . . 1198-1190 B.C.
        a.   Son of Tewosret, by Ramesses Siptah

IX.   Tewosret . . . . 1198-1190 B.C.
         a. Coregency with son, Merneptah Siptah
         b. Effaced Amenmesses' monuments

X.   Usurper . . . . 1190-1186 B.C.
         Possibly Bay (Ramesse-Khamenteru) or a foreigner

See bar graph, Chapter IX, for the relationship between Egyptian pharaohs and Hebrew patriarchs.

The "enigmatic time" part of Dynasty XIX after the death of Meriamon Merneptah, has left precious few Egyptian records. These give only a glimmer of fact to vaguely determine what actually took place during this period.

The only inscriptions of important historical content from the reign of Ramesses-Siptah are the graffiti of his viceroys in Nubia (Ethiopia), especially those at Wadi Halfa.

CHAPTER VII

Flavius Josephus' Accounts of Israelite History

It is ironic that the historical work totally unassociated with the Judaeo-Christian Bible provides us with the necessary information that unwittingly reveals the mythical origin of the "Exodus-of-the-Israelites story". It was written by none other than a Judean-Hebrew historian who was attempting to prove the credibility and antiquity of Hebrew/Israelites.

The extracts that are being quoted are from the books titled, *The Works of Flavius Josephus, Antiquities of the Jews,* and *Against Apion.* This last book is not really written against the Egyptian Apion, as is the first part of the second book, but against those Greeks who would not believe Josephus' former accounts of what he claimed were the very ancient origin of the Hebrew/Israelites.

Before proceeding with the examination of *Against Apion*, some excerpts will be given from Josephus' *Antiquities of the Jews,* Vol. I, Book II, in which he recounts the details of what he claims are the Hebrew/Israelite clan history of their time in Egypt.

I   In Chapter IX, Josephus states:

[5] "Thermuthis was the king's daughter."

AUTHOR'S COMMENTARY
In this sentence, Josephus is relating the name of the pharaoh's daughter, who was supposed to have retrieved Moses from the river when he was a baby. (The story states only the daughter of pharaoh.) It seems quite strange that such detailed information as the very name of pharaoh's daughter would have been kept by Hebrew historians concerning their origin, yet never is there once a mention of the name of the pharaoh who is infinitely more important.

II   Then in Vol. I, Chapter XV, Josephus states:

> "[2] They [ISRAELITES] left Egypt in the month of Xanthicus, on the fifteenth day of the lunar month, four hundred and thirty (430) years after our forefather Abraham came into Canaan, but two hundred and fifteen years (215) years only after Jacob removed into Egypt. It was the eightieth year of the age of Moses …"

AUTHOR'S COMMENTARY

With Sety I as a pivotal point, a combination of patriarchal years in the Scriptures along with the events after Joseph's death and dating from the Egyptian king list reveals that Josephus' recounting of the time between the Exodus and Abraham's entry into Canaan is uncannily accurate.

The following graph will show this close relationship:

- Abram was 75 years when he entered Canaan.
  GENESIS 2:4-5

- Abram was 86 years when his wife Hagar bore Ishmael. . . . . 11 years
  GENESIS 16:16

- Abram was 90 years when Ishmael was circumcised. . . . . 4 years

  GENESIS 17:24

- Abram was 100 years when Isaac was born. . . . . 10 years
  GENESIS 21:5

- Isaac was 60 years old when his wife, Rebekah, bore Jacob. . . . . 60 years
  GENESIS 25:26

- Jacob was 130 years when he came before Pharaoh. . . . . 130 years
  GENESIS 47:9

- Jacob came to Egypt at the end of seven years of plenty, so
  lived in Egypt in time of famine for seven years. 7 years

- Joseph served under the 14 years of Sety I, then under
  Ramesses II for 66 years. . . . . 66 years

- Time between the death of Ramesses II (1234 B.C.) to the
  Exodus (1104 B.C.) will be revealed further in Chapter IX . . . . <u>130 years</u>

                                          TOTAL   418 years

So, the difference between Josephus' calculations from EXODUS to Abram's entry into Canaan and the author's calculations of the same is only 12 years (430-418 B.C.). Also, the difference between Josephus' calculations from Jacob's entry into Egypt and the Exodus is only 9 years (215-206 B.C.). The preceding would make it appear that Josephus' account about the antiquity of the Hebrew/Israelites has been verified by the author; however, what it does is place the Exodus much later in history, which makes the Hebrew/Israelites' antiquity much less credible because their remaining history does not fit into a chronological sequence of their own making. In essence, their history of the period of Saul to Solomon is shortened almost intolerably. It also places them in sequence of the historical account of the Hebrew/Semites' invasion into Canaan from lower Edom in the 10ᵗʰ Century B.C. (See Chronological Charts, Chapter IX.)

Now *Against Apion* (Vol. IV) will be examined. In this work, Josephus was using the Egyptian Manetho's account of the Hyksos to prove Hebrew/Israelite antiquity, which is clearly stated in paragraph 13: Josephus states:

> "Now the very same thing will I endeavor to do; for I will bring the Egyptians and Phoenicians as my principal witnesses, because nobody can complain of their testimony as false, on account that they are known to have born the greatest ill-will towards us:"

Hyksos Account

Josephus quotes Manetho in paragraph 14:

> "Now, this Manetho, in the second book of his Egyptian History, writes concerning us [Hebrew/Israelites] in the following manner. *I will set down his very words, as if I were to bring this very man himself into court as a witness:* [for us] 'There was a king of ours [Egyptian] whose name was Timaeus. Under him it did come to pass, I know not how, that God [Amun] was adverse to us, and there came, after a surprising manner, men of ignoble birth out of the eastern parts, and had boldness enough to make an expedition into our country, and with ease subdued it by force, yet without our hazarding a battle with them. So, when they had gotten those that governed us under their power, they afterwards burnt down our cities, and demolished the temples of the gods, and used all the inhabitants after a most barbarous manner; nay, some they slew, and then led their children and wives into slavery. At length they made one of themselves king, whose name was Salatis; he also lived at Memphis, and made both the upper and lower regions pay tribute, and left garrisons in places that were the most proper for them. He chiefly aimed to secure the eastern parts, as foreseeing that the Assyrians, who had then the greatest of power, would be

desirous of that kingdom and invade them; and he found in the *Saite Nomos* [Seth-roite] [see map of Nile Delta Nomes, page 40] a city very proper for his purpose, and which lay east of the *Bubastic* channel, but with regard to a certain theologic notion was called *Avaris*, this he rebuilt, and made very strong by the walls he built about it, and by a most numerous garrison of two hundred and forty thousand armed men whom he put into it to keep it. Thither Salatis came in summer-time, partly to gather his corn and pay his soldiers their wages, and partly to exercise his armed men, and thereby to terrify foreigners. When this man had reigned thirteen years, after him reigned another, whose name was *Beon*, for 44 years; after him reigned another called *Apachnas*, 36 years and seven months; after him *Apophis* reigned 61 years, and then *Janias* 50 years and one month; after all these reigned *Assis* 49 years and two months And these six were the first rulers among them, who were all along making war with the Egyptians, and were very desirous gradually to destroy them to the very roots. [The total time of the Hyksos reign in the king lists was 150 to 160 years.] This whole nation was styled Hycsos – that is, "Shepherd-Kings". For the syllable, *Hyc*, according to the sacred dialect, denotes a *king*, as is *Sos* a *shepherd*. But some say that these people were Arabians."

At this point, Josephus departs from the text and introduces another version, without giving the authority, in order to prove his argument. He states in paragraph 14:

"Now, in another copy it is said that this word does not denote Kings, but, on the contrary, denotes *"Captive Shepherds"*, and this on account of the particle Hyc; for that Hyc, with the aspiration, in the Egyptian tongue, denotes the word *"Shepherds"*, and that expressly also: and this to me seems the more probable opinion, and more agreeable to ancient history."

Then, after introducing this unsubstantiated comment, Josephus proceeds to quote another excerpt from Manetho's writings, from which he extrapolates a conclusion from vague and faulty reasoning. Again, in paragraph 14, Josephus states:

"And this account of his [Manetho] is the truth; for the feeding of sheep was the employment of our forefathers [Hebrews/ Israelites] in the most ancient ages; and as they led such a wandering life in feeding sheep, they were called "Shepherds". Nor was it without reason that they were called *Captives* by the Egyptians, *since one of our ancestors, Joseph, told the king of Egypt that he was a captive*, and afterwards sent for his brethren into Egypt by the king's permission."

AUTHOR'S COMMENTARY

Nowhere in Hebrew Scriptures does Joseph refer to himself as a *captive*. This is a classic case of desperation to prove a point, where the evidence was invented to draw the conclusion that the Hyksos meant *captive shepherds*. By linking this particular non-existent statement to the previous totally unsubstantiated paragraph, Josephus absolutely failed to prove his claim.

Now Josephus returns to Manetho's text, quoting Manetho in paragraph 14:

> "These people, whom we have before named *kings* and called *shepherds* also, and their descendants," as he says, "*kept possession of Egypt five hundred and eleven years.*" [Actually 1720-1570, or 150 years.]

After these, he states:

> "That the kings of Thebais and of the other parts of Egypt made an insurrection against the shepherds, and that a terrible and long war was made between them."

He then states further:

> "That under a king, whose name was Alisphragmuthosis [Ahamos], the shepherds were subdued by him, and were indeed driven out of all the rest of Egypt, but were shut up in a place that contained ten thousand acres; this place was named *Avaris*."

Manetho states:

> "That the shepherds built a wall round all this place, which was a large and strong wall, and this in order to keep all their possessions and their prey within a place of strength; but that Thummosis, [Tuthmosis I, 1525-1508 B.C.], the son of Alisphragmuthosis, made an attempt to take them by force and by a siege, with four hundred and eighty thousand men, to lie round about them; but that, upon his despair of taking the place, by that siege, they came to a composition with them; that they should leave Egypt, and go without any harm to be done them, ... they went away with their whole families and effects, not fewer in number than two hundred and forty thousand, and left Egypt, through the wilderness, for Syria; but that, as they were in fear of the Assyrians, who had then the dominion over Asia, they built a city in that country which is now called Judea, and that large enough to contain this great number of men, and called it *Jerusalem*."

"63 ¶As for the Jēb'u-sītes the inhabitants of Jerusalem, the children of Jū-dah could not drive them out: but the Jēb'u-sītes dwell with the children of Judah at Jerusalem unto this day."

Sethosis and Ramesses

Now another story will be examined, where Josephus quotes the historian, Manetho.

Josephus:

[15] "But now I shall produce the Egyptians as witnesses to the antiquity of our nation (Judeans). I shall therefore here bring in Manetho again, and what he writes as to the order of this case, and thus he speaks:

Manetho:

"When this people or shepherds were gone out of Egypt to Jerusalem, Tethmosis (Tuthmosis I), the king of Egypt, who drove them out, reigned afterward, twenty-five years and four months, and then died."

Manetho then gives a list of kings in *Against Apion*, Book I, page 201, as follows:

DYNASTY XVIII (MANETHO)

Tethmosis	25 years and 4 months	after him was
Chebron	13 years	after who came
Amenophis	20 years and 7 months	then his sister
Amesses	21 years and 9 months	after her came
Mephres	12 years and 9 months	after him was

Mephramuthosis	25 years and 10 months	after him was
Tethmosis	9 years and 8 months	after him came
Amenophis	30 years and 10 months	after him came
Orus	36 years and 5 months	then his daughter
Acenchres	12 years and 1 month	then her brother
Rathotis	9 years	then was
Acencheres	12 years and 5 months	then came another
Acencheres II	12 years and 3 months	after him
Harmais	4 years and 1 month	after him was

DYNASTY XIX

Ramesses	1 year and 4 months	after him came
Harmesses Miamun	66 years and 2 months	after him
Amenophis	19 years and 6 months	after him came

Sethosis and Ramesses

The total years in Manetho's king list is *333 years.* It will also be necessary to compare this list with the contemporary king list for reference in this Manetho account.

DYNASTY XVIII (CONTEMPORARY)

Ahmose	25 years	
Amenhotep I	21 years	
Tuthmosis I	12 years	
Tuthmosis II	4 years	
Hatshepsut	22 years	Amesses 21 years and 9 months
Tuthmosis III	54 years	
Amenhotep II	26 years	
Tuthmosis IV	10 years	
Amenhotep III	38 years	
Amenhotep IV }		

Akhenaten	}	17 years
Smenkhare		3 years
Tutankhamen		10 years
Ay		4 years
Horemheb		28 years

DYNASTY XIX

Ramesses I	2 years
Sety I	14 years (missing in Manetho's king list)
Ramesses II	65 years (Harmesses Miamun in Manetho's king list)
Merenptah	20 years (Amenophis of Manetho's king list)

The total years in this contemporary kings list is *375* years.

After his king list, the story continues:

Manetho:-

"After him [Amenophis, Dynasty XIX] came *Sethosis* and *Ramesses*, two brothers, the former [Sethosis] whose power lay in his cavalry and his naval force, and in a hostile manner destroyed those that met him upon the sea; but as he [*Sethosis*] slew *Ramesses* in no long time afterward, so he appointed another of his brothers [Harmais] to be his viceroy over Egypt. He (*Sethosis)* also gave him all the other authority of a king, but with these only injunctions, that he should not wear the diadem, nor be injurious to the queen, the mother of his children, and that he should not meddle with the other concubines of the king; while he made an expedition against Cyprus, and Phoenicia, and besides, against the Assyrians and the Medes [Medians]. He then subdued them all, some by his arms, some without fighting, and some by the terror of his great army; and being puffed up by the great successes he had, he went on still the more boldly, and overthrew the cities and countries that lay in the eastern parts [Persia and India]. But after some considerable time *Harmais,* who was left in Egypt, did all those very things, by way of opposition, which his brother had forbidden him to do, without fear; for he used violence to the queen, and continued to make use of the rest of the concubines, without sparing any of them; nay, at the persuasion of his friends he put on the diadem, and set up to oppose his brother. But then, he who was set over the priests of Egypt, wrote letters to *Sethosis*, and informed him of all that had happened, and how his brother had set up to oppose him; he [*Sethosis*] therefore returned back to Pelusium immediately and recovered his kingdom again."

AUTHOR'S COMMENTARY

A.H. Sayce states:
"The pharaoh Amenophis, the son of Ramesses and father of Sethos is Meneptah, the son of Rameses II and father of Sety II."

Josephus then states:

> "The country also was called from his name *Egypt*; for Manetho says that *Sethosis* himself *was called Egyptus*, as was his brother *Harmais called Danaus*."

According to Josephus, however, in Book I, paragraph 16 (it is now, strangely enough, 393 years) when he claims:

> "16. This is Manetho's account. And evident it is from the number of years by him [Manetho] set down belonging to this interval if they be summed up together, that these shepherds, as they are here called, *who were no other than our forefathers*, were delivered out of Egypt, and came thence, and inhabited this country [Judea], *three hundred and ninety-three years* before *Danaus* (of the above account called *Harmais*) came to Argos; [Greece] ..."

AUTHOR'S COMMENTARY

According to the modern pharaonic king lists, the period of years between the expelling of the Hyksos under Ahmose (not Tuthmosis I) in 1570 B.C. and the death of Amenophis (Merneptah) in 1204 B.C. is 375 years. Regardless, when compared to Josephus' 393 years, it is still accurate for ancient calculations. Josephus continues to use ambiguous reasoning by assuming that the Hyksos were the Hebrew/Israelites just because Manetho states the Hyksos built Jerusalem. Also, it must be noted that Sety I, Dynasty XIX, is strangely missing from the Manetho king list.

Amenophis and Lepers

In *Against Apion*, Book I, paragraph 26, Josephus refers disparagingly to a story, detrimental to the Hebrews and Moses, which Manetho had written. Manetho, of course, is the very person he had quoted in earlier paragraphs to establish the veracity of Hebrew/Israelite antiquity. Concerning Manetho's story about an Egyptian king, Josephus states:

> "... now thus far he [Manetho] followed his ancient records; but after this he permits himself, in order to appear to have

written what rumors and reports passed abroad about the Hebrew/Israelites, and introduces incredible narrations as if he would have the Egyptian multitude, that had the *leprosy* and other *distempers*, to have mixed with us, as he says they were, and that they were condemned to fly out of Egypt together; for he mentions Amenophis, a fictitious king's name, though on that account he durst not set down the number of years of his reign, which yet he had accurately done as to the other kings he mentions; ..."

AUTHOR'S COMMENTARY

As was mentioned earlier, Josephus quotes Manetho's list of kings of Dynasty XVIII and XIX. There are two named Amenophis listed as the third and eighth kings in Dynasty XVIII, with reigns of 20 years and seven months and 30 years and 10 months, respectively. Then another Amenophis is also mentioned, listed as the third king of Dynasty XIX, with a reign of 19 years and six months. So when Josephus states "fictitious king" he would again be denying his own authority, and he has already stated that Manetho is a credible source. Josephus is also using Amenophis as the last king of Manetho's list with his years of reign just prior to Sethosis and Ramesses, and in their reign was Danaus, who was Harmais.

Now a review:

A.   The reign of Manetho's Amenophis and that of Merneptah are practically identical.

B.   The time between Manetho's Amenophis and the expelling of the Hyksos, (333 or 393 years) is almost identical to the interval, established by modern dating, between the expelling of the Hyksos under Ahmose and Merneptah: 375 years.

C.   There is little doubt that Amenophis is not fictitious and that Manetho's Amenophis is Baenre Merneptah, the fourth king of Dynasty XIX (see king lists, Chapter I.)

Also in paragraph 26, Josephus states:

> "... how he [Manetho] had already related that the departure of the shepherds for Jerusalem had been five hundred and eighteen years before; for Tethmosis was king when they went away."

AUTHOR'S COMMENTARY

Previously, in paragraph 14 of *Against Apion*, Josephus quotes Manetho as saying: "[the shepherds] kept possession of Egypt 511 years." Now Josephus states in paragraph 26 that what he said in paragraph 14 is really 518 years, from Tethmosis to Amenophis (to be realistic, seven years difference is of little importance this anciently).

Now the contemporary king list shows:

Expelling of Hyksos (shepherds)	1570 B.C.	
Dynasty XVIII	1570-1314 B.C.	256
Dynasty XIX (to Merneptah)	1314-1222	92 years
	Total	348 years

However, if the years of Dynasty XVIII are added to	
the four kings of Dynasty XIX and these to	348 years
the years of Hyksos occupation (1720-1560 B.C.),	160 years
the total is	508 years

So, the confusion of Josephus' statement in which Manetho claims that the Hyksos kept possession of Egypt for 511 has been cleared. The Hyksos occupied Egypt for approximately 150 to 170 years, and when added to the years of Dynasty XVIII and part of Dynasty XIX, the total is 508 years. This is the same as Manetho's account.

With this information in mind, an examination of the next account will begin to take on definite clarity.

Manetho's Leper Account

Remaining in paragraph 26, Josephus continues a preface to Manetho's account of the lepers with:

> "… for Tethmosis was king when they went away. Now, from his days, the reigns of the intermediate kings, according to Manetho, amounted to three hundred and ninety-three years, as he [Manetho] says himself, till the two brothers Sethosis and Hermeus; [Aramis not Ramesses]

> AUTHOR'S COMMENTARY
> This is similar to the two brothers, Sethosis and Ramesses (see the Manetho account in paragraph 15) only Ramesses is not part of this account. He had been killed by Sethos (Sethosis), so only his other brother, Harmais (called Danaus), is brought to the story (the 393 years attest to this conclusion.)

Josephus continues Manetho's account:

> "… the one of whom, Sethos [Sethosis] was called by the other name of Egyptus; and the other, Hermeus by that of Danaus. He [Manetho] also says that Sethos cast the other [Haramais] out of Egypt, and reigned fifty-nine years, as did his eldest son, Rhampses, reign after him sixty-six years. When Manetho therefore had acknowledged *that our forefathers* were gone out

of Egypt so many years ago he introduces his fictitious king Amenophis, and says thus: ..."

Josephus then proceeds with his paraphrase of Manetho's history: *The First Lepers' Account:*

"This king Amenophis [Merneptah] was desirous to become a spectator of the gods, as had Orus [ninth king of Dynasty XVIII in the Manetho list, and excludes the other two named Amenophis because they precede Orus] one of his predecessors in that kingdom, desired the same before him; he [Merneptah] then communicated his desire to his namesake Amenophis who was the son of Papis and one that seemed to partake of a divine nature, both as to wisdom and the knowledge of futurities. Manetho adds how this namesake of his told him that he might see the gods, if he would clear the whole country [Egypt] of the *lepers* and *other impure people.* The king [Merneptah] was pleased with this information and got together all that had any defects in their bodies out of Egypt, and that their number was eighty thousand; whom he sent to those quarries, which are situated on the east side of the Nile, that they might work in them and be separated from the rest of the Egyptians." He said further, there were some learned priests who were affected with *leprosy,* but still Amenophis (the wise man and prophet), fearful lest the vengeance of the gods should fall both on himself and on the king, if it should appear that violence had been offered them, added this also in a prophetic spirit; that certain people would come to the assistance of these polluted wretches, and would conquer Egypt, and hold it in their possession for thirteen years. These tidings, however, he dared not to communicate to the king, but left in writing an account of what should come to pass, and then destroyed himself, at which the king was fearfully distressed. After which he writes thus verbatim: After those that were sent to work in the quarries had continued for some time in that miserable state, the king was petitioned to set apart for their habitation and protection the city of Avaris, which had been left desolate by the Shepherds; and he granted them their desire. Now this city, according to the ancient theology, was Tyho's (Typhonian) city.

"When these men had taken possession of the city, and found it well adapted for a revolt, they appointed over themselves a ruler out of the priests of Heliopolis, one whose name was Osasiphars, and they bound themselves by oath that they would be obedient. Osasiphars, then in the first place enacted this law, that they should neither worship the Egyptian gods, nor abstain from any of those sacred animals which the Egyptians hold in the highest veneration, but kill and destroy them all, and that they should connect themselves with none but such as were of that confederacy. ... When he had made such laws as these, and many more such as were mainly opposite to the customs of the Egyptians, he then gave orders that they should employ the multitude of hands in rebuilding the walls about the city, and hold themselves in readiness for war with Amenophis the king, whilst he took into his confidence and counsels some others of the priests and *unclean persons.* Then he sent ambassadors to the city called Jerusalem, to those Shepherds who had been expelled by Tethmosis, whereby he informed them of the affairs of himself and of the others who had been treated in the same ignominious manner, and requested they would come with one consent to his assistance in this war against Egypt. He also promised in the first place to reinstate them in their ancient *city and country Avaris,* and provide a plentiful maintenance for their host, ... and informed them that they could easily reduce the country under dominion. The Shepherds received this message with the greatest joy, and quickly mustered to the number of two hundred thousand men, and came up to Avaris.

"... And now Amenophis [Merneptah] the king of Egypt, when he was informed of their invasion, was in great consternation. Remembering the prophecy of the son of Papis, he assembled his armies, and took counsel with the leaders, and commanded the sacred animals to be brought to him, especially those which were held in the greatest veneration in the temples, and charged the priests to conceal the images of their gods with the utmost care. And his son, *Sethos,* who was also called *Ramesses* from his father *Rampses,* being five years old, was committed to the protection of a friend. And he marched with the rest of the Egyptians being three hundred thousand warriors, against the enemy, who advanced to meet him; but he did not attack them, thinking it would be to wage war against the gods. He returned to Memphis, where he took Apis and the other sacred animals, and retreated into Ethiopia together with his army, for the king of Ethiopia was under obligation to him ... and took care of all the multitude that was with him ... He also allotted to him cities and villages during his exile, which was to continue from its beginning during the predestined thirteen years ... While such was the state of things in Ethiopia, the people of Jerusalem, having come down with *the unclean of the Egyptians*, treated the inhabitants with such barbarity, that those who witnessed their impieties believed that their joint sway was more execrable than that which the Shepherds had formerly exercised ... It is said also that the priest, who ordained their polity and laws, was by birth of Heliopolis, and his name Osasiphars, from Osiris the god of Heliopolis: but that when he went over to these people his name was changed, and he was called *Moyses*.

But still Manetho goes on:

"27 ... after this, Amenophis returned from Ethiopia with a great force, and *Ramasses* also, his son, with other forces, and encountering the Shepherds and the *unclean people at Pelusium* [earlier referred to as Avaris], they defeated them and slew multitudes of them, and pursued them to the bounds of Syria."

Diodorus Siculus – Second Leper Account

Next to this Manethonic account, we shall place the Greek conception of the matter as is found in the works of Diodorus Siculus (XL:3 taken from *Hecataeus of Abdera* and also in an earlier passage, XXXIV:I, without his authority being given). Diodorus says:

"When, says Hecataeus, a *plague* once broke out in Egypt most people believed that it was a punishment sent by the gods. For since many strangers of diverse races dwelt among them, who practiced very anomalous customs, with respect to the sacred things and to the sacrifice, it came to pass that hence their own ancient worship of the gods declined. Therefore, the natives feared there would be no end to the evil, if they did not remove those who were of foreign extraction. *The foreigners were, therefore, quickly expelled.* The best and the most powerful of them united together, and, as some people say, were driven away to Greece and other places, under distinguished leaders, of whom, Danaus and Cadmus, were the most famous. But, the greater mass withdrew to the country which is now called Judea, situated not far from Egypt, which was at that time barren and uninhabited. The leader of this colony was "Moses", who was distinguished by the power of his mind, and by his courage. He captured the country, and besides other towns, built *Hiersolyma*

[Jerusalem] which has now become so famous. He also founded the temple, which was so peculiarly holy in their eyes; taught them the worship and the service of their deity; gave them laws, and regulated their constitution. He divided the people into twelve tribes, because this is the most complete number, and agrees with the number of months in the years [previously it was shown that the Ionians had already established this practice; the Hebrews merely copied their practice]. But, he set up no image of the gods, for he did not believe 'that God had a human form, but that he is one God who embraces heaven and is Lord of all things' [Moses would have followed the same concept of a supreme creator, like the deity Aten of Amenophis (Akhenaten IV)]. He regulated the sacrifice and the usages of life very differently from those of other nations; since, in consequence of the banishment, which they had themselves experienced, he introduced a misanthropic [hatred of mankind] mode of life, hostile to strangers."

Third Leper Account

The statement in the earlier passage of Diodorus Siculus (XXXIV:1) sounds even more biting where it states:

"That they [the Hebrews/Israelites] alone among all nations scorn any intercourse with others and look upon everyone as their enemy. [see EXODUS 34:12-13] Their forefathers, also were driven out of Egypt as disgraced and hated by the gods; and *in order to cleanse the country*, those *attacked with the white sickness and leprosy* had been collected and cast beyond the frontiers as an accursed race. But, the expelled people had conquered the country round Jerusalem, had formed the nation of the Hebrews/Israelites and transmitted to their descendents, a hatred of mankind. On that account also they had adopted perfectly anomalous laws, neither to eat with any other people, nor to show them any kindness."

* * * * * *

The remaining selections by early historians available to support the accounts given previously, showing that the story of the Exodus of Hebrew/Israelites was based in part on the expelling of unclean Hebrews from Egypt are as follows:

Historian Choeremon – Fourth Leper Account

"That, at one time, the land of Egypt was *infected with disease*, and through the advice of the sacred scribe, Phritiphantes, the king caused the *infected people* (who were none other than the brick making slaves known as the *children of Israel)*, to be collected and driven out of the country." (See J.B. Pritchard, *Ancient Near Eastern Texts Relating to the Old Testament*, page 74; S.F. Dunlap, *Vestiges of the Spirit History of Man*, page 40; and I.P. Cory, *The Ancient Fragments*, pages 80-81.)

AUTHOR'S COMMENTARY

The preceding historical records are the basis for the author's conclusion that the Exodus story was based on the expelling of lepers within the latter half of Dynasty XIX and possibly even somewhat earlier events. These conglomerate facts were deftly molded together by later Hebrew historians to develop their more spectacular origin.

Lysemachus – Fifth Leper Account

"*A filthy disease broke out in Egypt*, and the Oracle of Ammon, being consulted on the occasion, commanded the king to purify the land by driving out the Judeans (*who were infected with leprosy*), a race of men who were hateful to the gods. The whole multitude of the people were accordingly collected and driven out into the wilderness." (See S.F. Dunlap, *Vestiges of the Spirit History of Man*, page 40, and J.B. Pritchard, *Ancient Near Eastern Texts Relating to the Old Testament,* page 75.)

S.F. Dunlap, in his *Vestiges of the Spirit History of Man,* states: "All persons afflicted with leprosy were considered displeasing in the sight of the Egyptian Sun god, Horus."

Concerning Leprosy and the Misunderstood Swine

The historian, "Aelian", quotes Manetho as saying:

"One who tastes sow's milk is so infected with *Leprosy* or Scall. The Egyptians hold that the sow is abhorred by both the Sun and the Moon.

AUTHOR'S COMMENTARY

Within this statement is embodied the basis for the Hebrew/Israelite's unreasoning religious abstinence from pork. Tacitus (circa 56-117 A.D.) maintains that the Hebrew/Israelites did not eat pork, because it carried a kind of leprosy. Since there was a lack of understanding about the causes of disease, some other illness was probably meant because, although the pig carries tapeworms and other types of worms and, of course, trichinosis (a dangerous disease which frequently causes blindness and death), none of these can be called leprosy.

The best explanation was by Antonius:

> "As the pig is valuable to the settled farmer only, the nomads,
> who have always felt superior to the farmer, came to despise
> the pig, as well as the farmer who bred it. In due course,
> they developed religious prohibition against the animals they
> themselves could neither breed nor keep."

There is little doubt that a variety of diseases similar to leprosy were attributed to the anciently dreaded affliction, primarily if they were contagious, where any contact meant contraction, and because the science of prevention was non-existent, meant rapid spread.

In the cultural mythology of the swine, first to spring to mind are those legendary fearsome boars who were pitted against various classical heroes such as Hercules, who vanquished the Erymanthian Boar; Meleager and Atalanta, who took on the indestructible Calydonian Boar; and Theseus, who slew the Wild Sow of Crommyon. These are more than simple Greek tales of demi-deity exploits that involve hogs, for they each seem to spring from a common origin beyond the ancient Greek religious beliefs.

According to Cretan legend, Zeus himself, in one of his earliest manifestations, was said to have been suckled by a sow and was later killed by a boar. As a matter of fact, being killed by a boar appears to have been an occupational hazard among ancient deities.

Adonis, who was first worshipped by the Syrians and later by the Greeks, was killed by a wild boar while hunting, as also was Attis, a Greek deity of vegetation. Under similar circumstances, a boar was supposed to have killed the Egyptian deity Osiris, who personified the corn-spirit. In all three cases, the devotees of these deities religiously abstained from hog meat. Attis, Adonis, and Osiris were all three worshipped as deities of vegetation and fertility, all three were celebrated as deities of death and resurrection who regularly rose from the dead each year, and the worshippers of all three broke their general hog meat abstinence only during their annual rituals when the pig was slain as a representative of the deity and consumed sacramentally. Indeed, the sacramental killing and eating of an animal implies that the animal is sacred and that, as a general rule, it is spared.

One such fairly familiar deity-hog linkage has to do with the Greek female deity, Demeter, and the rites surrounding her and her daughter, Persephone. Demeter was the corn deity to whom the pig was sacred; in art, she was portrayed with a pig in tow or carrying a pig or something similar. Originally, though, according to Sir James G. Frazer, in *The Golden Bough*:

> "The pig was the embodiment of the corn deity herself."

This same kind of interchangeability between hog and deity originally applied as well to the other deities mentioned – the ones who were supposed to have been killed by boars – for, as Frazer, states:

> "It may almost be laid down as a general rule that an animal which is said to have injured a deity was originally the deity himself."

The idea of pig divinity is supported all the more strongly here by virtue of the fact that the pig was eaten annually by the worshippers of Osiris in Egypt, a land where, ordinarily, the pig was regarded as unclean and untouchable. If an Egyptian so much as brushed shoulders with a passing pig, he was supposed to step into the river fully clothed to wash off the taint (this makes one wonder how tall the Egyptians were). Frazer states:

> "…also favors the view of the sanctity of the animal. It was believed that the effect of contact with a sacred object must be removed by washing before a man is free to mingle with his fellows, who, apparently, conceived of holiness as a sort of dangerous virus."

Insofar, then, as everyday pig-touching was concerned, the Egyptians' belief imply that the animal was looked on not as a filthy and disgusting creature but as a being endowed with high supernatural powers, and that as such it was regarded with that primitive sentiment of religious awe and fear in which the feelings of reverence and abhorrence are almost equally blended. What is divine is simultaneously hazardous. (In a future book by this author, the reason that the pig was so revered is disclosed in a shocking revelation.)

In this kind of uneasy equilibrium, one or the other of these contradictory feelings is likely to prevail. In this case, Osiris eventually became anthropomorphic and his original relation to the pig was forgotten. And once this came to be so, people also lost track of the fact that the pig was unclean on account of his holiness, figuring instead that if it was unclean it must be because it was just dirty unclean. Hence, the official rationale for sacrificing a pig to the deity Osiris was that the creature was Osiris' enemy, who was Seth or Set.

In India, the Hindu mother-goddess Kali, who gave birth and death to all beings in the universe, has been presented as a black sow that sends forth her creatures only to consume them. A Buddhist sutra from the Ming Dynasty, about 1520 B.C., illustrates the Hindu trilogy of Brahma, Vishnu, and Siva borne through the clouds in a chariot drawn by hogs.

Moses and the Excluded Miracle

One remaining set of circumstances in the EXODUS story seems to lend even more credence to the accounts that reveal the Hebrew/Israelites in Egypt were, in large part, thought of as unclean.

Previously, in Chapter V Moses was left speaking to a voice he hears coming from a bush that appears to be burning but is not consumed, in which he envisions an angel. EXODUS 3:14-15 continues:

> 14 "And God said unto Moses, I AM THAT I AM: and he said, Thus shalt thou say unto the children of Israel, I AM *hath sent me unto you.*"
> [earlier it was "*the Most High God*"]

He is then told by the voice:

> "15 And God said moreover unto Moses, Thus shalt thou say unto the children of Israel, the LORD God of your fathers, the God of Abraham, the God of Isaac, and the God of Jacob, hath sent me unto you: this is my name for ever, ..."

Later, however, in EXODUS 6:3, Moses' voice tells him:

> "3 And I appeared unto Abraham, unto Isaac, and unto Jacob, by the name of God Almighty, but by my name JEHOVAH was I not known to them."

This is interesting for, as mentioned above, GENESIS 22:14 states:

> "14 And Abraham called the name of that place Je-hō′vah – jī′reh: ..."

Just before this, the definition of the phrase, "mount of the Lord" is given. Now this was Abraham's deity – he heard it and was led along by this deity's directions – so there is no doubt that his deity was one in the same as the "I AM" of Moses. How could Abraham name a mountain after his deity, JEHOVAH, if he had never heard its name, as it is claimed in EXODUS. This tends to reveal that the Scriptures were written by many authors and not divinely inspired.

While Moses was yet in Midian, listening and talking to "I AM", which was a flame of fire out of the midst of a bush, he heard it say, as reported in EXODUS 3:10:

> "11 Come now therefore, and I will send thee unto Pharaoh, that thou mayest bring forth my people the children of Israel out of Egypt."

Then, in EXODUS 3:19-20, "I AM" told Moses the bad news which was:

> "19 And I am sure that the king of
> Egypt will not let you go, no, not by a
> mighty hand.

> '20 And I will stretch out my hand,
> and smite Egypt with all my wonders
> which I will do in the midst thereof: and
> after that he will let you go."

In EXODUS 4:3, 6 and 9, "I AM" shows Moses three wonders, which he is to perform before pharaoh.

The first was:

> "3 And he said, Cast it on the ground. [Moses' rod]
> And he cast it on the ground, and it be-
> came a *serpent*; …"

The second was:

> "6 ¶And the LORD said   furthermore
> unto him, Put now thine hand into
> thy bosom. And he put his hand into his
> bosom: and when he took it out, behold,
> his hand was leprous as snow."

The third was:

> "9 And … it shall come to pass, if they
> will not believe also these two signs,
> neither hearken unto thy voice, that
> thou shalt take of the water of the river,
> and pour it upon the dry land: and the
> water which thou takest out of the river
> shall become blood upon the dry land."

Now, as the story relates it, when Moses came before the pharaoh, he strangely does not perform all the tasks that "I AM" (by then called JEHOVAH) commanded of him.

First:	Rod to serpent	(Moses performs)
Second:	Leprosy	(Moses does *not* perform)
Third:	Water to blood	(Moses performs)

Why the "leperous wonder" was not performed by Moses can only be speculated upon; however, it does give added credence to the Manetho Leper Account "that Moses was a leper" as well as many of his people.

Miriam Made Leprous

To add reinforcement to the hypothesis, another event is now added that seems more than mere coincidence. The Judaeo-Christian Bible, Book of NUMBERS 12:9-20 relates that after the Israelites had left Egypt and were at a place called "Kibrothhataavah", in the Sinai desert:

> "9 And the anger of the LORD was kindled against them; and he departed.

> "10 And the cloud departed from off the tabernacle; and, behold, Miriam be-came *leprous*, white as snow: and Aaron looked upon Miriam, and, be-hold, she was leprous."

Realizing that the individual books were written by many chroniclers, it can be seen that these two incidences about Moses and Miriam, taken separately, would not be an admission of a "leprous clan" in themselves, but combined together with the following passages, certainly produce ample evidence to support the author's conclusion.

Leper Accounts Supported by the Judaeo-Christian Bible

DEUTERONOMY 28:27

> "27 The LORD will smite thee with the *botch of Egypt*, and with the *emerods*[2] and with the *scab*, and with the *itch*, whereof thou canst not be healed."

DEUTERONOMY 28:60

> "60 Moreover, he will bring upon thee all the diseases of Egypt, which thou wast afraid of; and they shall cleave unto thee."

DEUTERONOMY 7:15

> "15 And the LORD will take away from thee all sickness, and will put none of the evil diseases of Egypt, which thou knowest, upon thee; but will lay them upon all them that hate thee."

---

[2] hemorrhoids

CHAPTER VIII

Who Built Jerusalem?

Commentary of Manetho's Hyksos Account

The first mention of Jerusalem is in the Old Testament of the Judaeo-Christian Bible, where GENESIS 14:18 states:

"18 And Mĕl-chĭz'e-dĕk king of *Salem* …"
(GENESIS 14:18)

This alone does not establish a geographical location, but it does establish a chronology showing that Salem was already in existence in the lifetime of Abraham (circa 14th Century B.C.), some 300 to 400 years before Moses, according to the fable (see Chronological Chart, Chapter IX). However, further along in the Old Testament, in PSALMS 76:2, the geography is narrowed down:

"2 In *Salem* also is his [YAHWEH'S] tabernacle, and
his dwelling place in Zion."

S*alem* is now recognized by all historians and scholars alike as *Jerusalem*. The city of Salem was named after the Hindu prefix, Sal, pertaining to the fossil shells with horns, called ammonites, found in the area and supposed by Hindus to be representative of Vishnu. It was also related to the Ammorites of Canaan, who were closely related to Hebrews. The fossil was an icon of the Egyptian deity Ammon, another name for the deity Jupiter, which was always represented with the horns of a ram. Because it was close to the Dead Sea, Salem also represented an allusion to salt.

Manetho's account has the Hyksos building the city of Jerusalem; there is, however, a misunderstanding. What is really meant is that the Hyksos, probably Arabians, could have conquered the city of Jerusalem, but it had already been occupied for many hundreds of years previously. Later, according to the story, the Hebrew/Israelites attempted to make old Salem their capital, but it was already called Jerusalem.

Archaeological work done at Jerusalem by Dr. J.W. Crowfoot has verified the fact that occupation of the site began in or before the Early Bronze Age, dating from about 2000 B.C. Among the potshards of the Middle Bronze Age were found two bearing the impression of early seals, one of a Babylonian cylinder and the other of two Egyptian scarabs of Dynasties XII and XIII (2000-1700 B.C.). The Hyksos were expelled from Egypt in 1570 B.C.

The defenses, relatively poor in the early part of the period, were greatly developed later, between 1900-1800 B.C., by the construction of an additional wall of large stones, 15 to 20 feet thick. Fragments of pottery and figurines found in Egypt, now in Berlin, Cairo, and Brussels museums, from the Egyptian Middle kingdom (2052-1786 B.C.), have the name of "Jerusalem" on them.

Uru-salim or Ur-salimmu, in ancient times, was the name for later Jerusalem. The Ammorite deity, URU, was worshipped there. It thrived as a trade and commercial center, and always under the control of the indigenous people of the area. In the Old Testament story, the Hebrew/Israelites were never able to seize control of the city, which was already in the hands of the Jebusites.

Chronological Study of Old Testament Account

Now let us determine the narrative in the Judaeo-Christian Bible to determine if the Hyksos built Jerusalem. To begin this examination, it is necessary to determine if the patriarch, Abram, in the early part of the Old Testament, is, in fact, one and the same Abraham in the latter part of the same book.

This can be seen in GENESIS 17:5, which states:

> "5 Neither shall thy name any more be called *Abram*, but thy name shall be *Abraham*; ..."

Next, it is necessary to present a genealogy of Hebrew patriarchs, with critical years accredited to their lives, which will reveal that even the Old Testament shows that Jerusalem was in existence long before the Hebrew/Israelites were supposed to have entered Canaan.

Genealogy

GENESIS 12:4 states:

> "4   ... and Abram was seventy and
> five years old when he departed of

Hâ′ran." [around 1500 B.C.]
(See Chronological Chart, Chapter IX.)

Then GENESIS 12:5 states:

"5 ...; and they went forth to go into the
land of Canaan: and into the land of Canaan they came."

Also, GENESIS 14:13 states:

"13 ..., and told Abram the Hebrew; ..."

So, there is no mistake that Abram was of Semitic extraction, as were the people, according to the story, slaves in the first part of Dynasty XIX in Egypt.

Certain clans of Semitic people were originally inhabitants of INDIA, who had migrated to the Arabian Peninsula in very ancient times. Among the cult heroes of the Indians as well as Persians was the figure of Abraham or Abram the Brahmin. This figure was eventually deftly appropriated by the Hebrews, who were the descendents of these people. (Higgins, G.: *Anacalypsis*, Vol. II).

GENESIS 14:18 states:

"18 And Měl-chĭz′e-děk king of Salem ..."

According to the story, this establishes that Salem was in existence at the time. This would be somewhere around eight years after Abram settled in Canaan.

The preceding information plainly reveals that the city of Salem (Jerusalem) was already a thriving trade center at least 400-500 years prior to the Exodus, so the Hebrew/Israelites certainly could not have built it. Archaeological evidence proves that Jerusalem was a thriving city around 1900-1800 B.C., and even if the Hebrew/Israelites were the Hyksos, they would not have been the builders of Jerusalem.

The Jebusites were a black race, originally in Africa, who had anciently settled the area around Jerusalem; however, they called the city Jebusi or Jebus, as stated in JOSHUA 18:28:

"28 ...   ...Jē-bu′sī,
which is Jerusalem..."

And in JUDGES 19:10:

"10 ...   Jē′bus, which is Jerusalem; ..."

Did the Hebrew/Israelites Possess Jerusalem?

According to the story, when the Hebrew/Israelites entered into Canaan to possess the land as commanded by their deity, they ran into trouble when they tried to possess Jerusalem. The city was well defended by its ruler. As it states in JOSHUA 10:1:

> CHAPTER 10
>
> "NOW ...   ...when A-dō′nĭ-zē′dĕc *king* of Jerusalem ..."

And JOSHUA 15:63 states:

> "63 ¶As for the Jē-bu′sītes the inhabi-
> tants of Jerusalem, the children of Jū-
> dah could not drive them out: but the
> Jē-bu′sītes dwell with the children of
> Jūdah at Jerusalem unto this day."

Even in the time of David, the Jebusites were still in control of Jerusalem as stated in II SAMUEL 5:6:

> "6 ¶And the king and his men went to
> Jerusalem unto the Jē-bu′sītes, the
> inhabitants of the land: ...   David
> cannot come in hither."

But in the next sentence, David overthrows the separate fortified site close to Jerusalem, as stated in II SAMUEL 5:7:

> "7 Nevertheless David took the strong
> hold of Z[s]ion: the same is the city of Da-
> vid."

Verification that *Jerusalem* and the *city of David* are separate sites can be found in I KINGS 8:1:

> CHAPTER 1
>
> "THEN Solomon assembled the elders
> of Israel, and all the heads of the tribes,
> the chief of the fathers of the children
> of Israel, unto king Solomon *in Jeru-
> salem*, that they might *bring up the ark* of
> the covenant of the LORD *out of the city of
> David*, which is *Z[s]ion*."

Zion

The name Zion is directly related to Indian mythology. Zion is the kingdom of Sion or Siam, of which Cristna was born to be king of the people of Sion in the city of Judia (G. Higgins, *Anacalypsis*).

II CHRONICALS 3:1 states:

> "THEN Solomon began to build the house of the Lord at Jerusalem in mount Mō-rī'ah, …"

The mount here is the Moriah of Isaiah and of Abraham, the Meru of the Hindoos, and is like the Olympus of the Greeks. Although Sion or Moriah, or the Syrian Meru, was a high place, we find high places everywhere in the Old Testament. Mt. S(z)ion is a mystic mount and comes from the Mount S(z)ion of the Burmese empire or of the kingdom of Siam. (Simon de La Loubére, *The Kingdom of Siam*).

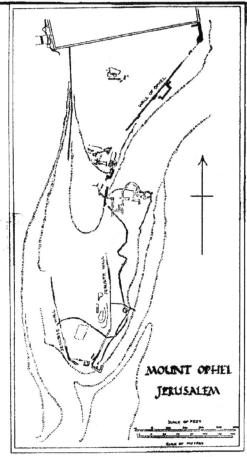

MOUNT OPHEL
JERUSALEM

SCALE OF FEET

SCALE OF METERS

Site of Jebusite Jerusalem on Mt. Ophel

Jerusalem.

Jos. x 1 [J].
Var. *LXX Ierousalem. EGN.* M.K. (*Syria*, viii 229-30)
'w-s-'m-m or *W-r-w-i-l-m* ; A (Kn. 287, 289, 290)
U-ru-sa-lim.

Loc. and Ident. The position of Jerusalem is determined by continuous tradition and almost uninterrupted occupation through 4000
years, from E.B.A. until to-day. The Jebusite city of L.B.A., which
figures in this narrative, occupied the narrow plateau of Mt. Ophel, to
the S.E. of the city (Pl. XXXVIII), upon the ridge between the Valley
of Hinnom (Wady el Nar) and the old Tyropoeon valley, now filled,
with its northern limit marked by the depression named the Zedek valley.
See Plan No. 9 ; also pp. 169 f. Its width averaged about 40 yards, and
its surface contained approximately 11 or 12 acres.

Excvns. on an extensive scale have been made for the P.E.F. in the
central part of the area, commenced by Prof. Macalister, assisted by the
Rev. Garrow Duncan, and continued by Dr. J. W. Crowfoot, during the
years 1926-28. At the southern end, above the pools of Siloam also, De
Weill, on behalf of the Baron Ed. de Rothschild, made considerable
clearances about the same time, and traced the city rampart on the E.
These researches leave no doubt as to the situation and growth of the
Jebusite city. Occupation of the site began in or before E.B.A. The
first line of defence on the exposed site to the N. was formed by a deep
rock-cut trench, dating from about 2000 B.C. Among the potsherds of
M.B.A. were found two bearing the impressions of early seals, the one of
a Babylonian cylinder, and the other of two Egyptian scarabs of the XIIth
and XIIIth Dynasties (*c.* 2000 B.C.). The defences, relatively poor in
the early part of the period, were greatly developed later by the construction of an additional wall of large stones, 15 to 20 feet thick, the space
between the ramparts apparently being kept clear as a measure of defence.
Similar features have been observed at Tell el Nasbeh, Gezer and Jericho.

JERUSALEM

CHAPTER IX

The Enigmatic Would-Be Pharaoh of the Exodus

Let us digress for a moment in order to make a final review of the EXODUS story before revealing the pharaoh who would have been reigning during that period, as determined by historical records and the Judaeo/Christian Bible.

When Joseph brought his father's (Jacob's) house into Egypt under Sety I (GENESIS 46:27), it numbered 70 men plus their households, which is verified by Josephus in Vol. I, Chapter IV. In GENESIS 47:6, Pharaoh then says to Joseph:

> "6 The land of Egypt is before thee; in the
> best of the land make thy father and
> brethren to dwell; in the *land of Goshen*
> let them dwell; ..."

And, later, in GENESIS 47:11:

> "11 ¶And Joseph placed his father and his
> brethren, and gave them a posses-
> sion in the land of Egypt, in the best of
> the land, in the *land of Ramesses*, as
> Pharaoh had commanded."

The seven years of plenty had expired; the seven years of lean began. Famine was throughout the Land of Egypt; the money failed. However, under Joseph's administration, he bought all the land of Egypt for Pharaoh by making "every man of the Egyptians sell his field" for seed to plant and then taxing them one-fifth of their harvest, Egypt survived the famine without rebellion or chaos.

The Hebrews fared well during this time, as stated in GENESIS 47:27:

> "27 ¶And Israel dwelt in the land of
> Egypt, in the country of Goshen; and
> they had possessions therein, and
> *grew and multiplied exceedingly.*"

At the end of the seven years of famine, Pharaoh Sety I passes into history to be replaced by the "Great Pharaoh" Ramesses II. Joseph continued to serve this Pharaoh as well for the next 66 years of his reign. Semitics were such a part of mainstream Egyptian life that the Hebrew children of Israel were not molested, since they were under the protection of Joseph.

After the death of Joseph, at the end of Ramesses II's reign, the absolute chronology of the story is interrupted, for EXODUS 1:6 states:

> "6 And Joseph died, and all his breth-
> ren, and all that generation."

AUTHOR'S COMMENTARY

This paragraph opens the *first time-gap* for it does not specify how many more years after Joseph's death it took for "that generation" to pass away. But considering that Joseph was said to be 110 years old at his death, everyone else of his generation must have been very close to expiring.

However, in EXODUS 1:7 this time gap lengthens into a time chasm, for it states:

> "7 And the children of Israel were
> fruitful, and increased abundantly, and
> multiplied, and waxed exceeding
> mighty; and *the land was filled with
> them.*"

The land mentioned here is obviously not all of Egypt, but refers to the eastern Nile Delta region. Regardless, to fill the land would take some time. As was mentioned previously, the story claims that during Joseph's administration in the seven years of famine and under the 66-year reign of Ramesses II – a total of 73 years – the "children of Israel" had been multiplying exceedingly. However, after Joseph's death the "children of Israel" continued to multiply until, as found in EXODUS 1:7:

> "7   … the land was filled with them."

The story does not give any hint as to how long it took for the Hebrews to fill the land but, starting with only 70 people, 73 years certainly would not be enough, for it is barely over one generation. To maintain the continuity of the story, some very interesting sleuthing must be undertaken if the Pharaoh of the EXODUS is to be found.

Next EXODUS 1:8 states:

> "8 ¶Now there arose a new king
> over Egypt, which knew not Joseph."

Now as has been established, Joseph died at approximately the end of Ramesses II's reign. The pharaoh who would assume the throne of Egypt after the Great Pharaoh was Merneptah. It must be remembered, however, that the waning years of Ramesses II reign were so indecisive, because of Ramesses' advanced age, that Merneptah had to be his co-regent.

It would then seem reasonable to assume that Merneptah was the "new king over Egypt, who did not know Joseph." Of course, assumptions can be deceiving and it is no truer than here, for, as previously commented, since Jacob's entry into Egypt, 73 years would not quite be enough to "fill the land" with Hebrew/Israelites. Here again clarity must be brought to the story, for the land mentioned would not be the whole Delta but only the "land of Goshen" and close vicinity.

What is needed at this point is to reveal the additional time in the story for the "children of Israel" to fill the land. So how can this be done without manufacturing circumstances to force the story to comply with the author's search? Here is where deduction solves the riddle.

The additional years sought come after the death of Ramesses II (1234 B.C.) and the end of Dynasty XIX in 1186 B.C., which would be 48 years. Certainly this deduction will be questioned, but valid reasons can be produced.

A   Pharaoh Merneptah, who followed the reign of Ramesses II (in which Joseph served) would have certainly been aware of Joseph's contribution to the stability of Egypt.

B   The remaining time in Dynasty XIX after Merneptah's reign was so filled with intrigues and conspiracies among the rulers and their offspring that little concern was expended upon insignificant Hebrew shepherds in the far-off eastern Nile Delta.

When the 73 years is then added to the remaining time of 48 years, it comes to 121 years. However, this places the story entering Dynasty XX. There are several more factors to be considered here, which are again logical deductions.

The "children of Israel" were not the only Hebrew slaves under suppression to build Pithom and Ramesses. This is given credibility by the words in EXODUS 12:38:

> "38 And a mixed multitude went up
> also with them …"

So it can be assumed that the Hebrew/Israelites were not the only Hebrews in the Land of Goshen. These other Hebrews, and probably other Hebrew/Semitic and Mediterranean peoples, had been under the protection of Joseph. If this were true, then these people would be considered as one, and they would have all been multiplying exceedingly and filling the "Land of Ramesses".

In 1186 B.C., a totally new dynasty arose out of the humiliating ashes of the remnants of Dynasty XIX. The short, two-year reign of the first pharaoh, "Sethnakht" (1186-1184 B.C.), was of little consequence to the story but does herald the reason for the Hebrew/Israelite oppression.

When Ramesses III (1184-1153 B.C.), the second pharaoh of Dynasty XX, came to the throne, he brought Egypt back to power, never looking back but only forward to a glorious future for the "Land of Ramesses". He would be the *king who knew not Joseph*. His first concern was to bring total control of the land back into pharaoh's hands.

In EXODUS 1:9-11, this is manifested with:

> "9 And he said unto his people, Behold, the people of the children of Israel are more and mightier than we:
>
> "10 Come on, let us deal wisely with them; lest they multiply, and it come to pass, that, when there falleth out any war, *they join also unto our enemies, and fight against us*, and so get them up out of the land.
>
> "11 Therefore they did set over them taskmasters to afflict them with their burdens. ..."

However, the pharaoh was unsuccessful, as stated in EXODUS 1:12:

> "12 But the more they afflicted them, the more they multiplied and grew."

This is when the pharaoh ordered all first-born males of the Hebrews to be "cast into the river". Right after this decree, Moses was born, and then shortly after, fetched out of the river by pharaoh's daughter. He was then nursed by a Hebrew woman until pharaoh's daughter brought him into pharaoh's house.

Then EXODUS 2:11 and 12 states:

> "11　And it came to pass in those days, when
> Moses was grown, …

> "12　… he slew the Egyptian, and hid him
> in the sand."

Moses would have probably been born in the reign of Ramesses III of Dynasty XX, about 1184 B.C.　When it states *he was grown*, it would probably make him anywhere between 18 and 25.　This would still place him in the reign of Ramesses III, about 1164 B.C.

EXODUS 2:15 states:

> "15　Now when Pharaoh heard this thing,
> he sought to slay Moses.　But Moses fled
> from the face of Pharaoh, and dwelt in the
> land of Mĭd'ĭ-an: …"

This is where Moses marries and shepherds the flocks of his fathers-in-law and communes with the deity of Abraham (I AM), who speaks to Moses, as represented in EXODUS 3:4 and 2:

> "4 …　out of the mist of the bush …"

that

> "2 …　　burned with fire, and the bush
> was not consumed."

Then, some time earlier, in EXODUS 3:23, the story relates only:

> "23 ¶And it came to pass in process of time,
> that the king of Egypt died; …"

Then EXODUS 4:19 states:

> "19 And the Lord said unto Moses in Mĭd'ĭ-
> an, Go, return into Egypt: for all the men
> are dead which sought thy life."

Moses returns to Egypt to demand that this new pharaoh release the "children of Israel" from bondage, as it states in EXODUS 7:7:

> "6 And Moses was fourscore years
> old, and Aaron fourscore and three
> years old, when they spake unto
> Pharaoh."

If Moses was approximately 20 years old when he fled Egypt, and he was 80 years old when he returned to Egypt, this means that 60 years had passed. Moses fled Egypt about 1164 B.C., and so in 60 years it would have been 1104 B.C. The pharaoh in Dynasty XX who was reigning in 1104 was Ramesses X (1109-1099 B.C.). So the pharaoh of the EXODUS story would have been **Ramesses X**.

Chronological Chart

This chart graphically shows the interrelationship between historical king figures of the Egyptian, Assyrian, Babylonian, and Hittite nations and Hebrew/Israelite patriarchal figures in a juxtaposed chronology during the period between 1600-550 B.C. (see Chronological Charts, pages 106-107).

The pivotal point in this chart is the beginning of Dynasty XIX at 1300 B.C. It is here that the story of the Exodus and historical records tie inextricably to Egyptian history by several facts, which are:

A   The Old Testament's admission that Jacob's family was given "Land of Ramesses" means the Exodus could not have taken place any earlier than Dynasty XIX.

B   The Old Testament's admission that Joseph bought all the agricultural land of the Nile Delta, then taxed the farms one-fifth of their crops.

C   The historian Herodotus reports that Sesostris (Sety I) (1303-1289 B.C.) divided the land into lots and gave everyone a square piece of equal size, from the produce of which he extracted an annual tax (Chapter IV).

Since the Exodus story uses the almost identical historical account of Herodotus' Sety I, who was the second king of the first Ramesside Dynasty, and since the years of Sety I's reign are identical to the story's plenty-and-lean 14 years, the figure of Joseph is axiomatically placed before Pharaoh Sety I in 1303 B.C. in Dynasty XIX. From this point, all chronological relationships – anterior and posterior – can be determined.

The following are other relationships set out in the Judaeo-Christian Bible:

I.   JUDGES 3:8 states:

> "8 Therefore the anger of the LORD was hot against Israel, and he sold them into the hand of Chū′shăn-rĭsh-a- thā′im king of Mĕs-o-po-tā′mĭ-a: ..."

Kashshu-nadin-ahi (1008-1006) was the third king of the "Second Dynasty of the Sealand". This period falls within the period of JUDGES in the Old Testament. The event happened during the reign of "Othniel", the first of the judges.

II   I KINGS 11:40 states:

> "40 Sŏlomon sought therefore to kill
> Jĕr-o-bō′am. And Jĕr-o-bō′am arose,
> and fled into Egypt, unto *Shī′shăk* king of
> Egypt, …"

Sheshonq (945-924 B.C.), the first king of the XXII Egyptian Dynasty, or Shī′shăk of the story, was a contemporary of Solomon.

AUTHOR'S COMMENTARY

The length of time between Chushaurishathaim and Sheshonq is approximately 70-80 years. These two kings fall at the beginning and end of the period containing Saul, Samuel, Judges, David, and Solomon, which, according to the Judaeo-Christian Bible, would have been a span of 300-400 years.

III   II KINGS 15:29 states:

> "29 In the days of Pēkah king of
> Israel came Tĭg′lăth-pĭ-lē′ser king of
> Assyria …"

Tiglath-Pileser III (744-727 B.C.) of Assyria was also a contemporary of Azariah, king of Judah.

IV   II KINGS 17:3 states:

> "3 Against him came up *Shăl-
> man-ē′ser* king of Assyria; and Hō-
> shē′a be- came his servant, and gave
> him pres-ents."

Shalmanesser (726-722 B.C.) of Assyria deported all the people of Samaria while Hoshea was king. Shalmanesser was also a contemporary of Ahaz, king of Judah.

V   II KINGS 18:13 states:

> "11 ¶Now in the fourteenth year of
> King Hĕz-e-kī′ah did *Sen-năch′e-
> rib* king of Assyria come up against
> all the   fenced cities of Judah, and
> took them."

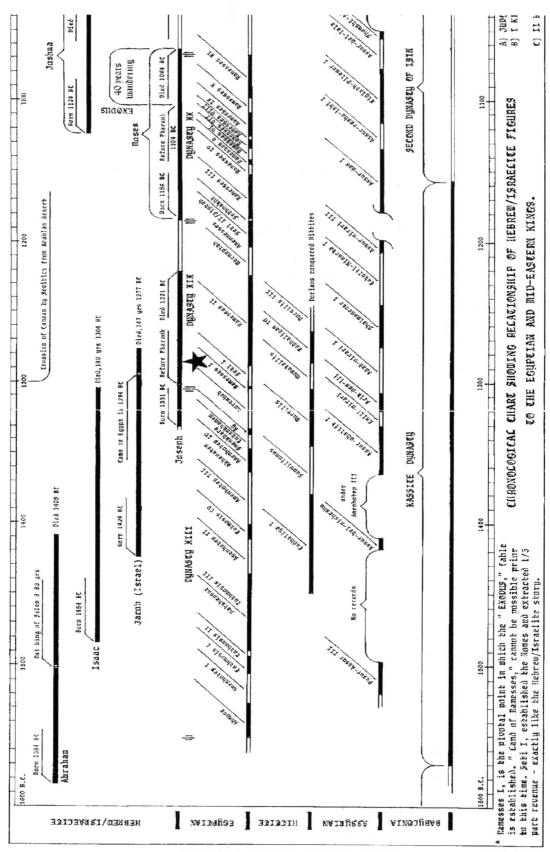

CHRONOLOGICAL CHART (LEFT)

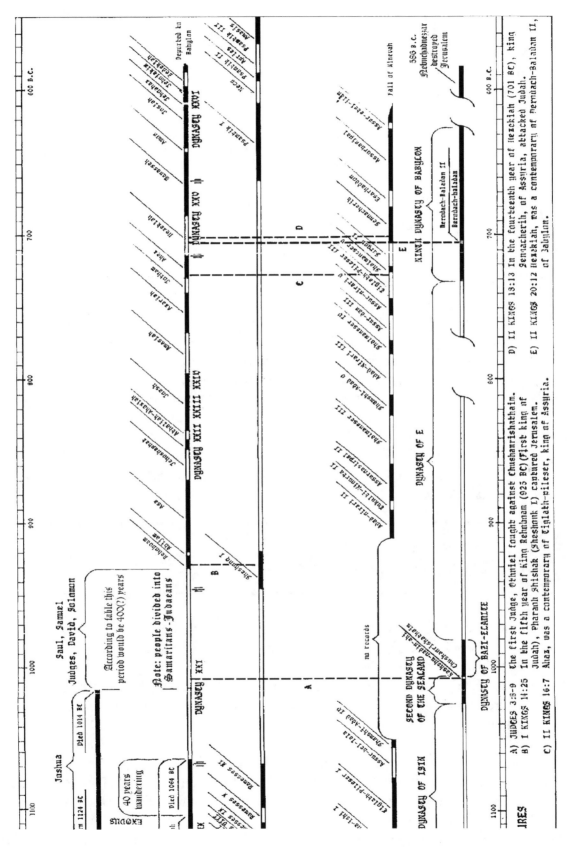

CHRONOLOGICAL CHART (RIGHT)

Sennacherib (705-681 B.C.) of Assyria was also a contemporary of Hoshea, king of Israel.

VI   II KINGS 23:29 states:

> "29 In his days Phâraōh-nēchōh king of Egypt went up against the king of Assyria to the river Eū-phrā′tēs: and king Jō-sī′ah went against him; ..."

Necho (Nekau, Wehemibra) (609-594 B.C.), second pharaoh of Dynasty XXVI of Egypt.

VIII   II KINGS 25:1 states:

> CHAPTER 25
> "AND it came to pass in the ninth year of his [Zedekiah] reign, in the tenth month, in the tenth day of the month, that Nĕb-u- chad-nĕz′zar king of Babylon came, he, and all his host, against Jerusalem, and ..."

Nebuchadnezzar (604-561 B.C.) destroyed Jerusalem in 586 B.C. and deported all the Hebrew/Judah clan.

COMMENTARY ON CHART
The chart discloses that Kashshunadin was contemporary with Othniel, the first of the Hebrew/Israelite judges, at approximately 1005 B.C.

The death of Joshua heralds the beginning of the period of Judges. Joshua, the son of Nun, was 110 years old (JOSHUA 24:29) when he died. Joshua's birth is not told, but by the third month after Moses led his people out of Egypt, he was already of fighting age, about 20 years, since he was sent by Moses to fight the Amalekites (EXODUS 17:9). This would place his birth about 1124 B.C.; therefore, his death would come approximately at 1014 B.C., the beginning of the era of JUDGES.

As can be seen, the remaining years from Joshua's death in 1014 B.C. until Rehoboam, first of the kings of Israel, and his contemporary, the Egyptian pharaoh Shoshenq (945-924 B.C.), is approximately 84 years. However, the collective time of JUDGES (Samuel, Saul, David and Solomon), is between 300 to 400 years. Since the Exodus date has already been established, the chronology of the 300-400 year period cannot be extended into the past to justify this lengthy fabled time. It cannot be pushed forward in time because the end of the

JUDGES Solomon period falls within the reign of the historical pharaoh Sheshonq (945-924 B.C.). Therefore, it is clear that this period was evolved from other stories of antiquity. In a future book by this author, this enigma will be explained.

CHAPTER X

Sites on the Exodus Fable Route

Before examining, at length, the remaining sites that were on the mythical journey of the Hebrews in the story EXODUS, it is necessary, at this point, to look at the pertinent phrases in the Judaeo-Christian Bible that reflect the locations along the path.

The story takes place over four chapters, 12–15, in The Second Book of Moses – EXODUS. In EXODUS 12:37, it is stated:

> "37 ¶And the children of Israel jour-
> neyed from Ram′e-sēs to Suc′coth, ...

EXODUS 13:17-19 states:

> "17 ¶And it came to pass, when
> Pharaoh had let the people go that God
> led them *not* through the *way of the
> land of the Philistines*, although that
> was near, ...

> "18 But God led the people about,
> through the *way of the wilderness of
> the Red sea* ...

> "19 ¶And they took their journey from
> *Suc′coth*, and encamped in *E′tham*, in
> the *edge of the wilderness*."

EXODUS 14:2, 9 & 21 and 15:22-23 states:

> "2 Speak unto the children of Israel, that they turn and encamp before *Pī-ha-hī'roth*, between *Mig'do*l and the *sea*, over against *Bā'al-zē'phon*: before it shall ye encamp by the *sea*.

> "9 But the Egyptians pursued after them, all the horses and chariots of Pharaoh, and his horsemen, and his army, and overtook them encamping by the sea, beside *Pī-ha-hī'roth*, before *Bā'al-zē'phon*.

> "21 And Moses stretched out his hand over the *sea*; and the LORD caused the *sea* to go back by a strong east wind all that night, and made the *sea* dry land, and the waters were divided.

> "22 ¶So Moses brought Israel from the *Red sea*, and they went out into the *wilderness of Shur*; and they went three days in the wilderness …

> "23 ¶And when they came to Marah, …"

* * * * *

Now the geographical sites, which are mentioned in the flight of the Israelites from Egypt, will be examined. The following are these locations in order of progression.

A	*Ram'e-sēs* (to)	
		EXODUS 12:37
B	*Suc'coth* (not through the way of)	
C	*Land of the Philistines* (led through the way of)	EXODUS 13:17
D	*Wilderness of the Red Sea* (then left from)	EXODUS 13:18
E	Suc'coth (encamped in)	EXODUS 13:20

| F | *Ē'tham* (wilderness) (turn and encamp before) | EXODUS 13:20 |

| G | *Pī-ha-hī'roth* (between) | EXODUS 14:2 |

| H | *Mig'dol* (and the *sea*) (over against) | EXODUS 14:2 |

| I | *Bā'al-zē'phon* (before it shall ye encamp by the sea) | EXODUS 14:2 |

| J | *Sea* (Israel went into the midst of) | EXODUS 14:9 |

| K | *Sea* (Moses brought Israel from the) | EXODUS 14:22 |

| L | *Red Sea* (went out into the) | EXODUS 15:22 |

| M | *Wilderness of Shur* (they came to) | EXODUS 15:22 |

| N | Ma'rah | EXODUS 15:23 |

Ram'e-sēs

In a preceding chapter, it was determined that the Ram'e-sēs of EXODUS 12:37 is not a town but an area located at the western end of Wadi Tumilat.

Suc'coth

The conclusion of most learned scholars (and also the author) is that Succoth is either an identical name for the Egyptian town of Theku (Tell el-Maskhuteh), at the eastern end of Wadi Tumilat, or in the immediate area. GENESIS 33:17 states:

> "17 … booths for his cattle:
> therefore the name of the place is
> called *Succoth*."

Ample proof has been offered to show that this area was the second most important access to Egypt from Sinai and Papyrus writings from the time of Merneptah describe the passage of Bedouin tribesmen from the desert, though Theku, to water their cattle at the Pools of PI-Tum (Pithom), which was in the area of Succoth. It would, therefore, seem a logical assumption that the Bedouin shepherds' cattle were corralled here while they temporarily pitched their tents.

The author would venture to guess from all evidence that Succoth is an area or precinct at the eastern end of the Wadi and that the actual fortress of entry was in proximity to the present Ismailia on Lake Timsah (see map of Wadi Tumilat, page 55). Succoth was also an Assyrian female-deity who was the equivalent of Venus. Her male counterpart was Sichaeus or Suchos, the Assyrian deity equivalent of Adonis.

Ē'tham

The Old Testament book, NUMBERS 33:6-8 states:

> "6 And they departed from Suc'coth, and pitched in *Ē'tham*, which is in the edge of the wilderness.

> "7 And they removed from *Ē'tham*, and turned again unto *Pī-ha-hī'rŏth*, which is before *Bā'al-zē'phŏn*: and they pitched before *Mig'dŏl*.

> "8 And they departed from before *Pī-ha-hī'roth*, and passed through the midst of the sea into the wilderness, and went three days' journey in the wilderness of *Ē'tham* and pitched in Ma'rah."

(See map of El Murra/Marah, page 121, for location of Marah.)

In looking at the word Etham", it will be noted that the word "Khetem" in Egyptian means "fortress". Etham undoubtedly alludes to the frontier of Egypt, since there were fortresses along that line. However, in NUMBERS it clearly states: "the wilderness of Etham," so it can readily be assumed it is the area east of the "Wall of Rulers". (See more information in examination of wilderness area in Chapter XI.)

Way of the Land of the Philistines

The ancient caravan route from Egypt to Hebron (in Canaan), beginning at the town of Sile (Tharu, Thel), modern el Qantara, between Horus Lake (modern Lake Menzaleh) and lake Ballah, proceeded northeastward past "the Migdol [fortress] of Merneptah", with Pelusium (Sin) a few miles to the north, then turned eastward and passed south of the shores of the tidal basin "Lake Sirbonis", then on to Rhinocorura (modern El'Arish). From this city, it continued up the coast of "The Philistine Sea" (Great Sea or Mediterranean) until it reached Canaan. This route was used primarily for all movement between lower Canaan and Egypt. Even though the desert sands of northern Sinai along the coast were hot and the water wells along the way brackish, the cooling winds from the ocean to the north made the journey less oppressive. Again, to give more credence to Marah's location where this author asserts, the myth verifies that the waters of Marah were brackish. This is identical to what is shown on the map of the area (see map of El Murra/Marra, page 121).

Way of the Wilderness of the Red Sea

EXODUS 13:17 states:

> "17… led them *not* through the *way of the land of the Philistines*, although that was near, …"

The above states where their deity does *not want* them to travel, but it is then followed by the route that *he does*! This description is given in EXODUS 13:18:

> "18 But God led the people about, through the *way of the wilderness of the Red sea* …"

First, it must be noted that it states that "the way of the land of the Philistines … was near; …" This again verifies that the Israelites would have been on or near the coast of the "Great Sea". This phrase is clearly explaining that the coast road would lead them directly to Canaan, where they would see immediate extinction of their clan by the indigenous peoples of the area, so they must return to "Edom", their brethren's homeland.

This route was to be "the way of the *wilderness of the Red sea*", also called "*Way of Shur*", which began on the eastern end of Wadi Tumilat at Lake Timsah and wound its way across the center of the Sinai Peninsula to "Edom" and the head of the "Gulf of Aqaba". To substantiate this claim, all that is needed is to refer to another section in the Judaeo-Christian Bible, titled I KINGS 9:26, where it states:

> "26…Ē'loth, on the shore of the Red sea, in the land of Ē'dom."

Ē'loth (modern Eilat; Elath) is a town at the head of the "Gulf of Aqaba". The ancient named land of Edom is north of that Gulf. Also, DEUTERONOMY 23:7 states:

> "7 Thou shalt not abhor an Edomite; for he is thy brother …"

The fable, at this point, alludes to traveling over this route directly to one of the Red Seas (now shown to be the Gulf of Aqaba); however, as will be seen, the site names take them north toward the Great Sea, then later they travel south to Edom, their ancestral homeland (see Chapter XI).

Wall of Rulers

Where the modern Suez Canal now exists was, for many centuries, the northeastern frontier between Egypt and the hated Asiatics (including everything from the Sinai Bedouins and all the countries beyond). To protect their country from invasion from the East, the Egyptians built a series of forts along a line from the "Sea of Egypt" (modern Gulf of Suez) to the "Great Sea" (Mediterranean). Between some of the lakes, randomly located along this same line, were dug wide channels or moats to connect them. These would act as a barrier after they had been filled with man-eating crocodiles.

The only pieces of surviving evidence relating to these canals or moats is from a relief in the Hypostyle Hall of Amon's temple at Karnak in Egypt, which shows Pharaoh Sety I (Dynasty XIX) approaching Egypt's northeastern frontier. The papyrus map in the Turin Museum in Italy depicts the triumphal return of Sety I from Syria and shows the road from Pelusium to Heroopolis and is embellished with quaint details (*Story of Maps* by Brown).

By looking at the map of frontier fortresses (see Wall of Rulers map, next page), it is readily apparent that the natural barriers across the land bridge between Egypt and Sinai (north to south) are:

A.   Lake Manzala / Horus Lake

B.   The swamp area to the east and southeast of Lake Manzala, which extends south to the area around Sile and modern El Qantara and southward to –

C.   Lake Ballah and swamp area south to –

D.   Lake Timsah

E.   Great and Little Bitter Lakes

The *first* of the artificial barrier canals connected the lower section of the swamp area south of Horus Lake (Lake Manzala) to Lake Ballah. In ancient times, Lake Ballah was either connected to the swamp area or in proximity. The *second* canal would have extended from the southern tip of Lake Ballah to Lake Timsah. A *third*, not certain but very likely, would have extended from the southern tip of Lake Timsah to the Bitter Lakes. In more ancient times, the waters of the Egyptian Sea (Gulf of Suez) extended to the Bitter Lakes and possibly to Lake Timsah. At what period these waters receded cannot, or has not been, nor cannot be, determined.

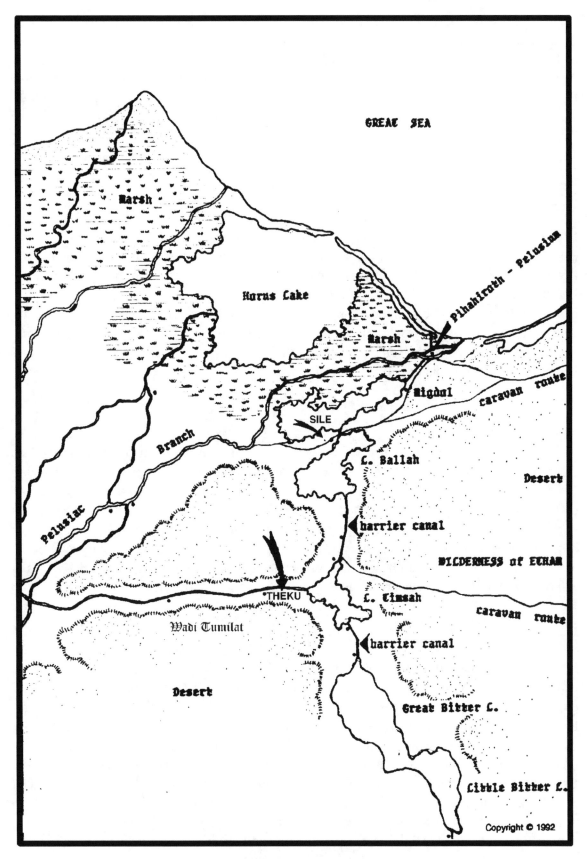

WALL OF RULERS

The early historians – Aristotle, Diodorus, Strabo, and Pliny – wrote that Sesotris (Sethos or Sety I) commenced the digging of a canal between the Bitter Lakes and the Sea of Egypt (Gulf of Suez) so that his extensive navy would have free access to navigate the Arabian Gulf (Red Sea) and beyond. He desisted, being afraid of the high level of the Gulf. By the very latest investigations, the Gulf of Suez (referred to as the Red Sea) is approximately 3 feet higher than the Mediterranean Sea. It was next undertaken by Nekos, the son of Psammeticus (Dynasty XXVI) about 663 B.C., but his death terminated the project.

Fortresses

As we have discussed earlier, the two major ports of entry to Egypt through this frontier were Thel (Tharu, Sile) at Tel Abu Sefeh, near modern El-Qantara and, Tjeku (Theku), Tell el Maskhuteh. Sile was located at the eastern end of a narrow tongue of land that remained between the lagoons, southeast of the Horus Lake (Lake Menzalah) and Lake Ballah. The dry ground of this strip was broken occasionally by reed-filled waterways. To traverse this area, it had become necessary to span the channels with bridges, thereby adding considerable security to this major point of entry into Egypt. This is the reason for the name, El Qantarah, or, more precisely, Gisr el-Qanatir, "The Crossing of Bridges" (see Wall of Rulers map, previous page).

Mĭg'dŏl

The only remaining fortress mentioned in Egyptian historical records (as well as Hebrew) is the Migdol of Sethos I (later renamed Migdol of Merneptah). The historian Hecataeus of Miletus lists Magdolus (Migdol) in his _Itinerarium of Antonini_ (a list of cities of a Roman general). It was located 12 Roman miles south of Pelusium and 10 miles northeast of Sile at modern Tell el Hēr (see map of Northeastern Corner of Nile Delta, page 36). At strategic points between Sile and Theku (at Lake Timsah) were watchtowers on the canal. There is also strong archaeological evidence that these towers were also between Lake Timsah and the Bitter Lakes, and on to the Sea of Egypt (Gulf of Suez).

Bā'al-zē'phŏn

Of the remaining pair of locations on the Hebrew Exodus route, Baal-zephon will be examined first. The mythological association of Baal-zephon to the Canaanite god Baal and other mideastern Semitic deities is so vast in detail that it is beyond the scope of this work. It will be left to the more serious scholars to investigate this subject to their satisfaction and clarification. It would be of value to note that there was discovered at Ugarit (Ra's Shamrah) on Syria's Mediterranean coast in 1930-33 A.D., at the Temple of Baal, a hoard of long lost Canaanite literature on clay tablets, mostly religious, written in the 14th century B.C. The phrase, "Baal upon Zaphon's summit", is frequently used in referring to the holy mountain in that area, which was anciently revered by the religious people of that land. The Hebrews copied the reverence of "High Places" (mountains) and absorbed the practice into their cultic observances by choosing the peak they called "Horeb, Hor, Mount Carmel, Mount Sinai" (the mountain of God), as well as others in the land of Canaan.

This Semitic and Canaanite mythology played a great part in the naming of cities and towns along the Mediterranean where these peoples settled and the religion assimilated. Otto Essfelt has shown in his book, *Baal-Zapho-Zeus Cassios*, that French archaeological finds have revealed the "Baal-zephon" of the EXODUS story to be "Mont Cassius", a sand hill on the west end of the Sirbonian Sea (Lake) (see map of Baal-zephon, next page), 15 kilometers to the east from the ruins of Pelusium. Essfelt also states: "In Roman times, the Pelusiac Amūn (Egyptian sun deity) was called Zeus Kasios (connected with Baal Sephon). His temple was excavated in the middle of the western mound of Tell Farameh (Pelusium, Sin). Baal Sephon (the Canaanite deity of seafarers) had a temple at Perunefer, the naval station near Memphis".

The Canaanite deity, "Baal", as known in the Hyksos period writings, became prominent in Egypt in Dynasty XIX, under Ramesses II and his successors, about the time of the story of the Hebrew/Israelites. More writings uncovered have shown that "Baal of Gaza", in lower Canaan, is identified with Zeus Krētagenīs. (*Cambridge Ancient History*, Vol. II, page 224.)

The Lycian and Carian (peoples of ancient southern Turkey) who settled in the Nile Delta are responsible for the introduction of the worship of the deity "Zeus". In a further connection of the area with "Zaphon", a stela was found near Sheih Saad, east of the Sea of Galilee, showing Ramesses II offering to "Adon-Zaphon, Lord of the North." Adonis was the vegetation deity worshipped by the Canaanites in spring and winter. This is revealed in Hebrew scriptures because their deity was also called "Adonis" (rendered in English as "Lord").

An extant map (El Murrah/Marah, page 121), produced as late as 1940 A.D., shows that "Mons Casius" (modern Katib el Qals) is located on an enlarged portion of the sand barrier separating the Serbonis Lake from the Mediterranean Sea, halfway between the eastern and western edges.

An itinerary of the Roman general Titus (68 B.C), traveling east from the city of Alexandria, Egypt, not far from the mouth of the Canopic branch across the Nile Delta to Canaan, mentions the following stops:

A.   Tanis,
      to the second station:

B.   Heracleopolis (Parva)
      then to the third station:

C.   Pelusium (refreshed for 2 days) then on the third day pitched his camp at temple of:

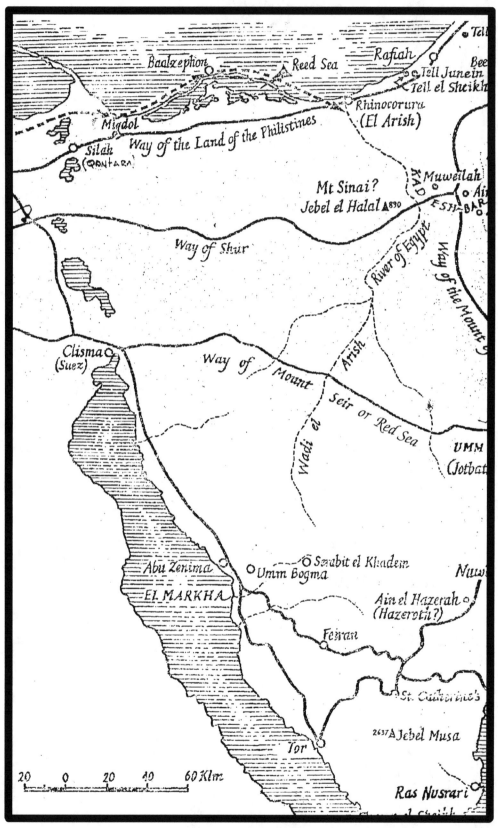

BAAL - ZEPHON

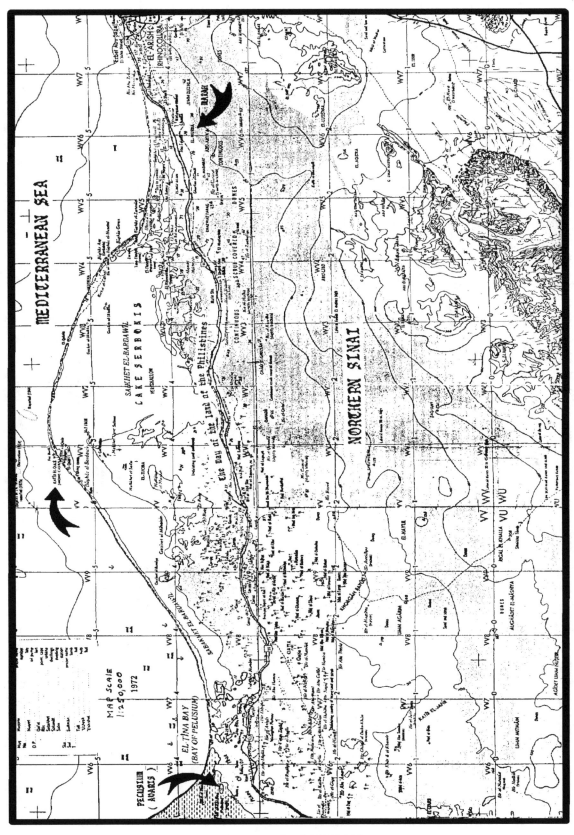

EL MURRA / MARAH

D.   *Zeus Kasios* (Baal-zephon)
       then to:

E.   Ostrakine (see map, next page)
       then "after that to":

F.   Rhinocorura (modern El Arish)

The Enigmatic Pī'-ha-hī'-roth

The last site to be examined on the route of the Israelite's exodus story is the mysterious "Pi-hahiroth," which has never been located by archaeologists or historians. An ambiguous title at best, holding its secret of identification so defiantly, scholars seem intimidated in their efforts to discover its exact whereabouts. This is because to do so will unequivocally challenge the popular belief about the 40 years of wandering into southern Sinai.

The etymology of this name has absorbed more time and pages than is reasonable or practical, so the author will not attempt to add more. If the serious student wishes to study the subject further, he or she will undoubtedly come to the same conclusion as the author. "Pi-hahiroth", Pelusium, Avaris [Abaris], or Sin are one in the same, if for no other reason than all evidence points directly to this conclusion. Only some of that overwhelming evidence is given as follows. Manetho's Hyksos account relates:

> "Saltis, the first King of the Hyksos, fortified the
> eastern boundaries of the Egyptian Delta against
> Assyrian invasion by founding Abaris (Avaris),
> situated to the *East* of the Bubastic arm in the Saitic
> Nome."

This should read "Sethroitic Nome," since all scholars agree the Saitic Nome is in the Eastern Delta. In later times, Strabo (pg. 804, and Ptolemy IV.5.53), who was born in Egypt, both locate the Sethroitic Nome eastward along the northern part of the Bubastic, or Pelusic, arm of the Nile. Later, in Manetho's leper's account, it is mentioned as an "Old Typhonic Town." (See map of Nile Delta Nomes, page 40.) The capital of the Sethroitic Nome was Heracleopolis (Parva) and *Pelusium.*

The site of Bā'al-zē'phon has been established, and the story plainly states: "beside Pī-ha-hī'roth, before Bā'al-zē'phon". The only site or town in that vicinity is old Avaris or Pelusium; therefore, an obvious conclusion is – Pelusium is Pī-ha-hī'roth.

The Sea

Without doubt, the "sea" which is referred to in EXODUS as "the waters were divided" (EXODUS 15:21) has been examined and quarreled over in minutiae for so many

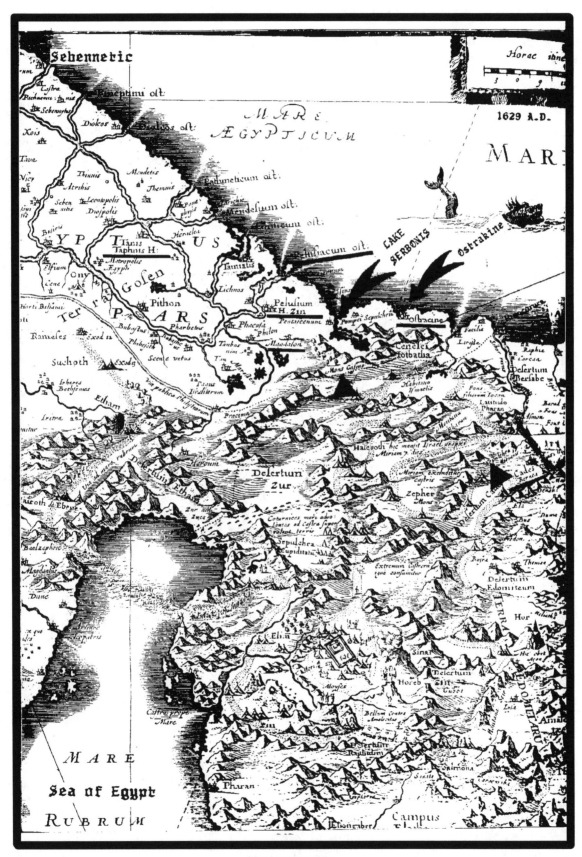

OSTRAKINE

centuries that it is time all argument was put to rest. The reason for such confusion is simply there is more than one body of water in contention.

In EXODUS, Chapter 14, where the Hebrews actually leave Egypt, only the word "sea" is used; however, in 15:22, it is noted as "Red sea". The "sea" of Chapter 14 has no outward identity – the body of water could be anywhere. Because the paragraph places the "sea" at Baal-zephon, and it has already been established that this site is on the coast of the Mediterranean, conversely, this "sea" must be in the same location. Most scholars are now generally agreed that the word "suph", meaning "sea", includes *inland bodies of water*.

The "Red sea" of Chapter 15 is now interpreted as "Yam Suph". "Yam" denotes reed or papyrus, so the name signifies a sea or swamp of papyrus or reeds, or "Sea of Reeds". In the same verses, 22-26, it continues:

> "22 ¶So Moses brought Israel from the
> Red sea, and they went out into the wil-
> derness of Shur; …"

"Shur" is located to the northeast of Egypt, beyond the Wilderness of Etham (see map, Chapter XI). So the "Red sea" mentioned here is not the Egyptian Sea (modern Gulf of Suez), nor the body of water to the south, properly called the "Red Sea", but is close to the shores of the Mediterranean Sea in northern Sinai.

* * * * * *

There is another "Red sea" mentioned, which has caused interminable confusion amongst scholars. That "Red sea" is, however, the modern "Gulf of Aqaba". This is amply substantiated at two locations in the Judaeo-Christian Bible. First, in the book I KINGS, Chapter 9, verse 26:

> "26 ¶And king Sŏlomon made a navy of
> ships in Ĕ′zĭ-on-gē′ber, which is be- side
> Ē′lŏth, on the shore of the *Red sea*, in the
> land of Ē′dom."

The second is in DEUTERONOMY l:1:

> CHAPTER 1
> "These be the words which Moses
> spake unto all Israel *on this side Jordan*
> in the wilderness, in the plain over
> against the *Red sea*, between Paran, …."

It has already been established that Eloth (Eilath) is located at the northern tip of the modern Gulf of Aqaba. The land of Edom (Idumaea) extends from the Gulf of Aqaba to the southern tip of the Dead Sea. Its eastern border was modern Wadi al'Araba, extending westward into the Arabian Desert.

EXODUS, Chapter 23:31 states:

> "31 And I will set thy bounds from the
> Red sea even unto the sea of the Philis-
> tines [Mediterranean] …"

This corresponds to the western boundary of the "Promised Land" given to Moses by his cult deity, Jehovah, meaning from the Gulf of Aqaba to the Mediterranean Sea (NUMBERS 34:3-5; JOSHUA 15:2-4).

The remaining body of water that needs definition because biblical scholars have forced it into a mold – which would conform to their concept of a miraculous "Parting of the Waters" – is the modern Gulf of Suez.

At the northern end of the Red Sea, the Sinai Peninsula acts as a knife-like wedge, dividing that body of water into the "Gulf of Aqaba," extending northward along the eastern coast of Sinai, and the Gulf of Suez, running along the western side of the Peninsula.

In ancient times, the tongue of water separating Egypt from Sinai was always referred to as the "Sea of Egypt". This is substantiated in ISAIAH 11:15, where it states:

> "15 And the LORD shall utterly destroy
> the tongue of the *Egyptian sea*; and …"

Simply through misunderstanding, the Egyptian Sea was thought to have been the Red Sea. To make a more impressive story, biblical scholars (mis)interpreted the "Reed Sea" (Yam-Suph) in EXODUS 15:22 as "Red Sea," probably because a large body of water was necessary to satisfy their vision of a mighty sea miraculously parting. This then would seem to give more credibility to the story, they hoped, of how 600,000 Israelites were miraculously able to wander aimlessly around in a burning desert landscape totally hostile to human intrusion for 40 years.

Yam Suph – Reed Sea, not Red Sea

Now the time has arrived to identify where the body of water is through which the Israelites were supposed to have come across on dry ground. From the preceding evidence presented, it should be of little surprise that this site is none other than the Sirbonian Sea (Lake).

To substantiate this claim, let us work in reverse. EXODUS 15:22 states:

> "22 ¶So Moses brought Israel from the
> *Red sea*, and they went out into the *wil-*

> *derness of Shur*; and they went three
> days in the wilderness, and found
> no water."

The wilderness of Shur borders the Sirbonis Sea, then stretches south to Etham. The Red sea here should be interpreted as "sea of reeds". The Sea of Sirbonis was then a shallow, reed-filled tidal flat. As previously shown, Baal-zephon was the last site by which the Israelites camped prior to going through the "sea". It was located on the sandbar dividing Lake Sirbonis from the Mediterranean or Great Sea (see map, page 120).

As a remaining corroboration of this claim, some historical records are presented which reveal that this site contains the geographical and historical properties that the fable has incorporated to construct the incident of the "Parting of the Sea".

> "British Major C.S. Jarvas, one time governor of Sinai, describes
> Sirbonis as an enormous salt-encrusted clay pan about 6 to
> 10 feet below the level of the Mediterranean Sea, separated
> by a narrow strip of sand 100 to 300 yards in width. Strong
> northwesterly gales cause waves to break through the narrow
> spit of sand at a half dozen places, and in a short time flood
> the whole salt pan several times a year. Forty-five miles long
> and thirteen miles in width, *this area saw military disasters in
> Helenistic times.*"
>
> G.H. Higgins, *Anacalypsis*

The Helenistic time was just prior to the period that the Hebrews had been taken in slavery to Babylon. Later, the Hebrews began to develop their own individualistic religious identity by reconstructing various Middle Eastern mythologies and histories into a miraculous version of their own origin to cover the ignominious past of being only a small, obscure sector of the Semitic conglomerate that had settled in Edom and lower Canaan and eventually had been taken into slavery in Egypt after the many Egyptian conquests in that area.

Study of other ancient religious myths and historical writings to see the similarity of passing through bodies of water, such as the stories of *Bacchus and Alexander the Great*, will reveal that this same type of performance was readily used by writers of the time to confer credibility on their folk heroes. To demonstrate how old this mythology really is, a review of Crishna's childhood in the ancient Indian Bhagaret Pooraun will be sufficient (see Thomas Maurice, *History of Hindostani*).

Route of the Exodus Story

Now that all of the sites have been identified and located that were on the mythical Exodus route, the author can finally describe where the fabled children of Israel would have gone, according to the story. EXODUS 12:37:

> "37 ¶And the children of Israel jour-
> neyed from Ram′e-sēs to Suc′coth, …

The route would have commenced in the *District of Ramesses* of *the Bubasites Nome* at the western end of Wadi-Tumilat within a pasture area called *Goshen*. Then the host would have proceeded eastward into *Wadi-Tumilat*, passing by the settlement of *Pithom* and into the *District of Succoth*. NUMBERS 33:6:

> "6 And they departed from Suc′coth,
> and pitched in *Ē′tham*, which is in the
> edge of the wilderness."

Then, after passing through the District of Succoth, the host would have come against the fortifications of the "Wall of Rulers" at the town of *Theku*. Since the host comprised a great number of people, they would have swarmed over the barrier like an army of ants. Then the mass of humanity spread out into the desert called the *Wilderness of Etham*. NUMBERS 33:7:

> "7 And they removed from *E′tham*, and
> turned again unto *Pī-ha-hī′roth*, which is
> before *Bāal-zē′phŏn*: and they pitched
> before *Mig′dŏl*."

The story had stated earlier that Moses' deity was not to have Moses take his people to Canaan along the coastal road of the Great Sea because of danger from attack by enemies in lower Canaan. EXODUS 14:9:

> "9…Pharaoh, and his horsemen, and his
> army, and overtook them encamping
> by the sea, beside *Pī-ha-hī′roth*, before
> *Bā′al-zē′phon*."

Then, according to the story, pharaoh and his army came into sight – vengence on their minds – ready to recapture their former slaves and return them to servitude. EXODUS 14:21:

> "21 And Moses stretched out his hand
> over the *sea*; and the LORD caused the
> *sea* to go back by a strong east wind all
> that night, and made the *sea* dry land,
> and the waters were divided."

Here the story states that in order to escape the pharaoh's army, Moses' deity makes the *Reed Sea* divide by a strong east wind at night. It could not have been the Great Sea so it had to be the Sea of Reeds (Lake Sirbonis). EXODUS 14:27-28:

> "27 And Moses stretched forth his
> hand over the sea, and the sea returned
> to his strength when the morning ap-
> peared; and the Egyptians fled against
> it; and the LORD overthrew the Egyp-
> tians in the midst of the sea."

> "28 And the waters returned, and cov-
> ered the chariots, and the horsemen,
> and all the host of Pharaoh that came
> into the sea after them; *there remained*
> *not so much as one of them.*"

As mentioned earlier, there are historical accounts of military contingents being lost in the same tidal flat. EXODUS 15:22:

> "22 ¶So Moses brought Israel from the
> *Red sea*, and they went out into the *wil-*
> *derness of Shur*; and they went three days
> in the wilderness ..."

When the host crossed over the land bridge between the Sea of Reeds and the Great Sea, they spread into the *Wilderness of Shur*, which is the desert area bounded on the north by the Great Sea, on the west by the *Wilderness of Etham*, on the east by the *Wilderness of Zin* or *Sin*, and, to the south, by the endless sands of the *Wilderness of Sinai*. EXODUS 13:18:

> "18 But God led the people about,
> through the *way of the wilderness of*
> *the Red sea ...*"

Once in the wilderness, the host headed south toward their ancestral homeland in Edom, north of the Gulf of Aqaba. For this route, see Exodus Route Map, next page.

There is no doubt that the Israelite/Hebrews of the fable did not go to Canaan but returned to their homeland in Edom, because YAHWEH (God) led them by the "Way of the Wilderness of the Red Sea" (Gulf of Aqaba).

If the story *were true,* then the Hebrew/Israelites would have left Egypt in the late 12th century B.C. Ironically, it was in the 10th century B.C. that waves of Hebrew/Semitics swept out of Edom, invaded lower Canaan, and, with some success, established a foothold in the mountainous areas of that country. It is obvious that the chroniclers of the story used this period as the time of the 40 years of wandering and Joshua's invasion of Canaan.

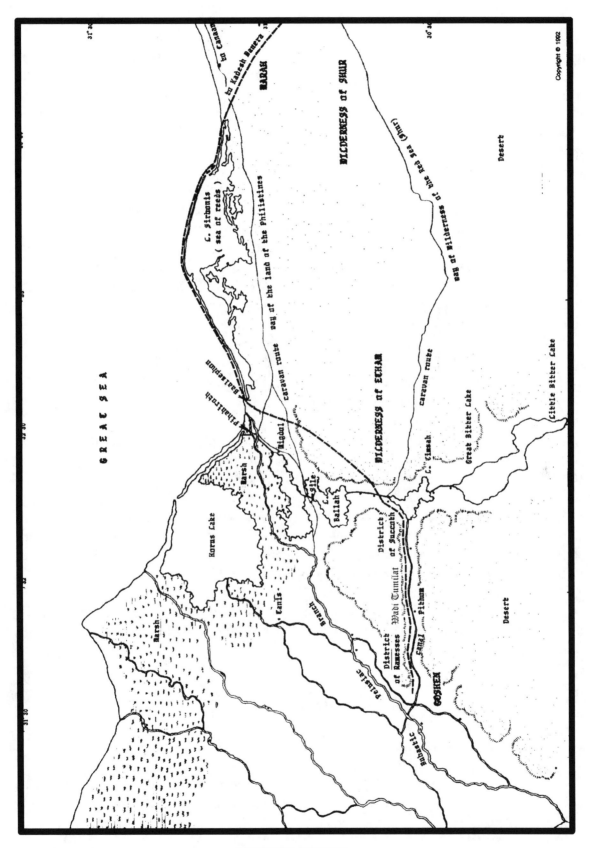

EXODUS ROUTE

The People Moses Led from Egypt

Although it is not common knowledge in the Judaeo-Christian community, the number of people in the Exodus taught by the clergy to its members for many centuries, is the astronomical figure of 600,000 souls (EXODUS 12:37). The logistics of moving, feeding, and caring for this staggering number of individuals has never been a factor in deterring the average believer from accepting this obvious anomaly. This figure by itself seems highly questionable because of the chronological period in which it was supposed to have taken place and the geographical area in which these people were to traverse.

In preceding chapters, it was shown that for this number of people to penetrate the heavily fortified frontier of Egypt was very improbable, but this, of course, can be questioned. However, when the figure of 600,000 is compared with the best estimates of the total population of Egypt at the beginning of the 14th century B.C., which would have been only four to five million, it seems almost impossible. If this were true then it would seem there would be no reason for the Israelites to leave when they could have taken control over the Land of Ramesses.

But does the Judaeo-Christian Bible really represent the total number of people in the EXODUS as 600,000? Is the number of people in the EXODUS really 600,000, or has the clergy perpetuated a protracted misunderstanding?

A careful examination of the Old Testament in the Judaeo-Christian Bible reveals facts that heretofore have simply been overlooked or, perhaps, purposely ignored because the revelation would cause the whole story to be questionable.

The book of EXODUS states how many of *his* people that Moses led out of Egypt. Somehow, according to popularly taught tradition, the Israelites passed unhindered (except for a pursuing Egyptian army) through the frontier fortifications and out into the blistering, waterless desert wasteland wilderness of the Sinai Peninsula.

But then after two years of tasting the fruits of desert living and "in the second year after they were come out of the land of Egypt" (NUMBERS 1:1), Moses was directed by the "Lord" in NUMBERS 1:2-4:

> "2 Take ye the sum of all the congrega-
> tion of the children of Israel, …"

However, Moses' deity is more specific by stating further:

> "2 … by the house of their fathers, with
> the number of their families, every male
> by their polls;

> "3 *From twenty years old and upward,*

all that are able to go forth to war in Israel: Thou and Aaron shall number them by their *armies*.

"4   And with you there shall be a man of every tribe; every one head of the house of his father."

Several facts are patently clear from these passages: that the count includes only males 20 years old and above and that these men were to constitute only the army of the Israelite clan.

This, then, is a synopsis of the counting by tribes as recorded in NUMBERS 1:20-45:

Reuben	46,500		Ephraim	40,500
Simeon	59,300		Manasseh	32,200
Gad	45,650		Benjamin	35,400
Judah	74,600		Dan	62,700
Issa-char	54,400		Asher	41,500
Zĕbulun	57,400		Naphtali	53,400

The total is then given at the conclusion of the counting (NUMBERS 1:46):

"46   Even all they that were numbered were six hundred thousand and three thousand and five hundred and fifty." [603,550]

After the total of the Israelite army is established, Moses' deity assigns him one more task, and that is to count the Levites, those dedicated to keeping charge of the tabernacle and by priests of the "Lord".   NUMBERS 3:14-15:

"14   ¶And the Lord spoke unto Moses in the wilderness of Sīnaī, saying,

"15   Number the children of Levi after the house of their fathers, by their families;   every   male from a month old and upward shalt thou number them."

The total is then given at the conclusion of the counting (NUMBERS 3:39), where it states:

"39 All that were numbered of the Lē-

vītes, which Moses and Aaron numbered at the commandment of the LORD,
throughout their families, all the *males*
from a month old and upward, were
twenty and two thousand" [22,000].

This passage again plainly states that Moses is to count only the *male Levites*.

So concludes the Old Testament account of the numbering of the children of Israel who came out of Egypt.

AUTHOR'S COMMENTARY

The number of Israelites that were counted comes to a sum total of 625,550. But a closer examination raises some bewildering questions.

Only *males* of 20 years of age and older are counted to constitute the army and only *males* a month old and upward are counted of Levi. Then what happened to the other people who came out of the land of Egypt: the mothers and fathers, the wives and children, the camp followers, the mixed multitude, as well as the host of others that hang on to a rebellious horde, as noted in EXODUS 12:37-38:

"37 ¶And the children of Israel jour-
neyed from Ram'e-sēs to Suc'coth,
about six hundred thousand on foot
that were men, beside children."

"38 And a mixed multitude went up
also with them; and flocks, and herds,
even very much cattle."

It would not be too presumptuous to conclude that each male in the army would be of fighting age, probably putting him between the ages of 20 years to 35 years. Then it could be reasonably surmised that each male would have a *mother* and *father*, or at least one of them, and that each male would have a *wife*, or at least most of them. So to turn this into understandable statistics, it might be presented as follows:

A	A mother and father to 50% of the males	603,550 (thousand)
B	A wife of 50% of the males	301,275
C	One child of 50% of the males	301,275
D	Unmarried women (30% of the males)	181,065
	TOTAL	1,387,165 (million)

The total of males 20 years and older   603,550

This staggering total represents only a conservative estimate   1,990,715 (million)

This is followed by a similar statistical study of the Levites:

A	A mother and father to 50% of the males	22,000
B	A wife of 50% of the males	11,000
C	One child of 50% of the males	11,000
D	Unmarried women (30% of the males)	6,600
	TOTAL	50,600

Added to the total of males in Levi   22,000

72,600

Then added to this count is the number of camp followers and others
that tag along for one reason or another. Conservatively, this could be: 50,000

This conservative estimate of the true total of Israelites and others who came en masse out of the land of Egypt would be somewhere around 2,000,000 people, plus the unspecified number of mixed multitude with them. This would constitute approximately 50% of the total population of Egypt, which, again, was four to five million.

Again, it must be emphasized that this figure has been reached from the evidence derived from the Judaeo-Christian Bible itself. It certainly casts a grave shadow over the veracity of the Exodus story by the simple conclusion that to move 2 million people out of Egypt and take them into the deserts of Sinai for any length of time, much less the popularly believed 40 years – eating manna all the while – is quite beyond believability, if not ludicrous.

CHAPTER XI

Traveling to the Promised Land

To conclude the thorough examination of the geography of the EXODUS, it is necessary to locate properly (and the author might add, for the first time) the larger remaining geographic areas that have an important bearing on the story in order to determine by process of elimination where the Israelites would have been and where they would have gone (see may of Sinai Wilderness Areas, next page).

Wilderness of Etham

Has been previously located.

Wilderness of Shur

GENESIS 25:18 states:

> "18 And they dwelt from Havilah unto *Shur, that is before Egypt, as thou goest toward Assyria*: …"

I SAMUEL 15:7 states:

> "7 And Saul smote the Amalekites from Havilah until thou comest to *Shur, that is over against Egypt.*"

Wilderness of Sin or Zin

NUMBERS 34:3 states:

> "3 Then your south quarter shall be from the wilderness of *Zin along by the coast of Edom,* …"

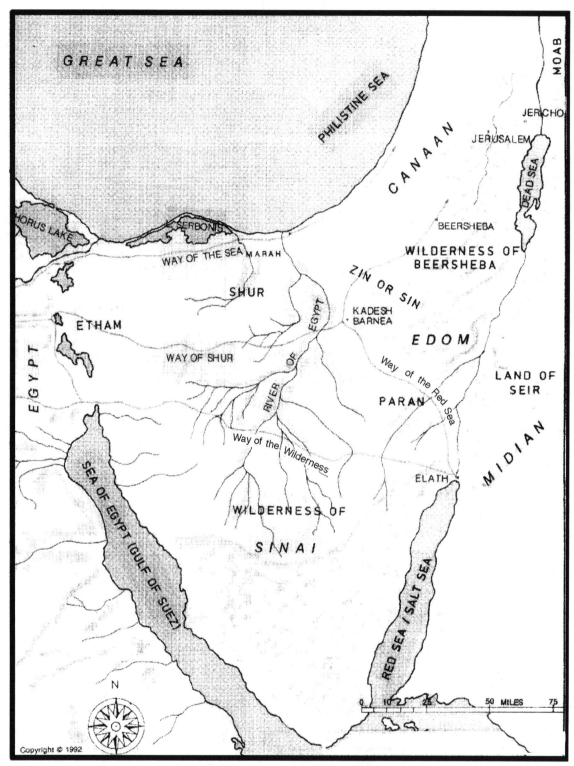

SINAI WILDERNESS AREAS

NUMBERS 20:1 states:

CHAPTER 20

"THEN came the children of Israel, even the whole congregation, into the desert of *Zin* in the first month: and the people abode in Kadesh; ...

NUMBERS 27:14 states:

"14   For ye rebelled against my commandment in the desert of Zin, in the strife of the congregation, to sanctify me at the water before their eyes: *that is the water of Meribah in Kadesh in the wilderness of Zin.*"

Kadesh [barnea] is located just west of Wadi el Arish approximately 50 statue miles south from the Mediterranean Sea. (See map of Kadesh-Barnea, next page.)

NUMBERS 33:11 states:

"11 And they *removed from the Red sea[3], and encamped in the wilderness of Sin.*"

In EXODUS 16:1, the story relates that the Israelites came from the sea and went out into the Wilderness of Shur; then they came to "Marah" (see El Murra/Marah map, page 121), then they came to "Elim. Then it states:

CHAPTER 16

"AND they took their journey from Elim, and all the congregation of the children of Israel came unto the wilderness of S[Z]in, which is between Elim and Sī'nai, ..."

Upon leaving the Reed Sea (Sirbonis) the Hebrew/Israelites traveled to Marah. They left Marah and came to the Oasis of Elim, which is called El Qus (as noted on map next page). Since it was only the second month after fleeing Egypt, they would have still been in northern Sinai, exactly where the Wilderness of Zin is located. (See map of Sinai Wilderness Areas, page 136.)

---

[3] Gulf of Aqaba

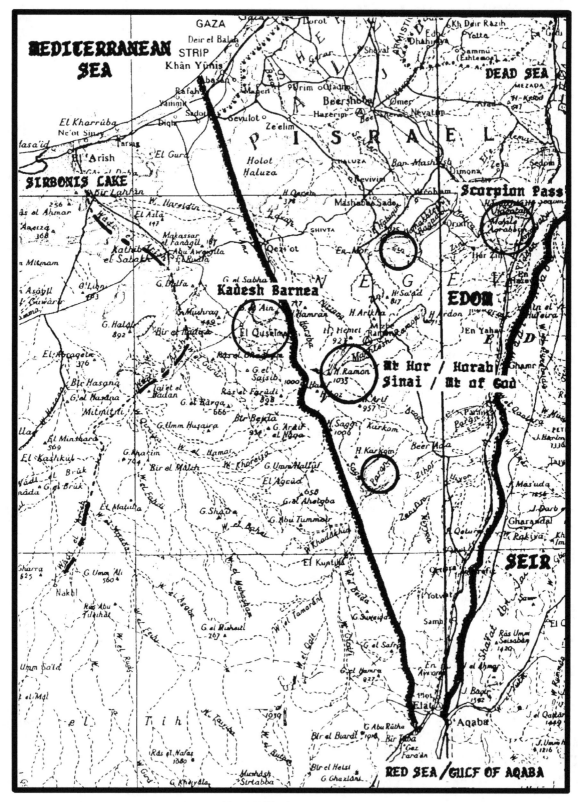

KADESH BARNEA

Land of Seir

GENESIS 32:3 states:

> "3 And Jacob sent messengers before
> him to Esau his brother unto the *land of
> Seir, the country of Edom.*"

Wilderness of Paran

NUMBERS 13:26 states:

> "26 ¶And they went and came to Moses,
> and to Aaron, and to all the congregation of
> the children of Israel unto the *wilderness
> of Paran, to   Kā'
> desh*; ..."

GENESIS 21 connects the Wilderness of Beersheba with the Wilderness of Paran, or they are in proximity.

Wilderness of Sinai

The Wilderness of Sinai constitutes all the remaining area in the Sinai Peninsula below the aforementioned Wilderness areas of Etham, Shur, Paran, and Zin or Sin.

* * * * * *

The Four Promised Lands

It is very doubtful that there was an Israelite attack upon Jericho, and there were only limited engagements with the indigenous peoples of the area. What did take place was a slow incursion into the Hill Country of Lower Canaan by Hebrew/Semitics, beginning, as has already been explained, during the 12th century B.C. Then around the 10th Century B.C., which would be time of kings in the story, another wave of Hebrews invaded lower Canaan and managed to achieve a tenuous hold upon the inhospitable Hill Country south of Jerusalem (Salem). At no time in history did the Hebrew/Semitics obtain complete control of what is the present-day State of Israel. In fact, the territory that contemporary Jews claim their deity, "Yahweh/Jehovah", promised to them has not been shown and cannot be shown in the Judaeo-Christian Bible to be that area.

In order to establish once and for all that the desert area now called "Negev" or Edom is the ancestral homeland of the Hebrew/Semitics – referred to in the Judaeo-Christian

Bible as the "Israelites" – it is necessary only to examine the Old Testament scriptures. These clearly verify not only that homeland, but that the Hebrews' traveled there after fleeing Egypt. If it can be shown that this was the only location that their deity Yahweh/Jehovah gave to them as their own in the story, then it will validate the evidence the author has presented previously.

There are several locations in their scriptures where the Hebrew/Israelite deity sets forth certain boundaries to the land that they will inherit. The texts presented below will be quoted only from those where their deity is directly relating these boundaries and not from texts where some of the Israelite leaders reiterate what has been promised in a former time.

First Promise

Conveniently forgotten from the teachings in the Judaeo/Christian houses of worship and also absent from the history books about the Israelite claim of their rightful boundaries, according to ancient tradition, is the Israelite deity's commanding promise to their patriarch, Jacob, in GENESIS 15:18:

> "18 In the same day the LORD made a covenant with Abram, saying, Unto thy seed have I given this land, from the *river of Egypt unto* the great river, *the river Eū-phrā'tēs*:"

(See map, Promised Land – First Promise, next page.)

Here, again, is another example of the selective recollection so common in the Judaeo-Christian amalgamation. But, as history has shown, the Arabs and Lebanese proved to be of a more invincible nature than the Israelite deity, Yahweh/Jehovah.

When the Hebrews developed this particular portion of their history, it did not seem preposterous to appropriate such a boundless territory in northern Arabia, originally the ancient homeland of the Hebrew/Semitic ancestors. Later, trapped by their own original writings, the reality that this region had become the permanent property of their stronger neighbors, Assyria and Arabia, was so obvious that the chroniclers of these scriptures artfully reconstructed the format of this promise to reflect the contemporary situation.

Second Promise

The *second promise* was drafted with deception in mind: The expanded text with the ambiguous locations was meant to confuse the reader into thinking that the previous promise was unchanged. In actuality, the second promise outlined a much restricted area for the Hebrews to share with other Semitic nomads.

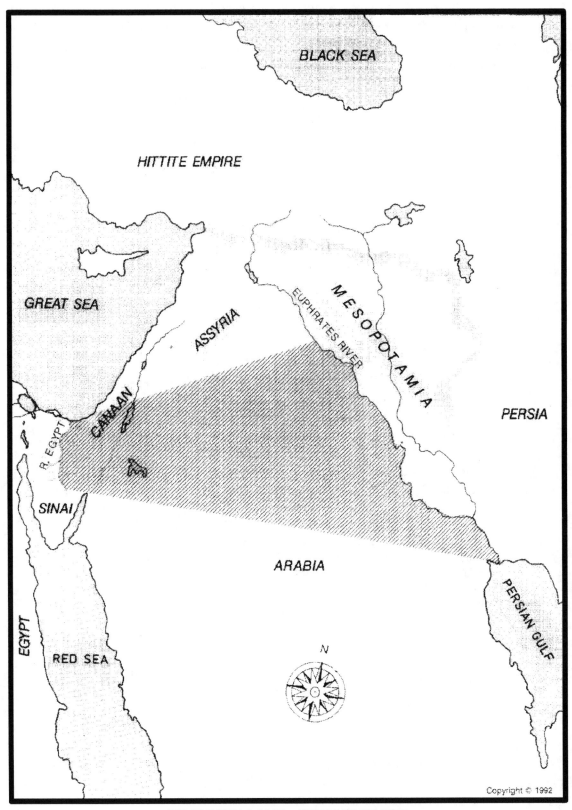

PROMISED LAND - FIRST PROMISE

In EXODUS, the Israelite deity extends the second promise to Moses on a mount called Sinai about two years after the Israelites left the country of Egypt. He heard his deity's voice coming from a thick cloud. Three days later, the "Lord/God" [Jehovah/Yahweh] appears to Moses and the Israelites in this fashion in Chapter 19:

> "16 ¶And it came to pass on the third day in the morning, that there were thunders and lightnings, and a thick cloud upon the mount, and the voice of the trumpet exceeding loud; so that all the people that was in the camp trembled.
>
> "18 And mount Sī'nai was altogether on a smoke, because the LORD descended upon it in fire: and the smoke thereof ascended as the smoke of a furnace, and the whole mount quaked greatly.
>
> "19 And when the voice of the trumpet sounded long, and waxed louder and louder, Moses spake, and God answered ..."

It states that the clan heard the voice also, but when it came to giving the details, Moses is called to the top of the mount for a private conference. So, "God/Lord" gives the promise to Moses, although in private (for his eyes only), because in Chapter 20, it states:

> "22 ¶And the LORD said unto Moses, Thus thou shalt say unto the children of Israel, Ye have seen that I have talked with you from heaven."

Then, after prescribing all manner of laws and rules, "God/Lord" tells Moses (EXODUS 23:31):

> "31 And I will set thy bounds from the Red sea even unto the sea of the Philistines, and from the desert unto the river: ..."

In all the scriptures, this paragraph gives the most condensed version of the promise. In preceding chapters, two of these locations were thoroughly examined so there is no doubt what their names actually mean: they are:

Red sea means: "Gulf of Aqaba".
Sea of the Philistines means: "Mediterranean Sea".

The confusion surrounding the other two esoteric locations can now also be dispelled because of the information offered before. These are:

Desert means: lower Sinai.
River: could be the Jordan or even the Euphrates.

To see the boundary limits of this area, as it is drawn using the locations described, see map, Promised Land – Second Promise, next page.

Third Promise

Forty years later, in NUMBERS, which is supposedly written by Moses because the scriptures state, most emphatically [in] The Fourth Book of Moses: "He hears God/Lord elaborate on the geography of their inheritance," where in Chapter 34:3-12 it states *the four cardinal boundaries*, by *cities*, *sites* and *area*, of the "Land of Canaan," which they were going to possess. They are presented in a more abbreviated form as follows:

Southern Border
    From the:
        Wilderness of Zin (along by the coast of Edom)
    To the:
        Salt Sea (outmost coast)
    Then turn from the south to:
        Ascent of Akrabbim (by coast of Amorites, popularly known as Scorpion Pass)
    And pass on to:
        Zin
    Going forth from the south to:
        Kadesh bar nea
    And pass on to:
        Azmon
    Unto the:
        River of Egypt
    Going out shall be at:
        The sea

Western Border
    Shall have the:
        Great Sea

Northern Border
    From the:
        Great Sea
    Point out for you:
        Mount Hor

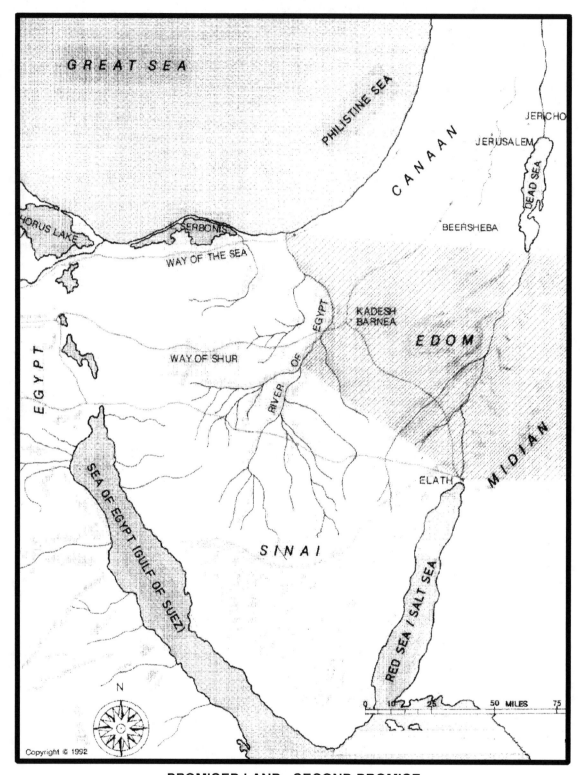

PROMISED LAND - SECOND PROMISE

Unto the entrance of:
> *Hamath*

Shall be to:
> *Zedad*

Shall go on to:
> *Ziphron*

Shall be to:
> *Hazarenan*

Eastern Border

From:
> *Hazarenan*

To:
> *Shepham*

To:
> *Riblah* (on the east side of Ain)

Shall descend and reach onto the side of the:
> *Sea of Chinnereth*

Border shall go down to:
> *Jordan*

Going out of it shall be at the:
> *Salt Sea*

Out of all of these locations, there are only a few that are positively known to this day; all others are totally conjecture. The known locations are:

Great Sea	is the	Mediterranean
Mount Hor (Sinai)	is in	Wilderness of Zin/Sin
Jordan	is the	Wadi Araba
Wilderness of Zin	is	Western Edom
Akrabbim	is in	Upper Edom
Kadesh bar nea	is in	North central Sinai
River of Egypt	is in	North central Sinai
Hamath	is	beginning of the south part of Canaan

The "Hamath" referred to here is not the "city of Hamath" in Syria. The phrase in NUMBERS 34:8 is:

> "8 From mount Hor ye shall point out your
> border unto the entrance of Hā′
> măth; …"

A similar phrase in II KINGS 23:33 states:

> "33 And Pharaoh-nechoh put him in
> bands at Rĭb′lah in the land of Hā′măth,…"

By examining these two phrases and determining that Riblah could be located east of Bethal (a few miles north of Jerusalem), then it becomes evident that this is the beginning of the "Land or Territory of Hamath," and here, it is claimed, is the northern boundary of the land promised by the Israelite deity. The author believes there are two other locations which have been interpreted incorrectly, and these are:

Sea of Chinnereth	is the	Dead Sea
Salt Sea	is the	Gulf of Aqaba

(See map, Promised Land – Third Promise, for location of this area, next page).

With the preponderance of known locations in "Edom" or in the lower "Hill Country of Canaan", then little doubt remains that here is where the ancestral home of the "Hebrew/ Semitic/Israelites" was located.

Fourth Promise

In the Judaeo-Christian Bible account titled, The Book of JOSHUA, the story becomes overly enthusiastic when the "Lord" (Jehovah) spake unto Joshua, repeating the "Promise" before the Israelites were supposed to have crossed over the Jordan River. It states in Chapter 1:

> "4 From *the wilderness* and *this Leba-non* even *unto the great river, the river Eū-phrā'tēs, all the land of the Hittites*, and *unto the great sea toward the going down of the sun*, shall be your coast."

AUTHOR'S COMMENTARY

As can be noted, it states, "this" Lebanon. Since the Israelites were across from the city Jericho, then this was southern Lebanon. It also states, "all the land of the Hittites," which would have included all the land north to southern Turkey; however, at the time of Joshua, the kingdom of the Hittites had totally crumbled, and they possessed no land as a contiguous nation.

The "great sea" is obviously the Mediterranean Sea. (See map, Promised Land – Fourth Promise, page 148.)

The Changing Route

During the years of study to prepare this book, several versions of the vintage and contemporary Judaeo-Christian Bible were used. In time, subtle changes began to be incorporated into the text. Of particular interest was a disconcerting modification to one of the maps tucked away into the posterior of every bible.

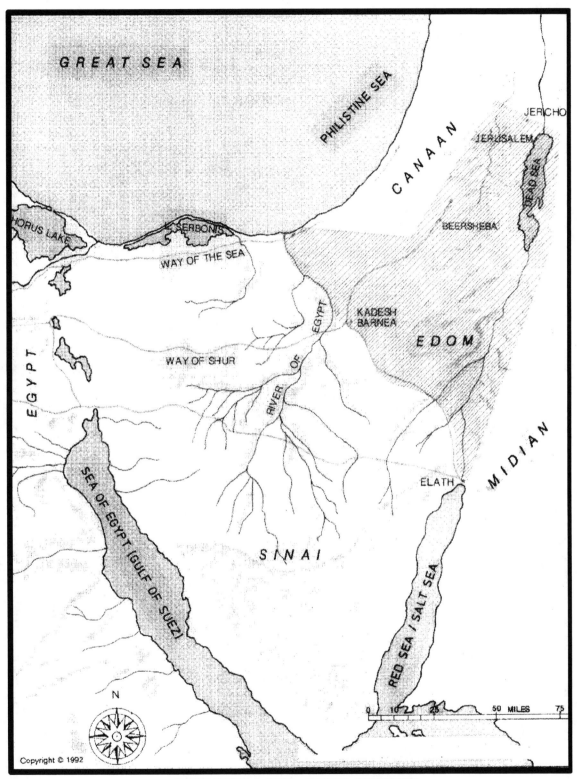

PROMISED LAND - THIRD PROMISE

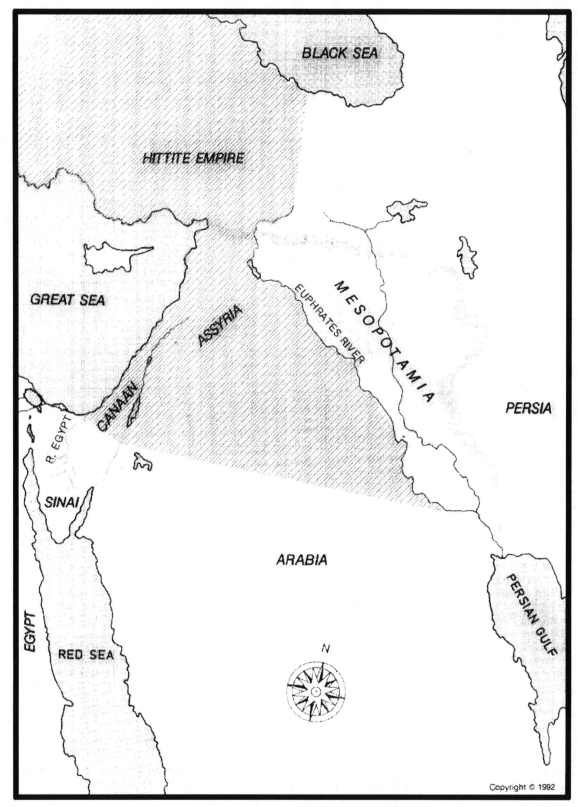

PROMISED LAND - FOURTH PROMISE

This map displayed the route of the Forty Years of Wandering of the Israelites in Sinai. It had been an undeviating hallmark incorporated into even the oldest bibles known. The typical map always displayed the same route with an unvarying bold red line. It originated in the eastern Nile Delta, then passed through the "Red Sea", at the head of the modern Gulf of Suez (old Sea of Egypt). Plunging southward to the location that the Christian church claims is Mount Sinai, it then abruptly reverses direction. The line continues a serpentine path northward until it finally terminates in Moab, opposite the town of Jericho (see 40 Years Wandering – Original Route map next page).

In the 1980s, the author discovered a new version of the bible that had changed the route (see 40 Years Wandering – Changed Route map, page 151). It can only be speculated, but perhaps knowledge of the discoveries in the eighteen and nineteenth centuries A.D. had finally found their way into the Christian community. This probably caused consternation among Bible scholars, resulting in the alteration of the map to reflect new archaeological and historical evidence.

These modifications reached such proportions that, by the 1990s, the red line was being drawn in alternative paths all over Sinai. Apparently, because scholars were unable to come to grips with the fact that the EXODUS story took place only in northern Sinai, they were unable to abandon their heretofore sacred beliefs (see 40 Years Wandering – Chaotic Route map, page 152).

Mount Sinai / Horeb

Many centuries ago, Christian monks established their monastery of St. Katherine on a very ancient holy site on Gebel Musa, a mountain in Lower Sinai. At some unknown period, these monks convinced the Roman church that Gebel Musa was the Mount Sinai in the story. It is no surprise why the site was chosen:

First: Because of its size and height, the mountain fulfilled the criteria as an appropriate setting where the Israelite deity gave the laws to Moses.

Second: If the Israelites had wandered (all two million) in the wilderness for forty years, this location at the extremity of the Peninsula would make it appear that the journey had extended over a great distance, thereby giving more credibility to the lengthy period.

If Gebel Musa is shown not to be the Mount Sinai of the story, then the forty years of wandering would be put into grave doubt. The proof has been offered previously that, after the EXODUS, the story actually relates that the Israelites traveled directly to Edom, their ancestral homeland. If this evidence is factual, then Mount Sinai would be in the vicinity of the country of Edom, not in southern Sinai. By carefully examining the story in regard to

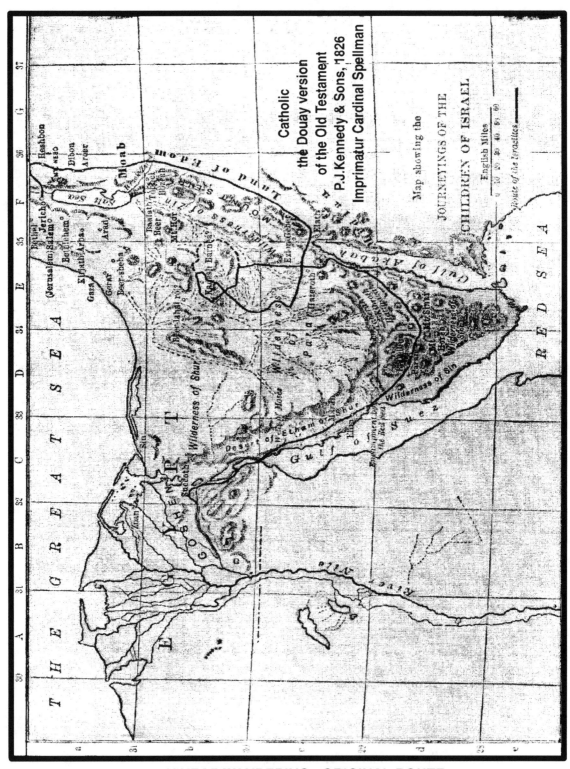

40 YEAR WANDERING - ORIGINAL ROUTE

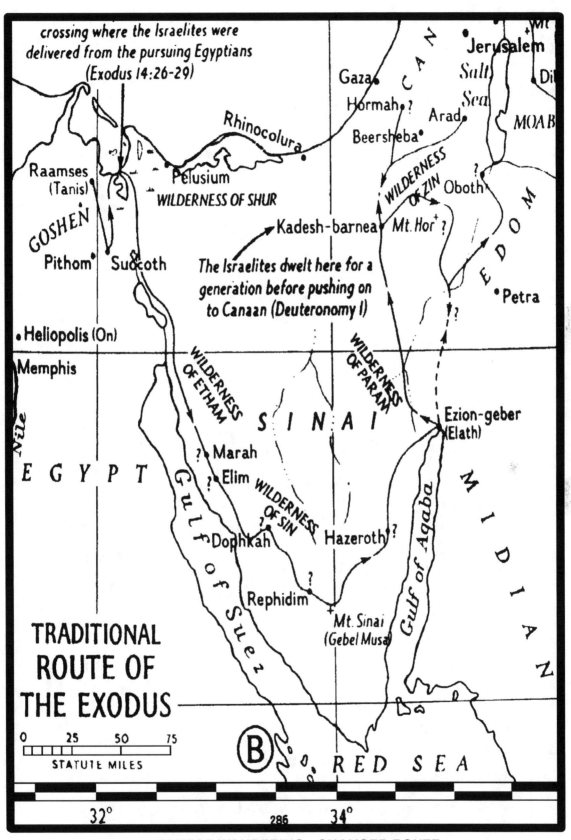

crossing where the Israelites were delivered from the pursuing Egyptians (Exodus 14:26-29)

Rhinocolura

Gaza

Hormah ?

Jerusalem

Salt Sea

Di

MOAB

Arad

Beersheba

Raamses (Tanis)

Pelusium

WILDERNESS OF SHUR

WILDERNESS OF ZIN

Oboth

EDOM

GOSHEN

Kadesh-barnea

Mt. Hor ?

The Israelites dwelt here for a generation before pushing on to Canaan (Deuteronomy 1)

Pithom

Succoth

Petra

Heliopolis (On)

Memphis

WILDERNESS OF ETHAM

WILDERNESS OF PARAN

S I N A I

Nile

Gulf of Suez

E G Y P T

Marah ?

Elim ?

WILDERNESS OF SIN

Hazeroth ?

Ezion-geber (Elath)

Gulf of Aqaba

M I D I A N

Dophkah ?

Rephidim ?

Mt. Sinai (Gebel Musa)

TRADITIONAL ROUTE OF THE EXODUS

0 25 50 75

STATUTE MILES

Ⓑ

R E D   S E A

32°

286

34°

40 YEAR WANDERING - CHANGED ROUTE

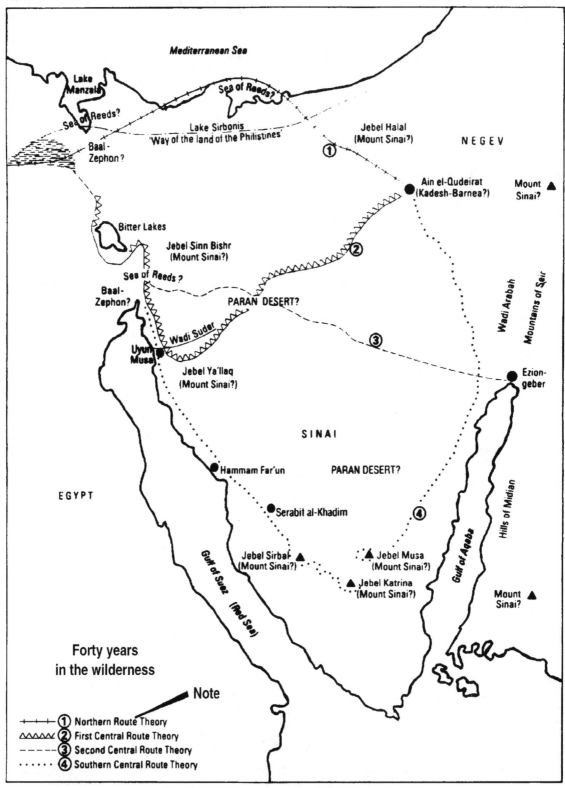

Forty years
in the wilderness

Note

+—+—+ ① Northern Route Theory
∧∧∧∧∧ ② First Central Route Theory
— — — ③ Second Central Route Theory
· · · · · ④ Southern Central Route Theory

40 YEAR WANDERING - CHAOTIC ROUTES

the location of Mount Sinai, then the following quotes from the Judeo-Christian Bible will confirm this fact.

When Moses was hiding from pharaoh in Midian, it states in EXODUS 3:1:

CHAPTER 3
"... and he led the flock to the backside of
the desert, and came to the *mountain of*
God, even to Hô′rĕb."

Midian was previously shown to be in the area of northern Edom. Later, Moses received the laws on a mountain, as stated in EXODUS 31:18:

"18   And he gave unto Moses, when
he had   made an end of communing
with him upon *mount Sī′naī*, two tables..."

While the Israelites were waiting for Moses at Mount Sinai, they made a golden calf to adore. But then in EXODUS 33:6, the Israelites repent of this act while still at Mount Sinai; however, the mountain is given another name.

"6 And the children of Israel stripped
themselves of their ornaments *by the
mount Hô′rĕb*."

It is again reaffirmed in Psalms 106:19, where it states:

"19 They made a calf *in Hô′rĕb*, and
worshipped the molten image."

It can be inferred that Mount Sinai is one and the same as Mount Horeb. Although the location of Mount Sinai is never given, it is possible to determine the site of Mount Horeb.

A short time after leaving Egypt, Moses brought forth water from "the rock of Horeb" [the mount of God (EXODUS 18:5)]. He thereupon names the place, as stated in EXODUS 17:7:

"7 And he called the name of the place
Măs′sah and Mĕr′i-bah, ..."

In NUMBERS 20:13-14, Meribah is identified with the same site:

"13 This is the water of *Mĕr′i-bah*; because the children of Israel strove with
the LORD, and he was sanctified in them.

> "14 ¶And Moses sent messengers
> from *Kā'desh* unto the king of *Ēdom*,
> Thus saith thy brother Israel, Thou
> knowest all the travail that hath be-
> fallen us:"

Earlier in the same chapter, Kadesh (Barnea) is placed in the wilderness of Zin (NUMBERS 20:1). The wilderness of Zin, of course, is in northern Sinai. However, even earlier, in NUMBERS 13:26, it states:

> "26 ¶And they went and came to
> Moses, and to Aaron, and to all the
> congregation of the children of Israel
> unto the *wilderness of Paran, to Kā'
> desh*; ..."

As can be seen in the map of the Sinai Wilderness Areas (page 136), the Wilderness of Zin, or Sin, and Paran are next to each other in northern Sinai and often overlap. The Wilderness of Paran is on the western border of Edom. This is finally verified in NUMBERS 20:16, where it states:

> " 16 ...
> and, behold, we are in *Kā'desh*, a city in
> the uttermost of thy border:" [Edom]

A summary of these findings is presented as follows:

1. Mount Sinai is Mount Horeb;
2. The mountain is at Kadesh, and is or by Meribah;
3. Kadesh is in the Wilderness of Paran;
4. The Wilderness of Paran borders the country of Edom;
5. Edom is in the far northeastern edge of the Sinai Peninsula.

The obvious conclusion is that Gebel Musa *is not* the Mount Sinai or mountain of God in the story.

CHAPTER XII

Did the Hebrew/Israelites Conquer the "Promised Land"?

As was mentioned earlier in Chapter II, the story of Exodus in the Old Testament about the Israelite/Hebrew nation being divided into twelve tribes is certainly astronomical mythology. This concept was borrowed from the ancient Ionians by the chroniclers of Hebrew Scriptures.

In Chapter X, it was shown that, according to the Exodus fable, the true number of Hebrew/Israelites who would have left Egypt was in the vicinity of two million people. This fact alone relegates the story to improbability. Then, when the Israelite 12 tribes are directed to possess 12 separate areas of the "Promised Land", the description is so ambiguous and the geographical area is so small, it would have been quite impossible to let that many people into the land and sustain them especially without driving out every other living soul, which the scriptures plainly reveal the Hebrew/Israelites did not.

According to the Old Testament, before the Hebrew/Israelites came into Canaan, the land was already completely settled by the indigenous tribes of the area. The only exceptions were the inhospitable mountainous areas of lower Canaan or northern Edom.

Earlier, Moses' deity told him about the land, as it states in EXODUS 3:8:

> "8 And I am come down to deliver them
> out of the hand of the Egyptians,
> and to bring them up out of that land unto
> a good land and a large, unto a
> land flowing with milk and honey. ..."

Before entering Canaan, Moses tells the clan of Israel that he is dividing up the land and giving each of the 12 tribes an area to possess. However, Moses' commands were easier to say than to carry out. The individual Israelite tribes soon discovered that somehow Jehovah/Yahweh was not going to gallantly march before them, vanquishing all who came into their path of conquest. The indigenous people of Canaan did not just lay down their arms and sheepishly give up to the Israelites, as the book of JOSHUA reveals. In the land given to the tribe of Ephraim, they went in (JOSHUA 16:10):

> "10 And they drave *not out* the Canaan-ites that dwelt in Gē′zer: but the Ca-naanites dwell among the Ē′phra-im-ites unto this day, and serve under tribute."

And the tribe of Manaseh (verse 12):

> "12 Yet the children of Ma-năs′seh could not drive out the inhabitants of those cities; but the Canaanites would dwell in that land."

And the tribe of Jūdah (verse 19):

> "19 And the LORD was with Jūdah; and he drave out the inhabitants [Jebusites] of the mountain; but could not drive out the inhabitants of the valley, because they had chariots of iron."

And the tribe of Benjamin (verse 21):

> "21 ¶And the children of Benjamin did not drive out the Jēbusītes that inhabited Jerusalem; but the Jēbu-sītes dwell with the children of Ben-jamin in Jerusalem unto this day."

And the tribe of Dan (verse 34):

> "34 And the Amorites forced the children of Dan into the mountain: for they [Amorites] would not suffer them to come down to the valley:"

The Hebrew/Israelites were never to conquer the "land of milk and honey", but tasted the bitter bile of co-habitation with the many clans who had already settled and possessed the land. As it states in JUDGES 3:1 and 3:

CHAPTER 3

"NOW these are the nations which the Lord [Adoni] left, …

"3 Namely, five lords of the Philistines, and all the Canaanites, and the Si-dō′ni-ans, and the Hī-vītes that dwelt in mount Lebanon, from mount Bā′al-her′mon unto the entering in of Hā′măth."

And again, in JUDGES 3:5:

"5 ¶And the children of Israel dwelt among the Canaanites, Hittites, and Amorites, and Pĕr′iz-zītes, and Hī′vītes, and Jēb′u-sītes: …"

So the Old Testament Scriptures plainly state that the Hebrew/Israelites could not drive out the other clans who did possess the land. Earlier in the fable, even before the "children of Israel" had come into the so-called "Promised Land", their deity, Jehovah, had told them, in DEUTERONOMY 31:16 and 17:

"16 ¶And the LORD said unto Moses, Behold, thou shalt sleep with thy fathers; and this people will rise up, and go a whoring after the gods of the strangers of the land, whither they go to be among them, and will forsake me, and break my covenant which I have made with them.

"17 Then my anger shall be kindled against them in that day, and I will forsake them, and I will hide my face from them, and they shall be devoured and many evils and troubles shall befall them; so that they will say in that day, Are not these evils come upon us, because our god is not among us?"

This prophetic warning by Jehovah was not a hollow promise, as the "children of Israel" were to become painfully aware. For they did exactly what they had been told *not* to do, as described in JUDGES 3:7:

> "7 And the children of Israel did evil in the
> sight of the LORD, and forgat the LORD their
> God, and served Bā'al-ĭm and the groves."

The *groves* referred to here are stone or pole circles that were used as setting references with the sun and stars to establish the festivals and ceremonies. These structures were similar to Stonehenge or even the much more ancient structures in India, from which the practice originated. For these transgressions, the fable describes how, from that time, the Israelites were put under subjugation by one foreign king after another.

First was King Chushanrisha (circa 1008-1006 B.C.) of Mesopotamia; next was Jabin, king of Canaan, himself under tribute to the Egyptian pharaoh; then came the Midianites of Midian; next followed the Philistines, the Syrians, the Babylonians, the king of Moab, and the Egyptians.

During this time, they were continually fighting among themselves and with other Hebrews in the land. Even David's armies fought against *the children of Israel* (JUDGES 20:14). The fable goes on to state that even in David's time the Jebusites still controlled the city of Jerusalem. The fable never states that Jerusalem was ever taken over by David's son Solomon, only that he built a temple. He certainly was no shining example of a monotheist, nor did he ever drive out the other clans from Canaan.

The Israelite deity had warned them not to worship other deities in the land; however, according to JUDGES 2:12, they continually:

> "12 And they forsook the LORD God of
> their fathers, which brought them out of
> the land of Egypt, and followed other gods,
> of the gods of the people that were
> round about them ..."

Along with a plethora of other evidence, this amply shows that the Hebrew/Israelites were never religiously monotheistic, but that only a select few had set themselves apart and were continuing to serve the male principle mythology without images that had been brought from the East. It was these few individuals who had strived to retain the purity of their ancient mythology and strove to make their clan remain under this religious persuasion but, as is evident, unsuccessfully.

The fable states that the Hebrew/Israelites soon broke into two groups, one, Samaria, and the other, Judah, as stated in I KINGS 16:21:

> "21 ¶Then were the people of Israel di-
> vided into two parts: …"

According to the story, in 725 B.C., in the ninth year of Hoshea, king of Samaria, Shalmaneser II (circa 727-722 B.C.), king of Assyria at Nineueh, conquered the Samaritans of northern Canaan. King Shalmaneser then took them from Samaria to Median (modern Arabia into Iran). The king then brought men from Babylon and other lands and placed them in the cities of Samaria. It must be noted that the so-called Samaritans were not just Hebrew/ Israelites but all manner of other indigenous clans. The fable does not state which Israelite tribes were deported, since the division of the Promised Land was totally ambiguous as to areas of possession. On very close examination, it will be found that the Samaritans were still faithful to the old holy site on Mt. Carmel, while the Judah clan took up worship in the new shrine around Jerusalem.

Finally, the fatal blow was struck to the remaining "children of Israel" when, in 586 B.C. (150 years later), in the 11th year of Zedekiah, King of Israel, Nebuchadnezzar (circa 604-561 B.C.), king of Babylon, took Jerusalem and conquered the remnants of the male principle worshippers. II KINGS 25:21 states:

> "21 And the king of Babylon smote
> them, and slew them at Rĭb′lah in the
> land of Hā′mǎth. So Judah was carried
> away out of the land."

The fable clearly states that all of the 12 tribes "were driven out or deported from Canaan". Since this was so, how do Biblical historians conclude that the "children of Israel" possessed the Promised Land?

One can only speculate as to how the Old Testament Scriptures were compiled if all the tribes were vanquished and everything they owned destroyed.

The following is a review of this conquest, as told in the Old Testament Scriptures.

Shalmaneser, King of Assyria, conquers Samaria, with
northern Israelite tribes and other clans of the area.
They are replaced totally.   725 B.C.

                                                                                139 years

Nebuchadnezzar, king of Babylon, conquers Jerusalem
and southern Israelite tribes, including Judah. Carried
away to Babylon.   586 B.C.

                                                                                 66 years

The Old Testament Scriptures claim that a few of the
Descendants of the Judah clan then returned to Canaan
66 years later.   520 B.C.

On their arrival, the country would have been occupied
by Semitic-speaking Hebrews of unassociated clans and
others from surrounding countries, so, if the remnants had   590 years
returned, they would have been only a small minority.
They would, again, be living with people who worshipped
other deities, just what their deity said not to do.

Romans conquer Judea and deport Judean insurgents.   70 A.D.
(See Chronological Chart, Chapter IX)

After the Romans occupied Judea, if there had been any
records about "the children of Israel" or Judeans, they would not
have survived. This time the conquest was final; however, the
newly developing faith of Christianity, that would tie itself
to the Israelite mythos, would eventually allow them to
resettle in Palestine in the 20th century under the title, "Jews".

The Story Ends – Nothing Remained

It is of interest to note that the Dead Sea Scrolls, which are records of many parts of the
Old Testament, including Moses, were written just before and shortly after the Julian period.
This period was when the Essenes or Carmelite monks collected the ancient scriptures that
were later used to develop Judean antiquity. After examining the chronology of the systematic
destruction of the Israelite clan, grave doubt is cast upon the survival of any sacred scripture.
According to the story, the whole clan was taken into captivity, which would almost certainly
mean that all scriptures would have been lost or destroyed.

CONCLUSION

The author hopes it is now clearly evident that the evidence given in this work depicts a totally different representation of the Exodus story from the version taught to Judaeo-Christian believers over many centuries.

It must be remembered that the author has not written his ideas of this tale, but has, for many years, compiled the individual records of scholars, presenting them here for the first time in one comprehensive account.

As the reader has seen, the EXODUS story was created from three great sources:

A.   Asian mythology
B.   Historical events
C.   Ancient historians' accounts

Then the story was cemented together with miraculous events. It was most cleverly written to be explicitly vague, yet at the same time the words virtually shout forth that the story does not relate the version that has been taught to Judaeo-Christian followers.

At the heart of this misunderstanding is an ambiguous part of the EXODUS story that relates how the king of Egypt placed the children of Israel under forced labor to build two cities (EXODUS 1:14):

> "14 And they made their lives bitter
> with hard bondage, in mortar, and in
> brick, and in all manner of service in
> the field: all their service, wherein they
> made them serve, was with rigour."

The story relates that this rigorous servitude was ordered because the king discovered that the children of Israel were more and mightier than the Egyptians (EXODUS 1:9). This made pharaoh afraid that the Israelites might continue multiplying and then, if Egypt were attacked, they would join with the enemy and fight against the Egyptians (EXODUS 1:10).

The pharaoh's decision was to "get them up out of the land" [Egypt] by placing taskmasters over the Israelites and forcing them to build the treasure cities of Pī'thom and Rā-ăm'sēs. But in opposition to pharaoh's directions, the Israelites were not removed from Egypt, and, instead of decreasing their number, they increased.

Upon examination, this part of the EXODUS story makes little or no sense. How could 70 Israelites increase to almost half of all the Egyptians, who numbered four to five million? Why would a pharaoh purposely kill off his labor force? Also, if the Israelites were becoming more numerous than the Egyptian inhabitants, they could have simply seized the Nile Delta.

However, hidden within the corpus of this ambiguous account is embodied, though vaguely, the elements of real history that were used to cleverly develop the EXODUS story.

If the reader will remember Manetho's Leper Account, Chapter VII, there can be seen all of the ingredients for the EXODUS story but without the miracles. Then, to add credibility to this observation, it is a Judean historian, Josephus, who paraphrases Manetho's history.

Here can be seen the king Amenophis (Merneptah) expelling the unclean and leprous from Egypt by banishing them to the quarries as laborers. Later, the king gives the unclean the city of Avaris (the old Hyksos capital). Then, the unclean appoint a former priest, Osasiphars, as their leader. In order to satisfy his hatred for being expelled from Heliopolis, he entreats pharaoh's Hebrew enemies in Canaan to join him for an invasion of Egypt.

In the story of EXODUS, the miraculous plagues were cleverly used to mask the fact that the actual Hebrews that fled from Egypt were lepers and thought to be unclean.

The miracle of Parting Waters was woven into the story by using the deeds of more ancient mythological characters of other societies.

Now it is up to readers to determine, through their own study and reflection, which route they will take to enlighten their own path.

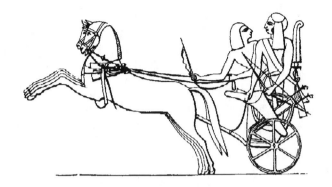

AFTERWORD

Reconstructed Climax of Dynasty XIX

It has been established that the latter half of Dynasty XIX was the basis for the Exodus fable. Now the author would like to reconstruct this fable by deleting the miraculous events and blending the historical facts of this period into a *natural and realistic historical fiction account.* This will be done by using the historical records of Merneptah's latter reign; by examining Manetho's, Diodorus Siculus', and Josephus' accounts of the period, side by side; and by reviewing all other records about the end of Dynasty XIX.

The author hopes that the reader will see that this is a natural and believable account, revealing that, in all cases, true-life events are always far more interesting and important than myth or fiction.

At the risk of perverting history, the author will now try to reconstruct, with as much reality as possible, the latter portion of Dynasty XIX, based on records of and about that time, with special attention to James A. Breasted's *Ancient Records of Egypt.*

******

Some time in the latter part of Merneptah's reign (1234-1222 B.C.), there broke out a universal plague of leprosy or the white sickness that resembled it, among the poorer and more unclean settlers of the Nile Delta. Many of them were Asiatics, which included the Semitic/Hebrews. Among these infected people were some learned priests of the Egyptian race.

Egyptians believed that inward uncleanliness and godlessness of the heart must necessarily be inseparably connected with outward uncleanliness and with leprosy, the most abhorred of the diseases sent by the gods. Merneptah, on this account, consulted the Oracle of Ammon (prophet) and was told that the deities had commanded that he must clear the whole country of these unclean people, but that he should not touch the priesthood.

Merneptah, who believed strongly in divining and dreams of predicting the future, obeyed the prophet's revelation and expelled all the afflicted peoples to the limestone quarries on the east side of the Nile from Memphis, where they had to work apart from the Egyptians. He defied the Oracle's words and also cast out the afflicted learned priests, who had been consecrated to the worship of Osiris–Ammon–Rē of Heliopolis. This action, however, had not solved the rampant spread of the disease; so Merneptah eventually gathered all the unclean people together and expelled them totally from Egypt.

Eventually, many of these banished unclean peoples sought refuge in the old Hyksos capital of Avaris, situated east of the Bubastic arm of the Nile in the Sethroite Nome, outside the line of frontier forts on the eastern Egyptian border. There they began to rebuild the crumbling ruins of the old town, which had fallen into disuse. Since Merneptah was well advanced in age, he cared little about these leprous peoples or their place of expulsion since it was no threat to Egypt at the time. So, they were forgotten.

Merneptah had two sons, Sethos and Ramesses, who were in line to assume the throne upon their father's death. In time, the king was struck down by a long illness with death seeming imminent. Swiftly, a cousin older than the brothers, whose mother was a daughter of Ramesses II, which gave him some legitimacy, took advantage of Merneptah's weakened condition and grasped the throne. Without investiture, he claimed kingship by necessity and thereupon conferred upon himself the august title of "Amenmesses."

Within a short time, the priesthood in Thebes, who disputed the ascendancy of Amenmesses, hatched a plot to place Sethos, the oldest son of Merneptah, in his rightful place on the throne. The intentions of the priesthood, however, were soon usurped by a powerful corrupt court faction that realized that the younger brother, Ramesses, could be manipulated to their advantage.

With a lightning stroke, Amenmesses' death was arranged over the protests of the priesthood, and Ramesses was conducted to the throne and given the title "Sefhaena Ramesses-Siptah". At the same time, he was given his sister, Tewosret, for his queen in hopes it would consolidate his power.

In his first year of reign, to ensure his tenuous position, the power behind Ramses-Siptah orchestrated a sham display of affection by appointing his young brother, Sethos, as Viceroy of Kush (Ethiopia). With all dispatch, Ramses-Siptah directed an official to escort Sethos out to his new post, as far as the city of Abu Simbel in southern Egypt, where a record of his appointment was recorded at Wadi-Halfa. Ramses-Siptah's supporters had another purpose in mind besides placing Sethos out of sight where he would no longer be a threat to Siptah's power; this was to place a visible head over the tribes in Kush, who had recently started a major revolt in WalWat in that country.

For three years, Sethos remained in Ethiopia, virtually a prisoner, but with all outward appearances of power with various titles: "Viceroy of Kush;" "Governor of the Gold-Country of Ammon;" and "Chief Steward of the King." During these years, Ramses-Siptah had commanded his chief treasurer, Bay (a man of some power), to keep a watchful eye upon the young Sethos lest he entertain any thoughts of returning to court by force. To give Bay more authority in this delicate position, Ramses-Siptah conferred upon him the official title of Ramses-Khamenteru (the spirit of pharaoh in Kush).

Fate, however, took a hand, for by placing the young boy as "Governor of the Gold-Country", it had put him in close communication with the powerful priesthood of Ammon, from whom so many usurpers had drawn their strength. In this case, however, the priesthood knew he was the rightful heir to the throne.

Bay did not perform his appointed task to watch Sethos well, for, in time, Bay came to like and respect the boy, because he was wise beyond his years and very bright. Later, those in Memphis, faithful to the old Merneptah, devised a plan to return Sethos to court in what they thought was his rightful place, but, more importantly, returning them to their original power, from which they had been excluded by Ramses-Siptah.

In time, Merneptah made a miraculous recovery but was prevented from resuming his throne because Ramses-Siptah forcibly reassured him that it would be best for Egypt if Siptah remained as king. Merneptah chafed under the knowledge that his favorite son had been virtually banished to Kush, and he would probably never see him again.

Merneptah's young son, Sethos, patiently bided his time in Kush, growing in wisdom and power. Then, at an opportune moment, Bay and the priesthood close to the young Sethos had Ramses-Siptah assassinated. With Bay envisioning a reward for performing the faithful act, Merneptah returned to the throne, and brought Sethos home.

While this intrigue was taking place, the all-but-forgotten unclean of Avaris had made the town habitable to their needs and were feeling more and more disgruntled for the hateful way in which they had been treated by the Egyptians.

From within their midst arose a dynamic personality by the name of Osasiphars, who was one of the leprous priests expelled by Merneptah. This enigmatic individual of great charisma was of questionable birth but, by request of pharaoh's daughter, was raised in the house of pharaoh as an adopted son. Although an exceptionally bright and imaginative boy, in his youth he had murdered a fellow Egyptian while attempting to prevent cruelty to a slave. Under sentence of death, he managed to escape punishment by fleeing into the deserts of Sinai. Eventually he eluded his pursuers, who believed that Osasiphars had died from thirst in the burning sands. Barely making it through the endless dunes and consuming heat by an undaunted spirit, his death was prevented when a daughter of a Midian priest found him while fetching drinking water. He finally settled in that country, which was between Edom and the western desert of Arabia. There, for a number of years, he lived an ascetic life in a monastery, dedicated to the service of Min, the desert moon deity.

In time, during Ramses-Siptah's reign, Osasiphars was found and told to return to Egypt under full pardon. Contrite and still haunted by guilt for taking a life, Osasiphars refused any high office befitting his station but asked only to continue living his life, dedicated to his deity, who, he claimed, was "the one and only creator" who had been waiting for eternity to find someone who would be his servant and carry his message to all humanity.

The tolerant pharaoh, Ramses-Siptah, in hopes of currying favor with the deities, granted his wish and appointed Osasiphars as a priest in Heliopolis. Once placed in the mind-stimulating atmosphere of political intrigue, he realized the full potential of his birthright as an adopted son of pharaoh. Greed began to take hold of him, as his ears were tantalized by the subtle wails of friends and cohorts who desired power, recognizing Osasiphar's potential as a path for their ambitions. Then, with crushing reality, Osasiphars appeared to have contracted leprosy. His usefulness at an end, Osasiphars was secretly ejected from the temple and forcibly transported to the quarries near Heliopolis along with several other priests similarly afflicted. After being cast out, he escaped and eventually joined with the other afflicted peoples who had taken up occupancy in Avaris. Because of his magnetic personality, the outcasts ultimately appointed the priest, Osasiphar, as their leader. After the inhabitants took an oath to be obedient to him in all things, he established laws for them, mainly opposite to the customs of the Egyptians. He commanded that they should not worship the Egyptian deities nor abstain from any one of the Egyptian sacred animals, which were held in highest esteem. He then bound them to an agreement whereby they should join themselves to no one but those that were of that confederacy. His greatest accomplishment was the institution of strict rules of cleanliness and abstinence, for he knew that, if his afflicted community was to survive, living in such close quarters in a town, these rules must be adhered to absolutely. When Osasiphars had completed these tasks, he gave orders to finish rebuilding the old walls about the city of Avaris for protection.

Gradually, Avaris grew in importance as other Hebrew nomads joined the disgruntled dwellers, seeking refuge from marauding desert bands.

Then, as if by a miracle, Osasiphars discovered that he did not have leprosy. With this revelation, his hopelessness vanished to be replaced by a spirit of consuming self-power. His seething anger over how he had been treated by pharaoh now turned to a thirst for revenge. Soon he began to plot insurrection from within Egypt.

Osasiphars had discovered from some of the banished priests with him that one of their kind in Heliopolis, called Danaus, was in fact of Hebrew descent, and, because of his close ties to the throne, had cast covetous eyes upon that position. Danaus, a cousin of Merneptah's son, Sethos, had power extending far beyond his role as priest of the Menervis cult there. His ancestry was mixed with Semitic blood, with which he had secretive ties. His brethren had baptized him with the name "Hermais". His designs upon the throne had been encouraged after the murder of his other cousin, Ramses-Siptah, but, with Merneptah's favored other son, Sethos, securely in line for the throne, Danaus saw his chances of kingship continually thwarted. Fortune, however, was patiently waiting around the corner for Danaus, and his time was close at hand.

A clandestine meeting was arranged between Osasiphars and Danaus. A sacred pact was sealed in which Danaus pledged to assist the people of Avaris to wrest power from the king when suitable conditions were right.

Osasiphars' plot of insurrection was hampered because his band of lepers were not warriors; at best, they could care only for themselves, but beyond that their ability to mount an armed rebellion had pitiful hope of success.

Then Osasiphars hatched a brilliant plan. Since his band was not able to fight, he would join with other Hebrews whom he had met years before while a fugitive in Midian. Because he had been in the house of pharaoh, he had always guarded a secret that was told to him by his mother: His father was of the Hebrew clan, working as an overseer of the other slaves building Pharaoh Merneptah's new cities of Pī'thom and Rā-am'sēs. He had come to think of himself as only Egyptian, but now he would use his father's ancestry to feign a kinship that could make for a beneficial alliance to achieve his plan.

After revealing his heritage to the others in his band, he immediately made arrangements to send emissaries to Edom to entreat his Hebrew cousins to join with them in making war on Merneptah and Egypt. His strategy was simple but ingenious. On arriving, his emissaries first explained to the Edom Hebrews how the others of their kind in Avaris had been treated. They then explained how the weakness and ineptitude of Merneptah made ripe the possibility for an invasion of the Nile Delta, with great wealth awaiting those who could make a successful campaign. In conclusion, Osasiphars' ambassadors reminded their Hebrew brethren about the humiliating expulsion of their ancestors from Egypt by Pharaoh Ahamos some 400 years earlier, so this was the time for their revenge. The ambassadors then said, at Osasiphars' command, that they should first conduct the army to Avaris, the town of their forefathers. Once there, Osasiphar' band would give them the protection and amply provide the troops with what they required. Finally, they could easily subject the country by having their fellow-conspirators inside Egypt start a rebellion to coincide with an invasion.

Greatly rejoiced by this news, the Edom Hebrews readily brought together some 200,000 men, and, after the hot desert march over the shore road of northern Sinai, they arrived at Avaris.

Such a large movement of men and arms never goes unnoticed, and so it was with the Hebrews' arrival at Avaris. Within a short period, spies had reported to Merneptah of these events and, undoubtedly, dire warnings were voiced. However, Osasiphars' co-conspirators, Danaus and other priests of the Apis cult in Memphis, did their job well by stilling the alarm and assuring the aged and retiring monarch that the deities of Heliopolis and Memphis had separately confirmed that this renegade band of Hebrews were of no threat to him or to the land of the Nile.

Unknown to the king and to the Egyptian army, which had been sorely neglected by Merneptah, was the fact that Osasiphars had secretly bribed the border guards in Theku, one of the fortresses protecting the eastern border of Egypt.

Finally, all the Hebrew warriors were in readiness in Avaris and, under cover of night, they slipped out of the city and into the desert of "Etham". They forced-marched south toward Theku at the entrance to Wadi Tamilat, which was the valley leading into the heart of Egypt. Their path took them parallel to the "Wall of Rulers", the series of fortresses that protected the eastern flank of the Nile Delta but well out of sight of the pickets manning the observation towers of the strongholds.

By the next evening, the Hebrew army was opposite the Wadi's mouth but out of sight behind the sand dunes and waiting to attack the fortress of Theku. As darkness fell, a few guards of Hebrew descent in the fort signaled the leaders of the army that the bridge over the barrier of the crocodile-filled canal was lowered and that the gates to their fortress had been opened.

An advanced chariot guard rushed the fort, slaughtering the garrison within. Then the Hebrew army crossed into Egypt and poured down the Wadi through the precinct of Succoth, past Pithom, destroying and pillaging everything in their path.

Even before the Hebrews had reached the town of Bubastis, at the western end of the valley, chariot-mounted messengers of the Egyptian army were clattering down the streets of Memphis to warn Pharaoh Merneptah of the invasion.

Upon hearing this calamitous news, the pharaoh was thrown into confusion. "How could this happen?" he agonized, still not realizing that he had been betrayed. When the army's messengers described the size and ferocity of the invading host, the king was grasped with fear. Old age overshadowed his ability to cope with this life-threatening situation, and he was frozen with indecision.

At this point, the second part of the treasonous plot unfolded; from out of the shadows stepped Danaus to the side of pharaoh. He reminded him that the deities had foretold that the Hebrews would have no courage in the face of Egyptian might and that the strength of pharaoh's arm, even in his old age, could easily overthrow these renegades. Then certain picked army generals came forward pledging their faithfulness and swords in defense of their pharaoh and to the destruction of his enemies. Little did the pharaoh know that these generals, who were of Hebrew and Semitic descent, were also party to the plot against him.

Danaus and the traitorous generals had planned with Osasiphar to convince Merneptah that he was invincible and then lead him into a trap while pretending to attack the Hebrew army, where the pharaoh would be killed. This would leave Egypt and its wealth in the hands of the plotters and their confederates.

The bait was swallowed by Merneptah, and a token army was mustered in short order by the generals to defend Egypt. The troops moved out of Memphis with the tottering pharaoh perched in his chariot at the lead, entertaining vision of a great victory similar to those of many years past, when he had crushed the Libyans, Syrians, and others who had threatened Egypt – just as these renegades were doing now.

As in all well-laid plans of men, this one, too, went awry for the pernicious plotters. On the eve of battle, as Merneptah was resting, one of his trusted counselors was able to slip past the surrounding clutch of conspirators insulating the king from the truth and warn him of the evil plan to take the pharaoh's life, which the counselor had overheard.

Thinking that he must have angered the deities in some way to be the recipient of such vehement treatment, Merneptah reflected over events that had brought him to this terrible situation. Suddenly, his anguished brain received a jolt of remembrance of the prophet's warning some years before, when he had written:

> You have angered the deities and kindled their wrath by casting consecrated priests into the quarries where they could be seen at common labor instead of service to their Benefactors. For this offense, the deities have decreed a curse on Egypt, because you are their representative of the Land. Certain people shall come to the assistance of the polluted wretches and conquer Egypt, and keep it in their possession for thirteen years.

A strong spirit grasped Merneptah, and he immediately summoned his personal guards to his side. With this shield of trusted soldiers, pharaoh purged the army of the conniving generals, broke camp, and swiftly retreated to Memphis. At the sight of what appeared to the Hebrews to be Merneptah's cowardly abandonment of the battlefield, the army, realizing they had won the day without battle and that Egypt and its wealth was theirs for the taking, went delirious with rejoicing. But the undisciplined Hebrew army made an all-too-familiar mistake of warfare. In their lust for spoils, they failed to pursue the enemy and destroy his army – a mistake later they would pay for dearly.

In all haste, Merneptah returned to Memphis, where he hoped to consult with the Oracles of Ammon for answers to this perplexing and dangerous situation. What awaited him on his return, however, was the glum-faced, but inwardly gleeful, Danaus and his fellow traitors, including the high priest of the Apis cult in Memphis, who had already received the news of his defeat from messengers assigned to spy upon the king and report back swiftly at the moment of his death. They were dejected only because the pharaoh had slipped from the trap and was not dead. But they were victorious on the field of battle, and it was only a matter of time before the deed could be consummated. Their insipid words to the king stung the old man, for their only suggestions were for him to flee the country.

Merneptah was reaching a state of paranoia, for he knew that assassins could be on all sides – what should he do? Still surrounded by his trusted guards, the haggard pharaoh proceeded to Ammon's Temple to hear what words the Oracle would receive from the deities about the future.

Danaus had hurriedly arranged the whole prediction with the Oracle, who was in his power. With pomp and mystic ceremony befitting the occasion, the pharaoh was informed, with all the proper amount of foreboding, that the deities were most displeased, and the only possible way for the monarch to receive absolution in his afterlife was to immediately end his own life – now, and with all dispatch.

Merneptah left the Temple of Ammon with a heavy heart and also a vial of noxious, life-removing potion, which, just by chance, Danaus had on hand and which he gave to the dejected pharaoh as he left.

In the privacy of his living quarters in the palace, the pharaoh lay down upon a comfortable lounge and prepared to end his life, resigned to the deities' will and his own fate. His family and close friends stood by his side to comfort him during the remaining minutes, attentive only to the old man's wishes. Danaus, squeamish about the whole affair, made himself conveniently absent, with an explanation that he must attend to temple affairs before the arrival of the enemy. Merneptah had, at this point, still not found out that Danaus and Cadmeus were his most dangerous enemies and the cause of his problems.

Fate – really luck – trod once again upon the stage for, as soon as Danaus was out of earshot and none of their spies were present, events took another tangential turn. As Merneptah lay on his death couch, ready to raise the vial of poisonous fluid to his lips, his son, Sethos, who had just returned from Sais in lower Egypt, entered and knelt down by his father's side weeping violently, he pled to the deities to lift this curse and not take his beloved father from him. From somewhere deep within the elderly gentleman, a spark of self-preservation flamed anew, consuming him with the thought: If he could live a little longer, he would be certain that his precious son would be safe from his enemies. Then a vision flashed before the king's eyes:

> He saw his son, Sethos, seated high upon a golden throne, with a gigantic figure of Ammon-Re behind him; and flanking the chair were the pantheon of deities protecting the young king. In front of the dais were multitudes of his enemies, their hands bound behind, kneeling in obeisance to Sethos. Placed on the head of each prisoner was the sandaled foot of an Egyptian soldier, with hand raised in praise of faithfulness.

This vision so shocked the old gentleman that he instantly sat erect with the gracefulness of a young man. Everyone, including Sethos, stood frozen in their place, totally stunned at Merneptah's actions and stared at the spilled liquid and broken glass of the vial on the floor, where it had slipped from the pharaoh's hand. The king began to issue orders in rapid succession, throwing everyone into confusion. There was strength in his voice and agility in his movements, something he had lacked for many a year; he felt renewed and burning with purpose. His thoughts were clear, and a plan of action had materialized in his mind, out of the former gray fog that had engulfed him.

Merneptah had everyone ushered from his presence except his son, Sethos. Then, in private, Merneptah told him what he intended to do. The king explained to Sethos that his father wished him to quickly remove the images of the deities from the temples and load them, along with the Sacred Apis Bull, on ships and sail up the Nile immediately to the protection of the king in their vassal state of Kush, who was still under obligation to Merneptah.

While Sethos was performing these tasks and preparing to sail to Ethiopia, Merneptah took care of affairs of state. His first order was to appoint a new, trustworthy general to head his demoralized army. His job was to mount a rear-guard action to delay the enemy as well as to attempt to save Memphis and Upper Egypt from invasion while the pharaoh made an orderly retreat to safety in the neighboring country to the south.

His remaining task was to appoint a titular head of state who would act in his behalf while he was in exile preparing an army, which he and his son would someday victoriously lead to regain the "Land of the Nile" for the Egyptians.

Although Danaus had again been disappointed, fortunately he had been successful in masking his treasonable actions from his monarch. Anyone who had the slightest chance of informing the pharaoh had been clandestinely removed. With an air of trustworthiness still surrounding him, he quickly wheedled his way past family and friends and convinced the pharaoh to place total confidence in him.

It was his plan that, when it came time for the king to depart Memphis, Danaus would already have maneuvered himself into being pharaoh's choice to act in his behalf during his absence, one which Danaus immensely hoped would never end.

A wail of anguish rose skyward from the throats of the assembled people on the docks of Memphis as the wind fills the sail of Merneptah's royal barge to take him into exile. The king's subjects were distraught that the earthly representative of their deities was being forced to leave "The Land". Now they would be destitute, with no way of reaching the deities to hear their pleas for deliverance. Danaus, however, along with his handpicked skeleton court, waved farewell to the disappearing royal vessel with smirks of glee upon their faces. Now the power had shifted into the hands of Danaus, and those hands were going to become very busy as he sought to consolidate his position.

Alone in what was now his royal palace, with his every command law and with none to answer to, Danaus began to rethink his agreements with Osasiphars and his Hebrew confederates. After all, they were lepers and detestable shepherds, and in his veins flowed not only the very strength of Egyptian blood but also the portent of greatness. Why should he share this power of Memphis and all of Upper Egypt? Let them have the swampy Delta as their reward for unwittingly assisting him to power – maybe even to the throne itself.

Consistent with his deceitful nature, Danaus thereupon made another pact with Osasiphars: If the Hebrews and their army remained away from Memphis, Heliopolis, and Upper Egypt, Danaus would hold the Egyptian army in check at the capital on the pretense that they must wait for the pharaoh's return before attempting to retake the Delta. The Hebrews of Edom, who were not really anxious to fight at all, were pacified with this reasoning. Osasiphars, however, was livid with rage for this treachery from his ally. Osasiphars, therefore, made every attempt to encourage his Hebrew confederates to press on to Memphis for the ultimate vengeance of which they dreamed. But his words fell upon deaf ears, for the soldiers and generals were only too happy to live off the fat of the Delta land, which was a vast improvement over the scrub-brush, dry, hill-country area of Edom whence they had come.

Left to their own designs, the invaders treated the people of the Delta so shamefully that the period of their government appeared to all who then beheld these impieties the worst of time. For they not only burned towns and villages and were not satisfied with plundering the sanctuaries of Pi-Ramses, Bubastis, and Sais and abusing the images of the deities, but they continually made use of those venerated and sacred animals that were fit to be eaten. They compelled the priests and prophets to become their butchers and destroyers, and then sent them away empty-handed.

After being betrayed, then flagrantly ignored, Osasiphars returned to his unclean of Avaris. There, with the magnetism of his personality and cunning nature, he began to build a society from the refuge of Egypt. Eventually, he was able to arrest, then totally halt, the spread of disease by the very force of his sanitary policies involving the use of anciently known cures and practices that he had learned while in Midian.

Osasiphars' reputation for success spread far and wide as a healer and saintly man. His sensitivity for his people and compassion for others was to make him famous throughout the Delta and into Syria. His own people finally decided to honor him with a name that would more befit his position and stature among the Hebrews. The one chosen was a common nickname given to a well-loved king, Moses.

Soon, more and more of the Hebrew invaders came to look upon Moses as their leader, admitting to him their sorrow for not taking his council to march on Memphis, for Danaus had become a tyrannical dictator, constantly issuing orders that were detrimental to the Hebrews.

After Danaus had made certain that Merneptah was securely exiled in Ethiopia, he proceeded to purge sympathizers from the old pharaoh's court and the army. His power became so absolute in such a short period of time that he began to have delusions of grandeur. Since he now possessed complete political power, there was nothing in his path to prevent him from grasping the position he had sought all along and it would give him divine power, a demi-deity on earth. An act so devious as this presented little difficulty to this man who had the keenest abilities to manipulate and an unquenchable ambition. He was already high priest of the Menervian cult in Heliopolis and his co-conspirator, Cadmeus, was high priest of the Apis cult in Memphis – how more perfect could the situation be? With great deliberation Danaus began to instigate the process that would eventually join him with the divinities themselves – as pharoah.

Surreptitiously, the plan unfolded, with revelations from the deities made by the "Oracle of Ammon" that Danaus was of royal blood and in the royal book of Heritage. And, so, with confirmation voiced loudly by his friend, Cadmeus, "The High Priest of Memphis", the installation of Danaus to the throne took place with the grandeur, pomp, and circumstance of some well-rehearsed stage play. After taking the royal symbols of office, Danaus assumed the Pharaonic title of "Amenmesses-Siptah", after his father, the former Amenmesses.

Sandwiched in between the Hebrews in the north and the still dangerous Merneptah in the south, there was little he could do to expand his compact kingdom. With no great deeds to perform nor countries to conquer, he instead took out his frustration by effacing Merneptah's old monuments and recording accolades to himself, and also praising what he wanted others to believe were *his* rightful ancestors.

Now that he was king, Amenmesses-Siptah was himself a target of intrigue for, unknown to him, a spy had remained in his court, a man who played the counter agent to a tee – Bay, the court treasurer and Sethos' old friend and mentor. He had promised Sethos and his father that he would remain behind and send messengers to Ethiopia in order to keep them apprised about events in Memphis.

The years dragged by for Merneptah and his son, Sethos. The king of Ethiopia supplied the troops that had followed pharaoh into exile with all the necessities of life. The king also afforded and assigned them as many towns and villages as would suffice during the time they were compelled to be deprived of their own comforts of home. Then he placed an Ethiopian army on the borders of Egypt as a protection for Merneptah and his followers.

Thirteen long years passed, until Merneptah felt that he had rebuilt his army and sufficiently trained his son in the skills of battle as well as in the wisdom of a great leader. Bay continually kept the old pharaoh informed of the atrocities that the Hebrew invaders had carried out and also about the despicable ways of Amenmesses-Siptah, with whom he had entrusted Egypt during Merneptah's long exile. Bay had also secretly made allies with a close and trusted group of supporters in Memphis who were faithful to the old pharaoh and his heir in order that they might pave the way for his triumphal return to reclaim his throne.

The time finally arrived when the aged and infirm Merneptah decided that he was ready to consummate the most important decision of his long life. It was the fulfillment of his dream, which was the return to Egypt with his son, Sethos, at the forefront of the army leading them on to the glorious liberation of his homeland.

The enthusiastic Egyptian army was mustered together and prepared for battle. To increase their strength and numbers, Merneptah requested assistance from his vassal ally, the king of Ethiopia. The king thereupon furnished several battalions of Nubian foot soldiers to march at the pharaoh's side, adding a substantially greater potential for Merneptah's success.

During their councils of war, the young, imaginative Sethos, having learned his war strategy well, conceived a brilliant plan to outwit their enemies. Instead of the host of warriors sailing down the Nile, where enemy spies, who were already aware that the pharaoh was gathering an army, would surely spot them, he plotted to deceive both the Hebrews and the usurper, Amenmesses-Siptah (Danaus).

Sethos' plan was to create a mock army of mannequin soldiers that would be placed aboard a flotilla of hastily constructed barges, manned only by a skeleton crew, thereby giving animation to the contrived assembly. The flotilla would proceed at a leisurely pace down the Nile, being very visible to the pickets who would surely report their movements as they gradually approached Memphis for battle. While this deception was being made, the main body of the army would board another flotilla of ships on the eastern coast of Kush, then rapidly sail north on the "Sea of Egypt" and land just below the head of that gulf. Upon disembarking, the army would rapidly march overland toward Memphis by way of the little used route from Sinai to Heliopolis, thereby totally surprising the enemy and outflanking them. They would be outwitted into believing that the mock flotilla on the Nile was filled with an army that was so overconfident that it need not keep its movement concealed.

Sethos' plan was to prove a stunning success. Amenmesses-Siptah's messengers had warned him of the approaching armada, which had remained at a safe distance from shore and close scrutiny. The usurper hurriedly appealed to the Hebrews to come to his assistance, lest Merneptah's army should defeat Amenmesses' small forces and retake Memphis and then the whole Delta again. As in the past, the Hebrews fell sway to the usurper's old power of persuasion and joined him to ambush what he believed was Merneptah's army.

Imagine the Heliopolian's surprise as Merneptah's army, with his son, Sethos, standing magnificently in his golden chariot at the lead, came charging like a whirlwind from out of the desert. When the Hebrews realized that this threatening multitude was no mirage emerging from the simmering heat waves over the desert sands, it was too late for a defense. The only hope possible was to run for their lives or be food for the sword blades and lances of pharaoh's warriors, who were screaming for their blood.

The moment the Temple City was subdued, Sethos shunned any congratulations on his victory and strategy. He paused only for a short time while he instructed the bearers of the portable couch on which his father lay to move him to the great Temple of Ammon-Ra. There, he tenderly placed the exhausted old man under care of the priests who were attending his army. Sethos admonished them to watch over his father and to offer prayers to the deities for continued victories so that he might return the images and the Apis to their rightful place. With anger in his eyes, Sethos then turned his face toward Memphis.

Sethos' victory over his enemies at Heliopolis preceded him to Memphis and to Amenmesses-Siptah, waiting in ambush by the Nile, south of the city. On hearing the news, Siptah's (Danaus') first reaction was anger, which was vented instantly upon the cowering messenger who bore the grim tidings. Even as the courier's bloody corpse was being dragged from Siptah's tent, he began raving at his generals for their stupidity and bungling. But this act of desperation could not and would not save the usurper from Sethos' vengeance. He and his wretched followers were caught between two armies, the flotilla (mock though it was) approaching from the south in sight on the Nile before him and another thundering down upon him from the north.

To Sethos, the deities gave him the victory he had asked for; however, vengeance was to be left in the hands of his heavenly divinities. Even though Sethos was to be denied the satisfaction of staring into the face of Danaus as he plunged his sword into the body of the man who had caused so many heinous crimes, the irony of fate, which results from the consequences of betrayal, was not to be denied.

Siptah's cloak of delusions of grandeur rapidly vanished as if he had just awakened from a somber sleep, leaving him naked to the truth that his world had just disintegrated, his power lost, and his hopes of immortality dashed. His generals had fled, along with the army, court friends, and minions – all had vanished like smoke in the wind. Alone in his tent, pressed in on all sides, Amenmesses-Siptah – conspirator, traitor, tyrant, usurper – stared at a vial, not unlike the very one he had handed to his pharaoh that night so long ago, when he had told the king:

"There is no hope – end it all now!"

Sethos' thirst for vengeance was unquenched. The usurper was dead, as evidenced by the charred remains of a royal, robed body placed in front of him as proof of Siptah's death – a death by his own hand and not by Sethos' blade. Siptah's mercenaries had either been put to the sword or sworn to the service of pharaoh. The major body of wretched Hebrew soldiers had escaped, however, under the cover of night. Sethos knew that to let the brigands escape unpunished would mean danger that they might have to be faced on the battlefield again.

The pharaoh's army had been on the move for days now, and his soldiers were exhausted, so even though Sethos was anxious to pursue his enemy, he realized that an army tired and hungry was not an efficient fighting machine. The boy placed his personal desires aside for the good of the troops. After their brief respite, Sethos was among his troops, inspiring them to move out and find the enemy that had pillaged and defiled their land.

With Sethos at the lead, pharaoh's army, like an angry swarm of hornets, was hot upon the heels of the retreating Hebrews. From Memphis, they rapidly marched northward, past Giza at the desert's edge, with the foreboding, monolithic Pyramid of Chephren looming in the sands beyond. South of Letopolis, the army crossed the turbid Nile before it branched into the Canopic and Sebennetic branches, then moved up the caravan road that ran along the eastern side of the Bubastic arm called "The Waters of Horus". Their march was interrupted only briefly for Sethos' hurried visit his father in the temple at Heliopolis to reassure himself that the failing pontiff was comfortable and quickly to describe his victories in the name of pharaoh. He hoped the old man would rest more easily with the knowledge that Merneptah had trained his son well, avenged his honor, and recaptured his throne.

Fortunately for Danaus and Cadmeus, they had made good their escape during the confusion of battle and ensuing panic of the Hebrew army retreat. Devious to the last, Danaus had arranged to murder an innocent soldier, dress him in royal attire, disfigure the body sufficiently to make identification doubtful so that Sethos would believe him dead, then join Cadmeus and flee for their lives. They successfully reached the town of Canopus, located on the western Delta coast of the "Great Sea" (Mediterranean) well ahead of pharaoh's troops, where a ship had already been provisioned and made ready for a hasty departure for the Ionian Sea across the horizon.

Bidding farewell to his father, Sethos rejoined the army, who were waiting only for his command to commence the relentless search for their enemies. Sethos was soon to be rewarded, for, when the army was just north of Liontonplis, his advance scouts returned with news that the Hebrew army was encamped at the western end of Wadi Tumilat and east of Pi-Sapdu (a town nicknamed Ramses, for the Great Pharaoh).

Sethos first divided his forces. A smaller contingent was to proceed up the Pelusiac arm and retake the towns of Bubastis and Pi-Ramses and then move on to Tanis. In the meantime, he would attack the main Hebrew army in the Ramses district.

Then, with all haste, Sethos advanced on his enemy. However, the Hebrew rear-guard scouts on patrol, not realizing that the Egyptian army was so close at hand, stumbled upon the pharaoh's troops. In mortal fear for their lives, they wheeled around and made a hasty retreat toward their comrades. When information of the approaching Egyptians reached the Hebrew soldiers, the news spread through the camp like wildfire and panic gripped the host. Tales of the mighty Egyptian armies that had swept through Canaan and Syria in years past and had viciously driven the Hyksos, their ancient ancestors, from the Delta centuries ago flashed through their minds, along with the recent tales of the furious vengeance by Sethos' army.

The route that ensued would have made the old pharaoh smile as the enemy blindly fled down the Wadi – baggage, tents, carts, utensils and armor were discarded to hasten their retreat -- past the "Wells of Merneptah" at Pithom in the area called Succoth, through the fortress town of Theku, across the bridge spanning the crocodile-infested canal built as a barrier to Asiatics such as these, and into the desert from which they had come that moonless night thirteen years before.

Close on their flanks, the Egyptian army, with Sethos standing proudly erect in his golden chariot tightly gripping the reins of the pair of magnificent white horses, was bearing down upon the withdrawing mass of uncontrollable troops and camp followers. The boy secretly hoped they would turn at the last moment like a trapped animal with its back against a cliff, but he had forgotten that the desert was home to these sand dwellers. Like a flash flood in arid landscape, the mass of humanity was swallowed up within minutes as they fled into the desert sand dunes of the "Wilderness of Etham".

His mission was not accomplished yet, for the hated old Hyksos capital of Avaris, remained untouched. Where the seeds of rebellion and treachery had originally been sown, this would be his next goal now that he had driven the invaders beyond the borders of Egypt.

When pharaoh's army reached Theku, Sethos loaded his army on barges and headed north toward Avaris. A few days later, the army reached the fortress of Thel (Sile), the other major entry gate to the Delta from Asia on the ancient caravan route from Egypt to Canaan. There, he rejoined the other contingent of his army, which had rapidly completed their mission to retake the other major towns of the eastern Delta.

After several days, the army was rested and resupplied. Sethos then laid plans for the siege of Avaris, since it was a fortified walled city. The army moved out of Thel and across the bridge spanning the large channel connecting Lake Ballah to Horus Lake. Within hours, by way of the caravan route, he joined the garrison at the "Migdol of Sethos" (named after one of his ancestors), some five miles south of Avaris, which lay opposite the Pelusiac (Bubastic) mouth. There, Sethos learned that many Hebrew soldiers had recently passed by the fortress, obviously on the way to Avaris. He then realized to his anger that many of the defeated Hebrews had returned to Avaris for protection, since traveling to Edom would be very dangerous without arms or provisions.

As the morning sun rose over the shadowy sand dune peaks – "Horus arising after his long night's journey through the underworld" – the Egyptian host was amassed in front of Avaris. The inhabitants had given the fortress a Hebrew name, "Pi-Hahiroth" (the house of Hah-Eiroth or Rising Sun), the conjunction of the female guardian deity from Syria and Sinai. From between the ramparts at the top of the walls around the city, Hebrew soldiers stared down at the legion of fighting men assembled to attack them.

Suddenly, to Sethos' surprise, the city gates opened, and from within appeared a man in long flowing robes. His countenance bespoke authority; he was erect, tall, with flowing white hair and beard. As he walked from the shadows of the portal and into the glaring sunlight, Sethos saw that the corresponding movement of the tall shaft, which he grasped tightly in his hand, followed his every step. Pharaoh's son watched the aristocratic-looking gentleman stride deliberately toward his tent, where the boy was sitting on a raised chair. As the enigmatic individual came to the front of the boy's tent, he halted without entering. He then began to speak in a stuttering, high-pitched voice totally out of keeping with the demeanor of his person:

> I am Moses! Leader of the people within the City, who
> now call themselves Israelites, after their ancestors. These
> people are no threat to the land of Egypt, and only wish to
> be left alone to live in peace. The Hebrew soldiers, whom
> we have recently given shelter, are dispirited, tired, and in
> fright for their lives from pharaoh's army. I believe I am
> the one that pharaoh seeks. If anyone should be punished
> for the harm that has befallen Egypt, then take me. I

place myself in your hands, Oh son of pharaoh, that your
vengeance may be satisfied.

He then stepped forward and placed his staff on the ground in front of pharaoh's son.
At first, Sethos felt something between perplexity and compassion for this anomalous person
standing in front of his tent. Then a flash of outrage surged through him for feeling anything
but hatred for this man and his band of revolutionists behind those walls a few hundred
yards away. This, he thought, was an obvious trap, like so many others, and he would not be
unwittingly duped any longer by these heathen. Sethos sat quietly for some time, then turned
to the aide by his side and whispered to him what to say, so that he would not have to speak
to this unworthy Asiatic. The aide stepped forward and delivered the boy's reply:

> The deities cannot be appeased so easily
> for the desecrations to the images and priests. Their wrath
> can be appeased only by retribution. Pharaoh's anger will
> be quenched only with the blood of his enemies, so go!
> Return to your wretched people and prepare to meet your
> death.

When Moses had returned to the city and informed its occupants of the death sentence
of pharaoh by his son, wails of anguish rose up from the people, for they knew that not if,
but when, the walls were breached all within would be put to the sword. In desperation, the
Israelites reverted to the old absolution ritual of attrition to their deities by sacrificing a first-
born lamb, then splashing its blood upon their front door jamb as prescribed by the anciently
practiced "Rite of the Threshold".

For three days, Sethos threw his troops against the tall eight-foot-thick mud walls
of Avaris but was unable to breach the ramparts at any point. Finally, the siege machines
arrived from Memphis and Sethos prepared for a final assault on the fortress.

When Moses saw the machines arrive, he realized that there were only hours before
his people would be slaughtered at the hands of the Egyptians. If he were to save his people,
action must be taken immediately. With the cunning that had long been his, he conceived
a plan to escape the impending doom. Calling a council of elders together, he revealed the
scheme to them. Almost from the very walls, west of the city was a treacherous swampy
area all the way to Horus Lake. On the south and east were pharaoh's soldiers, and on the
north was the Great Sea. No one would suspect them of slipping out of the city into that
swamp. Years ago, however, Moses had been shown a safe path through the swamp to the
seacoast. Once there, they could sneak eastward along the beach with the sand dunes above
the beach preventing their detection by the Egyptian sentries. When out of sight of the army,
the Hebrews could follow the narrow sand bar that acted as the outer barrier, between the
deep tidal pool of "Lake Serbonis" and the Great Sea. To traverse the wide breaks in the sand
bar that were open to the Great Sea at the east end, they must travel at night and wait for the
tide to flow out; then they could wade across. Once on the other side of these breaks, they

could disappear into the wilderness, where Moses knew of wells and oases from his travels to Midian years ago.

Under the protection of darkness from a moonless sky, the Israelites, with Moses at their head, followed the route that their leader had proposed. The hand of fate, however, again stirred the potion of trouble, for, on the beach that evening between the Israel clan and freedom was a gathering of Egyptian soldiers refreshing themselves in the cooling waters of the ocean breakers after a hot day.

With efficient skill, the Egyptians were dispatched without alarming their other comrades bivouacked only a short distance away, and the Israelites silently slipped past the army encampment and proceeded quietly ahead within the narrow confines of the shoreline. The only remaining barrier was the small settlement at the western end of Lake Serbonis, called "Baal-Zephon", with its temple sanctuary and monastery dedicated to the Syrian god "Zeus-Cassius". The Hebrews were again successful in eluding detection by anyone in the small community by wading through the shallow waters at the end of the tidal lake, hidden by the tall reeds that grew profusely along its shores. When the Hebrew band had succeeded in avoiding the only remaining obstacle to their freedom, they began the hasty trek over the confined, narrow, sandy land bridge, anxiously glancing from side to side at the ominous murky waves lapping the beach on each side only yards from their feet. When they finally arrived at the first break in the sand bar, their fears began to mount when they saw that the waters had still not receded from the gap in their pathway. Moses signaled a halt, and the Israelites began an apprehensive postponement.

Back in the Egyptian camp, the early morning pickets were reconnoitering and detected that there were no guards posted on Avaris' walls. Within a short time, they also discovered that the Hebrews had vacated the city, and the alarm was sounded to waken the army. Before the soldiers were in formation and horses hitched to war chariots, the murdered soldiers were found scattered upon the beach. Without hesitation, Sethos knew what had happened and set off in hasty pursuit.

Unknown to Moses, this particular night was the one that occurred every month in which the Great Sea was to experience its highest tide. Gradually, the waters rolled out of Lake Sirbonis as the Israelites waited impatiently to cross. The eastern horizon was beginning to lose its inky blackness, heralding the coming of dawn, when the waters had reached their lowest ebb. Bag and baggage, the Israelite clan tremulously waded across the first break to the island sand bar beyond. As the last of the thousands of people completed the first crossing, a cry of terror rang out from the stragglers at the rear. In the distance behind them could be seen hundreds of torches, whose light shone onto glittering metal. The Hebrews instantly knew this could only come from the swords and lances of the pursuing Egyptian army.

Panic struck again, but this time Moses was able to quell their fears with the power of his personality. With all the urgency born of fear for their lives, they blindly scrambled forward as rapidly as they could shuffle their feet through the wet, clinging sand. It seemed like an eternity before the Hebrews reached the second crossing. Moses lifted his rod toward the heavens, and then turned toward his band and shouted:

> Yahweh has delivered us this day from our enemies. He
> has parted the sea and let us pass through so that we may
> escape pharaoh's armies. Be afraid no longer; follow me
> to your deliverance, for pharaoh will surely not capture
> us this day!"

Moses thereupon wheeled about and, not looking back, strode to the other side through the swirling eddies remaining on the visible sea bed, the waves of the Great Sea on his one side, and the waters of Lake Sirbonis on the other, as the tide rapidly began to rise again to cover the ground.

When the Egyptians finally reached the first crossing in the sand bar, the sun was already climbing towards its zenith in the sky, and the waters of the Great Sea were beginning to swirl back into Lake Sirbonis. Sethos was hard pressed to restrain his troops at the sight of their enemy only a few miles ahead, so they plunged into the breach in the land bridge and onto the opposite island sand bar beyond. Before the forefront of the army could reach the second crossing, the waters of the Great Sea were pouring rapidly into the Lake, blocking their forward movement; the tail of the army was caught in the waters filling the other gap, drowning many of the soldiers and stranding the remainder upon the confines of the narrow sand bar island.

Sethos could only stand in his chariot and vent his frustration with anguished screams of rage. His enemies, the wretched Hebrews, had escaped with no way to pursue, and his army, totally isolated from him, were drenched, drowning, or dead.

After a time, Sethos had his chariot floated to shore and then returned to Sile to arrange for barges to rescue his bedraggled troops, huddled in the sand, surrounded by the waters of the Great Sea and "Yam Suph", the Reed Sea.

His army was soon rescued and placed in the hands of competent generals to direct their return by boat down the Pelusiac to Memphis. Sethos headed for Heliopolis by chariot. Although he had not been able to put all his father's enemies to the sword, at least they had been totally driven from Egyptian soil.

Sethos reigned in the lathered stallions as he wheeled in front of the Temple of Ammon-Ra in Heliopolis. His spirits were much higher with the anticipation that, within moments, his father's ears would listen to the news of his victories. As he bolted up the sweeping steps that rose to the pillared monument above, he was greeted by wails of grief, ushering from within the sanctuary. He instantly came to a halt upon surmounting the stairs, gripped by an invisible hand of impending doom.

Pharaoh Merneptah had passed into history without returning to his rightful throne. After order had been restored and the command given to begin the ritual of burial preparations for his father, Sethos decreed a period of mourning throughout Egypt for many months. Rebuilding what had been destroyed and reestablishing the images to their rightful places was not something to be ignored for long. Therefore, when the golden casket containing Merneptah's mummified remains was sealed within his secret tomb, work began.

If the deities were to sanctify their work and bring fruitfulness back to Egypt, there must be a new pharaoh to intercede for the land and its people. Among the tumultuous cheers for their liberator and chants of praise for long life, peace, and health to Merneptah's son and proper heir, the new pharaoh stepped from the Temple of Investment as "Sethos II, fifth and rightful successor to the throne of Dynasty XIX".

Although Sethos II's brief six-year reign was to prove unspectacular, he was able to carry out a certain amount of building. Apart from his tomb and a funerary temple, he built a small temple at Karnak, made additions to the Karnak temple of the goddess "Mut of Ishru", and completed the decoration of the temple of "Thoth" at Hermopolis, which had been begun by his grandfather, Ramses II, and of which the fabric had been completed by Merneptah. He also reestablished and expanded turquoise mining in Sinai.

Eventually, Sethos II's sister, Tewosret, was to engineer the position as the new pharaoh's consort. This was a reward for her faithful service to Sethos' father during the years in exile. As in so many other instances of reward, this one, too, was responded to with deception. Tewosret, daughter of Merneptah, being much older than her brother, had always been jealous of Sethos and possessed covetous designs upon the throne, believing it to be hers by virtue of succession by eldest.

Before the assassination of Merneptah's eldest son, Ramses-Siptah's, Tewosret, as his queen, had borne him a son. As deep-seated jealousy always grows with time, this one did as well. Tewosret, with the continual encouragement of those who were always grasping for wealth and power, began to realize that her son was the path to the throne.

In the sixth year of his reign, Sethos II was struck down by a grave, protracted illness – slow poisoning – and, with constant assistance from Tewosret at his side, Sethos was not to recover his health. During the long illness, Tewosret, to salve her conscience for causing such prolonged agony, gave to her dying pharaoh brother her very own tomb, which she had spent so long preparing and so much money to ensure her comfort during her afterlife. Death, however, terminates many contracts, so she took it back and buried Sethos in a cheaper crypt.

Before his death, Sethos II was to appoint his old and faithful friend, Bay, as "Great Chancellor" over the entire land of Egypt, a position which had come naturally, for Bay had assumed the political helm during pharaoh's sickness. Tewosret had been very careful to hide her treachery from Bay, so he was not aware that she was performing such a despicable act in order to acquire the throne. After Pharaoh Sethos's death, Bay had become very suspicious when Tewosret had made such haste to inter the body and thus remove it from scrutiny.

With Tewosret beside the throne, her son was handed the flail and crook of kingship along with the title "Ikhenre-Setepnere Merneptah Siptah". Tewosret was not to receive or dispense power during the eight years of her co-regency with Merneptah-Siptah, for Bay had forced her into an arrangement for the good of Egypt. Her son could have the throne, but matters of state would be under Bay's control. Bay's power gradually increased during those eight years, with Tewosret restricted to limited duties, and her inept, sickly son, Merneptah-Siptah, was all but reduced to an ineffectual pawn of his mother.

The harbinger of death was soon to claim Merneptah-Siptah, which removed any hope of Tewosret's ambitions being realized. Tewosret, however, was not to be deterred, and she continued to plot against Bay's authority.

The "Land of the Nile", however, needed strong and authoritative leadership, so, with this mandate, Bay was able to maneuver onto the throne a son of Sethos II, who assumed the reigns of state (under Bay's direction) until a dynamic personality of authority and lineage, called "Userkhaure Sethnakhte (1198 B.C.), was to appear. He would return Egypt to its former glory through a new period titled "Dynasty XX".

The demise of Dynasty XIX would herald the dying breath of Egypt, for after some 3,000 years as masters of the Middle East, this small land nestled snugly in the northeastern corner of the massive continent of Africa was but a flickering flame in the glaring light of emerging nations around the Mediterranean seacoast. The threatening societies of Mesopotamia and the old Zoroastrian country of Persia were now under the sway of an advancing faith, which claimed as its founder the prophet Mohammed.

Bibliography

Albright, W.F.
> *The Archaeology of Palestine*, 1956
> *From the Stone Age to Christianity*, 1957

Allegro, John M.
> *Sacred Mushroom and the Cross*, 1983
> *The Chosen People*, 1972

Anati, Emmanuel, *Palestine before the Hebrews*, 1962

Apuleius, Lucius, *The Golden Ass*, translation by W. Adlington, 1915

Arbuthnot, Foster, *The Mysteries of Chronology*, 1900

"Archaeological Discoveries in the Holy Land," *Archaeological Institute of America*, 1967

Bamberger, Bernard, *The Story of Judaism*, 1957

Batrick, Ebn, *Annals*

Bell, B., *The Dark Ages in Ancient History: I, The First Dark Age in Egypt*, 1971

Bietak, M., *Tell el-Daba II*, 1975

Bimson, J.J., *Re-dating the Exodus and Conquest*, 1981

Bonwick, James, *Egyptian Belief and Modern Thought*, 1956

Breasted, James H.
> *Ancient Records of Egypt, III*, 1906
> *A History of Egypt*, 1905

Brodsky, Alyn, *The King Departs* (Maccabee's), 1974

Brown, Lloyd A., *The Story of Maps*, 1949

Bryant, Jacob, *Analysis of Mythology*, 3 Volumes, 1775

Buck, Henry P., *Anthropology and Religion*

Budge, Sir E., *Tutankhamen, Amenism, Atenism and Egyptian Monotheism*, 1923

Burhams, Robert, *Celestial Handbook*, 1966

Burns, A.R., *Minoans, Philistines and Greeks; 1400-900 B.C.*, 1930

Butzer, Karl W., *Early Hydraulic Civilization in Egypt*, 1976

Cambridge Ancient History; Vol. I, II, and III, Cambridge University Press, 1973

Champollion, Recueil, *The Geography of the Exodus*, 1922

Clark, Dr. D, *Dr. Daniel Clark's Travels*, 1919

Clay, Albert, *Empire of the Ammorites*, 1896

Coles, M.R.,
> *Masculine Cross (A History of Ancient and Modern Crosses)*, 1891
> *Cultus Arborum (Phallic Tree Worship)*, 1890

Cory, I.P., *The Ancient Fragments*, 1876

Cook, Stanley A., *The Religion of Ancient Palestine*, 1908

Cornfield, F.M., *From Religion to Philosophy*, 1912

Crooke, W. (B.A.), *The Popular Religion & Folk-lore of Northern India*, Vol. I, II, 1968

Dentan, Robert G., *The Knowledge of god in Ancient Israel*, 1968

Die Phonizier, *Movers, F.C.*, Dr.

Dothan, T., *The Philistines and their Material Culture*, 1982

Dunlap, S.F., *Vestiges of the Spirit History of Man*, 1858

Dupuis, Charles, *The Origin of All Religious Worship*, 1872

Elisofon, Eliot, *The Nile*, 1964

Essfelt, Otto, *Baal-Zapho-Zeus (Cassios)*

Evens, A.J., *Mycenaean Tree and Pillar Cult*, 1901

Faber, George S., *The Origin of Pagan Idolatry*, 1816

Fairservis, Walter A., Jr., *The Roots of Ancient India*, 1971

Farrer, Austin, *The Rebirth of Images*, 1949

Fergusson, J., *Tree and Serpent Worship*, 1868

Field, H.M., D.D., *On the Desert*, 1883

Frankfort, Henri
>   *Intellectual Adventures of Ancient Man*, 1946
>   *Kingship and the Gods*, 1948

Frazer, J.G.
>   *The Golden Bough*, 1907
>   *Apollodorus*, 1921
>   *Folk Lore in the Old Testament*, 1919

Freund, Philip, *Myths of Creation*, 1964

Gaster, Theodor
>   *Dead Sea Scriptures*, 1956
>   *The Samaritans*, 1925

Gardiner, A.H. and Peet, T.E., *The Inscriptions of Sinai, 2 Vol.* (edited and completed by J. Cerney), 1952

Gardiner, A.H., *Egyptian Archaeology, 5, 6*, 1918

Gardiner, Patrick
>   *On Turin Papyrus*, Journal of Egypt Archaeology, 1887
>   *Theories of History*, 1959

Garstong, John, *The Foundations of Bible History – Joshua and Jude*, 1931

Georgius, Vide, *Alphabetum Tibetanum*, 1762

Ginzberg, Louis, *Legends of the Jews*, 1909

Glueck, Nelson, *Rivers in the Desert; Negev*, 1959

Godley, A.D., *Herodotus*, Volumes I-IV, Harvard University Press, 1920

Gray, J., *The Canaanites*, 1964

Green, Longmans, *History and Literature of Israelites*

Griffith, A.L., *The Antiquities of Tell el Yahudigeh*, 1890

Griffiths, J.G., *The Flight of the Gods before Typhon – Myth Hermes*, 1960

Grobel, Kendrick, *The Gospel of Truth*, 1960

Gunn, N. & Gardiner, A.H., "The Expulsion of the Hyksos," *Journal of Egyptian Archaeology*, 1870

Grene, David, *The History of Herodotus*, 1987

Harmon, A.M., *Lucian*, Volumes I-VIII, Harvard University Press, 1913

Heath, Sir Thomas, *Aristarchus of Samos*, 1913

Higgins, Godfrey Esq.
> *Anacalpysis* Vol. I, II, 1836
> *Celtic Druids*, 1827

Hodges, Richard E., *Cory's Ancient Fragments*, 1876

Hokins, E.W., *Origin and Evolution of Religion*, 1924

Holladay, J.S., *Cities of the Delta, Part III, Tell el Maskhuta, Preliminary Report on the Wadi Tumilat Project 1978-79*, 1982

Hooke, S.H.
> *Myth, Ritual and Kingship*, 1958
> *Babylonia and Assyrian Religion*, 1953

Imparati, F., *Hurriti*, 1964

James, Edwin O., *Tree of Life, An Archaeological Study*, 1886

Jastow, M. & Clay, *An Early Version of the Gilgamesh Epic*, 1861-1925

Jones, H.L., *The Geography of Strabo I (63 B.C.)*, 1917

Kees, Hermann, *Ancient Egypt*, 1961

Keller, Werner, *The Bible as History*, 1975

Kent, Charles F., *Growth and Contents of the Old Testament*, 1925

Kitchen, K.A., *Ancient Orient and the Old Testament*, 1966

Knight, Richard P., *Language of Ancient Art and Mythology*, 1836-1837

Kohler, Kaufman, *Origins of the Synagogue and the Church*, Vol. I and II, 1937

Kramer, Samuel N., *Sumerian Mythology*, 1944

La Loubére, Simon de, *The Kingdom of Siam*, New Edition, 1967

Lepsius, Dr. Richard, *Egypt, Ethiopia and Sinai*, 1852

Lindsay, Jack, *Sinai and Palestine*, 1883

Lippert, Julius, *Evolution of Culture*, 1931

MacQueen, J.G., *The Hittites and their Contemporaries in Asia Minor*, 1975

Madaurehsis, Apuleius, *The Golden Ass*, 1924

Maspero, Rapport S., *The History of Egypt;* Vol. II, 1900

Maurice, Rev., *Antiquities of India*, 1913

Mertz, Barbara
> *Red Land, Black Land*, 1990
> *Temples, Tombs and Hieroglyphs*, 1990

Michalowski, K., *KARNAK*, 1970

Montet, Pierre, *Everyday Life in Egypt in the days of Ramesses*, 1958

Moore, C.H. & Jackson, J., *Tacitus, The Histories;* Vol. IV and V, *The Annals*, 1931

Moret, Alexander, *The Nile and Egyptian Civilization*, 1927

Moshe, Davis, *Israel; Its Role in Civilization*, 1956

Muller, Max F., *Sacred Books of the East* (Series), 1880-1884

Muller, Max W., *Mythology of All Races*; Vol. XII, 1964
Murrey, Margaret A., *The Splendor that was Egypt*, 1964

Nassau, Robert, *Fetichism*, 1893
Naville, Eduard
        Goshen and the Shrine of Saft el Henneh, 1886
        The Store-City of Pithom and the Route of Exodus, 1975
Nibbi, Alessandre, *The Sea People and Egypt*, 1975
Nilsson, Martin P.
        The Mycenaean Origin of Greek Mythology, 1932
        Cults, Myths, Oracles and Politics in Ancient Greece, 1951

Oldfather, C.H., *Diodorus of Sicily*, Volumes I-VIII, Harvard University Press, 1933
Oren, E., "How Not to Create a History of the Exodus – A Critique of Professor Goedicke's Theories," *Biblical Archaeology Review*, 1981

Patai, Raphael, *The Hebrew Goddess*, 1967
Parkhurst, *Hebrew Lexicon*, 1792
Patten, Donald W., *The Biblical Flood and the Ice Epoch*, 1966
Peet, Eric T., *Egypt and the Old Testament*, 1922
Petrie, W.M.F.
        History of Egypt, Volumes 1-6, 1899-1901
        Researches in Sinai, 1906
        The Status of the Jews in Egypt, 1922
Phillips, Wendell, *Qataban and Sheba*, 1955
Phonizier, *Movers*
Pichler, H. & Schiering, W., *The Thera Eruption and late Minoan IB Destruction on Crete*, 1977
Pierret, Paul, *The Egyptian Pantheon*, 1881
Pietrie, William F.
        A History of Egypt, Volumes 1-6, 1896-1918
        Hyksos and Israelite Cities, 1906
Piotrozskii, Boris B. & Hogarth, J., *The Ancient Civilization of Urartu*, 1969
Potter, C.H., *The Story of Religion*, 1929
Pritchard, J.B., *Ancient Near Eastern Texts Relating to the Old Testament*, 1950

Rapport, *Myth and Legend of Ancient Israel*
Rawlinson, George, *Histories*, 1996
Redford, D.B.,
        A Study of the Biblical Story of Joseph, Genesis 37-50, 1970
        Essays on the Ancient Semitic World, 1970
        Egypt, Canaan, and Israel in Ancient Times, 1992
Reichen, Charles A., *A History of Astronomy*; Vol. V, 1963
Renouf, Prof., *Religions of Ancient Egypt*, 1884
Riencourt, Amaury de, *Sex and Power in History*, 1974

Rothenberg, Beno, *Gods, Wilderness – Sinai*, 1961

Sanford, E.M., *The Mediterranean World in Ancient Times*, 1951
Sayce, A.H.
    Carian Language and Inscriptions, 1885
    Early History of the Hebrews, 1897
Schiaparelli, G., *Astronomy of the Old Testament*, 1900
Scholem, G., *The Curious History of the Six Pointed Star*, 1949
Schonfield, Hugoh, *Secret of the Dead Sea Scrolls*, 1956
Seligman, C.G., *Notes on the Veddas*, 1911
Selincourt, Aubrey de, Herodotus, *The Histories* (translation), 1972
Seton, Lloyd, *The Archaeology of Mesopotamia*
Shaw, Ian, *The Oxford History of Ancient Egypt*, Oxford Press, 2000
Sibree, James, *Great African Island*, 1880
Smith, Robertson, *Religion of the Semites*
Smith, Sir William, *A Dictionary of the Bible*, 1948
Smith, W.R., *Lectures on the Religion of the Semites*, 1889
Sneh, A., & Weissbrod, T., "Nile Delta: The Defunct Pelusiac Branch Identified," *Science*,
    Vol. 180, pp. 59-61, 1973
Speiser, E.A., *Oriental and Biblical Studies*, 1967
Spence, Lewis, *Babylonia and Assyria*, 1874
Stanley, A.P., *Sinaitic Penninsula*, 1874
Stanley, A.P. & Murray, J., *Sinai and Palestine*, 1918
Stocking, G.W., Jr., *Researches into the Physical History of Man*, 1973
Starr, C.G., *The Origins of Greek Civilization*, 1961
Syme, Richard, *History in Ovid*, 1879

Taylor, Edward
    Primitive Culture, 1871
    Metamorphosis or Golden Ass, 1927
Taylor, Thomas, *The Eleusinian and Bacchic Mysteries*, 1875
Tompkins, Peter, *Secrets of the Great Pyramid*, 1971
Trumbull, Clay H., *Beginning of Religious Rites*, 1896

Van Seters, J., *The Hyksos: A New Investigation*, 1966
Vega, Garcilaso, *Commentaries*, 1961
Velikovsky, Immanuel, *Oedipus and Akhantion*, 1960
Vernes, M., *Sinai contre Kades*, 1915

Waddell, W.G., *Manetho's History of Egypt*, Harvard University Press, 1940
Walker, W.S., *Tales Alive in Turkey*, 1966
Wall, O.A., *Sex and Sex Worship*, 1919
Wasserstein, Abraham, *Flavius Josephus, Selections from his Works*, 1974
Weigall, Arthur, *Personalities of Antiquity*, 1928
Weinstein, J.M., *The Egyptian Empire in Palestine: A Reassessment*, 1981

Whiston, W.A.M., *Works of Falvius Josephus*; Vol. II and IV, 1979

Widengren, *Mesopotamian Elements in Manichaeism: King and Savior*, 1946

Wilkinson, John, *Manners and Customs of the Ancient Egyptians*, 1878

Wilson, Edmond, *Dead Sea Scrolls*, 1955

Wilson, Ian, *The Exodus Enigma*, 1985

Woodman, A.J., *The Annals of Tacitus*, Cambridge University Press, 1996

Woolley, Leonard Sir, *Ur of the Chaldees*, 1900

Yarden, L., *The Tree of Light (A Study of the Menorah)*, 1971

Zaehner, Robert, *The Dawn and Twilight of Zoroastrianism*, 1961

About the Author

Born into Roman Catholicism in the mid 1930's, Thomas Bordelon was instructed and lived under the traditional beliefs of that faith. In the late 1950's, he left that church because of unsettling changes that began altering the old form of worship. For years, nagging questions plagued him about what he had been taught but, like most followers, he continued a mechanical worship.

In the early 1960's, he joined a nondenominational charismatic Christian movement in Houston, Texas where he preached and taught bible text. With his unshakeable belief in every word written in the Judaeo-Christian bible, he sought to bring the very essence of the "Lord's word" to every listener by following the traditional interpretation. While preparing for a sermon on one particular mystical parable, which compared the mustard seed tree to heaven, he decided to research the subject. In the library, he stumbled upon the book, "The Sacred Mushroom and the Cross", which he felt compelled to read. That book ignited a flame of inquiry that totally consumed him and started him on a journey of discovery. Forty years of continual study have uncovered the information presented in this book.